WISCONSIN

Also in This Series

† *Arizona,* Malcolm L. Comeaux

† *Colorado,* Mel Griffiths and Lynnell Rubright

† *Hawaii,* Joseph R. Morgan

† *Maryland,* James E. DiLisio

† *Michigan,* Lawrence M. Sommers

† *Missouri,* Milton D. Rafferty

  Nebraska, Bradley H. Baltensperger

† *New Jersey,* Charles A. Stansfield, Jr.

† *Texas,* Terry G. Jordan with John L. Bean, Jr., and William M. Holmes

† *Wyoming,* Robert Harold Brown

Forthcoming Through 1986

Connecticut, Thomas R. Lewis and John E. Harmon

Illinois, A. Doyne Horsley

† Available in hardcover and paperback.

GEOGRAPHIES OF THE UNITED STATES
Ingolf Vogeler, General Editor

Wisconsin: A Geography
Ingolf Vogeler
with Harold Mayer, Brady Foust, and Richard Palm
and with editorial assistance by Sharon Knopp

"America's Dairyland" is the favorite image of Wisconsin, but as this book explains, the state is as rich in culture as it is in agriculture, as diverse as it is bountiful. Popular impressions as well as the historical and contemporary landscapes are examined in this systematic and well-illustrated geography of Wisconsin.

Over 160 photographs, sketches, graphs, and tables reflect the state's variety—the red and white farmsteads, the abandoned ore mines of the Gogebic Range, the beauty of the Chequamegon National Forest, the small-town ethnic festivals, and the busy streets of Milwaukee—and delineate Wisconsin's geography, a landscape made diverse by the massive glaciers that covered most of the state more than 10,000 years ago. Within this environment, three distinctive historical landscapes evolved: the boreal riverine fur-trading empire, the settler era, and the nationalist stage of railroads and factories.

In considering the state's three regions, close attention is paid to the differences that have characterized Wisconsin's growth. In the Northwoods region, the use of natural resources by the Indians and logging and mining companies is contrasted with the practices of agricultural settlers and urban recreationalists. Although famous for its dairy farms, the southern agricultural area also provides a wealth of specialty crops such as tobacco and cranberries. The state's small towns and urban areas make up the third region. Particular attention is paid to Milwaukee and its ethnic neighborhoods.

Wisconsin provides a thorough look at a state marked by contrasts and, in so doing, gives depth to our image of America's dairyland.

Ingolf Vogeler, associate professor and chair of the Department of Geography at the University of Wisconsin–Eau Claire, is also the series editor for *Geographies of the United States.* **Harold Mayer** is professor of geography at the University of Wisconsin–Milwaukee. **Brady Foust,** professor, and **Richard Palm,** assistant professor, teach at the University of Wisconsin–Eau Claire. **Sharon Knopp** is associate editor of the *Journal of Geography.*

To the geographer
in all of us

WISCONSIN

A GEOGRAPHY

Ingolf Vogeler
with contributions by
Harold Mayer, Brady Foust, and Richard Palm
and with editorial assistance
by Sharon Knopp

Westview Press / Boulder and London

Geographies of the United States

Cover photo courtesy of U.S. Soil Conservation Service

Chapter 1: Charlie Maguire granted permission to reprint lines from "Getting in the Cows," copyright 1978 by Charlie Maguire; published by Chinook Music; all rights reserved.

Published in 1986 in the United States of America by Westview Press, Inc.; Frederick A. Praeger, Publisher; 5500 Central Avenue, Boulder, Colorado 80301

Library of Congress Cataloging in Publication Data
Vogeler, Ingolf.
  Wisconsin, a geography.
  (Geographies of the United States)
  Includes index.
  1. Wisconsin—Description and travel. I. Title.
II. Series.
F581.V63 1986   977.5'04   85-13907
ISBN 0-86531-186-2
ISBN 0-86531-492-6 (pbk.)

Printed and bound in the United States of America

10   9   8   7   6   5   4   3   2   1

CONTENTS

List of Figures ix
List of Tables xiii
Preface and Acknowledgments xv

INTRODUCTION 1

1   IMAGES OF WISCONSIN 4

Water Recreation 4
Beer 9
Dairying 15
Frank Lloyd Wright 21
Selected References 22

2   PHYSICAL PROCESSES AND PATTERNS 24

Climate 24
Focus: Wisconsin Thunderstorms 29
Landforms 30
Vegetation 45
Water 49
Selected References 50

3   HISTORICAL LANDSCAPES 51

The Boreal Riverine Empire: Indian Culture Areas and
    European Fur Trading 51
The Settler Empire: Miners, Agriculturalists, and Loggers
    on the National Frontier 56
Focus: Ethnic Festivals in Wisconsin 71
The Nationalist Empire: Railroads and Factories 77
Selected References 80

4   THE NORTHWOODS REGION 84

Indian Reservations 87
Logging and Lumbering, 1840s–1910s 92

Focus: Lumberjack Lingo 93
Northern Mining, 1880s–1960s 97
Cutover Agriculture, 1910s–1950s 103
Northern Recreation After the 1950s 115
Selected References 121

5   THE SOUTHERN AGRICULTURAL REGION 124

Wisconsin's Agricultural History 124
Dairying in Wisconsin Today 127
Focus: Dairy Farming: A Hard Row to Hoe 132
Specialty Crops 136
Selected References 145

6   THE URBAN REGIONS 147

Historical Evolution of the Urban Pattern 147
Central Places: The Size and Spacing of Cities 154
Manufacturing 162
Conclusion 170
Selected References 171

7   THE MILWAUKEE METROPOLITAN REGION 172

The City's Location and Site 172
Historical and Cultural Heritage 177
Milwaukee's Major Areas 183
*Focus: Greendale, Wisconsin: Federal City Planning
    During the Great Depression* 185
The Metropolitan Economy 190
The Service and Utility Infrastructure 201
Milwaukee's Future 203
Selected References 205

Index 209

FIGURES

Counties of Wisconsin (map)..xvii

1.1   Chicago recreational travelers per average summer day (map)..................5
1.2   Government fishing advertisement..6
1.3   National Freshwater Fishing Hall of Fame, Hayward (photo)...................7
1.4   A Door Peninsula scene...8
1.5   The Wisconsin Dells recreation area (map)..................................10
1.6   Downtown Wisconsin Dells (photo)...11
1.7   "The Strip," Lake Delton (photo)...11
1.8   U.S. malt-beverage consumption by state (map)..............................12
1.9   Wisconsin breweries, 1850s–1970s (map).....................................12
1.10 Wisconsin breweries terminated by 1932 (map)...............................13
1.11 Wisconsin breweries and production, 1933–1980..............................13
1.12 Beer labels of Wisconsin's regional breweries..............................14
1.13 U.S. brandy consumption by state (map).....................................15
1.14 Prime cropland as a percentage of total area by county (map)...............16
1.15 Display on a dairy farm (photo)..17
1.16 English barn type..18
1.17 German barn type...18
1.18 Barn styles..18
1.19 Round Barn Restaurant (photo)..20
1.20 A Frank Lloyd Wright house...20
1.21 U.S. distribution of buildings designed by
      Frank Lloyd Wright, 1887–1953 (map)..21
1.22 Wisconsin distribution of houses designed by
      Frank Lloyd Wright, 1887–1953 (map)..22

2.1   Air masses in Wisconsin (map)..26
2.2   Cold and warm fronts...27
2.3   A forecast map of the United States (map)..................................28
2.4   Annual average thunderstorms across the United States (map)................29
2.5   Major tornado tracks in Wisconsin (map)....................................29
2.6   Annual average snowfall (map)..30
2.7   Polar front jet stream (map)...30
2.8   Generalized distribution of bedrock in Wisconsin (map).....................34
2.9   A glacial landscape (photo)..36
2.10 Wisconsin glacial deposits (map)...37

2.11   Ages of glacial deposits (map)... 38
2.12   Areas susceptible to acid rain (map)....................................... 40
2.13   Physiographic regions of Wisconsin (map)................................... 41
2.14   Castle Rock at Camp Douglas (photo) 43
2.15   An esker in the glaciated Eastern Ridges and Lowlands (photo)............. 45
2.16   Vegetation types of Wisconsin about 1850 (map)............................ 47

3.1   Boreal riverine empire in Wisconsin (map)................................. 52
3.2   Fur-trading settlements at Portage (map)................................. 55
3.3   Long-lot survey, Prairie du Chien (map) 57
3.4   Indian land lost to European expansion, 1815–1848 (map).................. 58
3.5   The township and range survey in southwestern Wisconsin (map)............ 59
3.6   The Wisconsin lead-mining district (map)................................. 61
3.7   Wisconsin land offices, 1830s–1900s (map)................................ 64
3.8   Percentage of German-born population by county, 1890 (map)............... 67
3.9   *Fachwerk* barn (photo).. 68
3.10   Number of Norwegian-born persons by county, 1890 (map)................... 70
3.11   Alpine yodelers (photo) 71
3.12   New Glarus Swiss land uses (map)... 72
3.13   The Old North and New North in Wisconsin in the 1860s (map).............. 74
3.14   Number of Finnish-born persons by county, 1920 (map)..................... 75
3.15   Evolution of Wisconsin's railroad network, 1853–1900 (map)............... 78

4.1   Major land-use types in Wisconsin (map).................................. 85
4.2   The Northwoods region (map).. 86
4.3   Indian reservation institutions, 1928 (map).............................. 88
4.4   Indian reservations and settlements, 1980 (map).......................... 90
4.5   Lac Court Oreilles Reservation (map and photo)........................... 91
4.6   Indian cemetery on the Red Cliff Reservation (photo)..................... 91
4.7   Indian poverty and white wealth (photo).................................. 91
4.8   Logging camp (photo)... 92
4.9   Log hauling (photo) 94
4.10   Driving logs on the Chippewa River in 1906 (photo)....................... 94
4.11   Lumber production in Wisconsin, 1869–1909 95
4.12   Logging towns and the Cutover region, 1850 (map) 96
4.13   The Gogebic Iron Range (map)... 98
4.14   Annual iron-ore production from the Wisconsin section of the
        Gogebic Range, 1885–1965 98
4.15   Individual mine production on the Gogebic Range (map) 100
4.16   Population of the Gogebic Range communities, 1980 (map)................. 100
4.17   Montreal, Wisconsin, 1921 (map)... 102
4.18   Foreign-born persons on the Wisconsin portion
        of the Gogebic Range, 1900 104
4.19   Bountiful harvest in the Cutover (photo) 105
4.20   County immigration committees in Wisconsin (map)....................... 105
4.21   Stump clearing, Medford, Taylor County, 1895 (photo) 106
4.22   Sawyer County lies at the center of urban markets (map)................ 108
4.23   Wisconsin Colonization Company house plans............................. 109
4.24   Clearing the land with explosives (photo).............................. 111
4.25   Tax delinquency rates by township, 1936 (map).......................... 113

4.26 Age-sex pyramid for Price County, 1958 114
4.27 The Chequamegon Resort Hotel, Ashland, 1882 115
4.28 Seasonal homes as a percent of total housing units (map) 117
4.29 Cottage ownership regions in northwestern Wisconsin (map)..............118
4.30 Recreational land per county (map)...119
4.31 Hotel and motel rooms per capita (map)..................................120

5.1   Wheat acreage and milk cows, 1866–1930 125
5.2   Cartogram of U.S. dairy farms (map)....................................127
5.3   Dairy farm landscape (map) 128
5.4   Grade A milk production and market areas (map)........................129
5.5   Milk production by month..131
5.6   Climatic conditions and agricultural work 131
5.7   A dairy farmstead...133
5.8   Cross-section and floor plan of a dairy barn 134
5.9   Cheese regions (map)..135
5.10 Vegetables harvested for sale by county in the United States (map)..........137
5.11 Source area and travel patterns of Wisconsin's migratory
          agricultural workers (map)..139
5.12 Topographic map of cranberry bogs (map) 140
5.13 Drainage in a cranberry bog...141
5.14 Cross-section of a cranberry bog in summer and winter...................141
5.15 Tobacco farms in the southern district (map)...........................143
5.16 Cross-section of a tobacco barn 143
5.17 U.S. tobacco-curing regions (map) 144
5.18 Wisconsin tobacco regions (map) 145

6.1   The Wisconsin urban system, 1850 (map)................................148
6.2   The Wisconsin urban system, 1870–1900 (maps).........................149
6.3   The Wisconsin urban system, 1910–1940 (maps).........................150
6.4   The Wisconsin urban system, 1950–1980 (maps).........................151
6.5   A model of urban growth..153
6.6   Spacing and size of Wisconsin urban centers (map).......................155
6.7   Market-area "nesting" 156
6.8   Functional size versus population size at the lower levels of the
          Wisconsin urban hierarchy...156
6.9   Hierarchical levels in the upper Midwest...............................158
6.10 Hierarchical levels of Wisconsin's urban system (map) 159
6.11 Reilly's Law: calculation example......................................160
6.12 Primary wholesale-retail market areas in Wisconsin (map)...............161
6.13 Logging camps and contractors (map)...................................165
6.14 Papermills (map)..166
6.15 Aerial view of the Pope and Talbot papermill in Eau Claire (photo)........166
6.16 Vitreous china casting in a Kohler plumbing fixtures plant (photo)..........167
6.17 Fabricated metal products (map)..168

7.1   Physiographic features in the Milwaukee region (map)..................174
7.2   Eroding bluffs along the Lake Michigan shoreline at Cudahy (photo)........175
7.3   The north end of the Inner Harbor (photo).............................175
7.4   Lake Michigan shoreline (photo)..176

7.5   The residential growth of Milwaukee, 1850–1980 (map)..................... 178
7.6   The Pabst brewery (photo).. 180
7.7   Percentage of foreign-born and blacks in the Milwaukee SMSA,
        1870–1970.. 181
7.8   Ethnic and racial groups in Milwaukee (map) 182
7.9   Duplex houses in the university district of northeast Milwaukee (photo)..... 184
7.10   A planned unit development in northwest Milwaukee (photo)............... 184
7.11   Low- and high-income areas in Milwaukee (map)......................... 186
7.12   The Menomonee Industrial Valley (photo) 187
7.13   The Performing Arts Center in downtown Milwaukee (photo).............. 188
7.14   Milwaukee's civic plaza (photo).. 189
7.15   The General Motors plant in Oak Creek (photo).......................... 196
7.16   The Allen-Bradley plant in Walkers Point (photo)......................... 196

TABLES

1.1 Major states producing malt beverages 11
1.2 Production capacity and market share of Wisconsin breweries 14

2.1 Temperature and precipitation for six Wisconsin cities 31
2.2 Generalized geologic history of Wisconsin 35

3.1 Wisconsin's population in 1850 65
3.2 Ten leading industries by value of manufactured products, 1880–1920 80

4.1 Indian reservations in Wisconsin, 1980 89
4.2 Colonization companies in the Chippewa Valley, 1910–1920 107
4.3 The Wisconsin Colonization Company improvements in
     southern Sawyer County, 1917–1920 110

5.1 Evolution of Wisconsin agriculture by region 124
5.2 Wisconsin's vegetable crops, 1981 138

6.1 Thresholds for selected functions in Wisconsin 156
6.2 Examples of settlement-building functions for
     selected cities in Wisconsin 161
6.3 Wisconsin manufacturing employment 163
6.4 Location quotients for Wisconsin industries 164

7.1 Metropolitan Milwaukee's largest regional shopping centers 190
7.2 Manufacturing employment by major industry group, Milwaukee SMSA 191
7.3 Employment by category, Milwaukee SMSA and all SMSAs
     in the United States 192
7.4 Median family income for large SMSAs 193
7.5 Large manufacturing firms that normally employ 2,000 or more
     workers in metropolitan Milwaukee 194
7.6 Industrial and office parks and districts, metropolitan Milwaukee 198
7.7 Total employment and manufacturing production workers,
     Milwaukee SMSA, 1960–1979 199

PREFACE AND ACKNOWLEDGMENTS

Wisconsin: A Geography is not a comprehensive encyclopedia, but rather an interpretative essay. Dominant themes in the past and present geographies of the state are explored. A complete coverage of topics and places through time would be impossible, and even if attempted, the sheer quantity of details would make for dull reading. Consequently, teachers are encouraged to add depth to the topics covered and to supplement the book with topics and case studies of their own interests. Indeed, the book is written in such a way that local case studies can be based on the more general material presented. For example, if poultry farming is important in your county, assessor's farm statistics, topographic maps, platbooks, and fieldwork can be used to construct the geography of poultry farming. We hope you—teachers and students—will use the *ideas, concepts,* and *techniques* in this book to explore the geography of your locale.

Many individuals helped produce this book.

I specialize in rural and cultural-historical geography at the University of Wisconsin–Eau Claire. I organized, edited, and provided most of the illustrations and maps. I also wrote Chapters 1, 3, and 5 and the sections in Chapter 4 on agriculture in the Cutover region and Indian reservations.

Harold Mayer, an urban and transportation geographer at the University of Wisconsin–Milwaukee, has spent a considerable part of his professional career studying the Chicago-Milwaukee conurbation. His contribution is Chapter 7.

Brady Foust teaches economic and urban geography at the University of Wisconsin–Eau Claire. He is responsible for Chapter 6 as well as the section on Northwoods recreation in Chapter 4. An earlier, shorter version of Chapter 4 was originally published in *Wisconsin Dialogue,* no. 3 (Spring 1983), by the University of Wisconsin–Eau Claire. Brady Foust, Anthony de Souza, and I would like to express our appreciation to the University of Wisconsin–Eau Claire for permission to use this material.

Richard Palm, climatologist and physical geographer at the University of Wisconsin–Eau Claire, contributed Chapter 2.

Sharon Knopp is an educational psychologist, curriculum and instruction consultant, and associate editor of the *Journal of Geography.* She edited this volume for consistency and educational appropriateness.

Several other individuals also made contributions to this project. Arnold Alanen, cultural geographer in the Department of Landscape Architecture at the University of Wisconsin–Madison, wrote the section on mining in Chapter 4. Anthony de Souza, an eclectic geographer, who edits the *Journal of Geography* at the University of Wisconsin–Eau Claire, wrote the section on logging in Chapter 4.

Rick Pifer, archivist at the University of Wisconsin–Eau Claire, provided material for Chapter 4 on the colonization companies of northern Wisconsin. Roland Nichols, a recreational geographer at the University of Wisconsin–Eau Claire, provided material for the section on recreation in Chapter 4. Adam Cahow, a physical geographer at the University of Wisconsin–Eau Claire, provided advice and assistance in preparing materials for Chapter 2.

David Schiltgen, a geography major at the University of Wisconsin–Eau Claire, drew many of the maps. Judy Jacobi, a cartographer and human geographer at the University of Tennessee, lent her considerable cartographic skills to the revision of numerous maps. Mary Farr drew the illustrations for the book. Yvonne Plomedahl applied her outstanding skills in typing several versions of this volume.

Several persons contributed materials that could not be used because the final manuscript had to be shortened. Margo Conk and James Cronin, who teach social and urban labor history at the University of Wisconsin–Milwaukee, and Stephen Meyer, who is an historian of technology at the Illinois Institute of Technology, wrote about West Allis. Thomas Detwyler, an environmental geographer at the University of Wisconsin–Stevens Point, submitted a case study on corporate colonization of central Wisconsin.

To all my fellow contributors—many, many thanks.

Ingolf Vogeler
Eau Claire, Wisconsin

Counties of Wisconsin

INTRODUCTION

Wisconsin: A Geography is more than a book about Wisconsin. It is also an introduction to geography as a social science. For most people, geography is the study—indeed memorization—of where rivers, hills, towns, and cities are located and where major commercial products are produced. But professional geographers are interested in more than what can be found in a comprehensive atlas. Fundamentally, they try to answer the broad question: *Why* is it *where* it is?

In studying places, such as Wisconsin, geographers use three different yet related approaches: regionalization, human-environmental interactions, and spatial analysis. (1) Geographers compare and contrast places, such as cities, agricultural areas, states, and countries. Identifying the unique characteristics of areas results in *areal differentiation* or regionalization. (2) In the human-environmental tradition, the interactions of people with the physical elements of their environment are studied. Environmental perception and attitudes toward natural resources are critical in explaining why certain people and activities are located where they are. Human-environmental geographers use the concepts of *site,* or absolute location, and *situation,* or relative location, to describe and explain human landscapes. (3) Geographers who use spatial analysis are concerned with the most abstract characteristics of places. They focus on the basic geographic concepts of direction, distance, shape, and size and assume an *isotropic surface,* a theoretical surface devoid of cultural and physical attributes. They want to know how important the geometry of human settlements is in accounting for human behavior.

All three approaches constitute the academic discipline of geography. Each approach has its own contributions to make in understanding our world. Concerned with the character of places, spatial patterns, and the relationships between people and environments, geographers provide a broad interdisciplinary understanding of specific places in everyday life. We shall apply the geographer's perspective to the study of Wisconsin.

Wisconsin, the political state, is an artificial, arbitrarily created region, but over time this state has developed characteristics and a sense of place that now exists independent of state boundaries. Fundamentally, all kinds of regions, whether soil and forest types, urban milk sheds, or ethnic neighborhoods, are "artificial," or mindsets about the real world. Geographers, and other scientists, classify reality to describe, explain, and ultimately to predict future geographies. The geographer's distinctive form of classification is regionalization, whereby the earth's natural and human features are grouped in systematic and logical ways.

Traditional regional geographies treat major physical and human components of the landscape as separate pieces of a puzzle. Description is the hallmark of this approach. But to seek explanation in regional geography, as in all sciences, requires an integrative approach. Relating relevant human and physical aspects of a region makes for a more demanding task and provides for a more rewarding intellectual experience but commonly results in disagreements. *Wisconsin: A Geography* hopes to spark your curiosity in the cultural and physical landscapes of the state and in the field of geography itself.

The study of one place, such as Wisconsin, is useful for its own sake: learning little things from little places. This is called the *idiographic* approach. But regional study is also important for what it reveals about other places and times: learning big things from small regions. This approach is called the *nomothetic* approach. Both the idiographic and nomothetic approaches to the study of regions are necessary to fully appreciate and understand places. Wisconsin is a unique state, but it also shares many characteristics with adjacent states and indeed with the United States as a whole.

We all classify and compare places in order to understand our world. Hence, we speak of lumber towns, resort towns, downtowns, and ghettos. These places, regardless of *where* they are found, have more in common with each other than with other places, whether near or far away. For example, Madison, where the state capitol and a land grant university are situated, has more in common with East Lansing, Michigan, than with Janesville, which depends heavily on the auto industry, even though East Lansing is 400 mi (644 km) away and Janesville is only 50 mi (80 km) away.

This book focuses on ordinary people—rather than on famous decision makers and politicians—who shaped the changing geography of Wisconsin and whose experiences are linked with events in other parts of the United States. The geography of any state is largely about these ordinary people in everyday places: factories, shops, houses, parks, cities, and farms. Senators, governors, and wealthy individuals also played

their roles in the historical geography of Wisconsin, but the "movers and shakers" of cultural landscapes are the people who are rarely considered in history books.

This book explores, describes, and explains a complex and dynamic geographical reality filled with conflict: between Indians and white traders and settlers; between "old" and "new" immigrant groups; between lumberjacks and farmers and lumber barons, railroad builders, bankers, and politicians; between laborers and their industrial bosses; between rural and urban people.

Several general themes emerge from the study of the making of the Wisconsin landscape. First, human beings make geography—we are not passive bystanders merely responding to impersonal human and physical forces and events. The human geography of Wisconsin is the result of the labor of millions of people, who created the wealth and institutions of this state, not just the efforts of a few prominent Wisconsinites. The clearing of the land; the planting of crops; the building of transportation lines, houses, and factories; and the producing of goods and services: All these are the achievement of generations of Wisconsin people. These accomplishments are expressed in the landscape and deserve to be remembered, appreciated, and celebrated.

Second, Wisconsin did not develop in isolation. International and national events have shaped and changed the history and geography of the state. Wisconsin has likewise influenced the nation. Third, the development and growth of capitalism in Wisconsin did not affect everyone in the society equally. Those who owned the land, the factories, and the banks tried to use their financial and political power to create a state that many farmers, industrial workers, politicians, and social reformers opposed. Throughout Wisconsin history, many women and men struggled to create a society that reflected the democratic interests of social justice for all people.

The human geography of Wisconsin reflects the great transformations that occurred in the last 300 years. Reading the cultural landscape allows us to appreciate the importance of the work of all classes of people. The working and living conditions and experiences of the vast majority of people, after all, constitute the raison d'être of U.S. democracy. Because geographers study ordinary landscapes, geography is particularly pertinent to understanding and appreciating Wisconsin.

IMAGES OF WISCONSIN

Wisconsin! What an intriguing state: "Lakes," "beer," and "cows" are the three words that capture the popular images of the state for residents and visitors alike. These images are fostered by the Wisconsin Division of Tourism's recreational advertisements, by private commercial promotional literature available at interstate rest stops and restaurants, and by the actual experiences of visitors while traveling through the state. A less well known but equally distinctive image of Wisconsin is as the birthplace and home of famed architect Frank Lloyd Wright.

WATER RECREATION

Wisconsin is Chicago's playground. In every county of the state residents of metropolitan Chicago are the single largest group of travelers. In fact, 56 percent of all vacationers in the state come from Illinois, and of these, 80 percent are from the Chicago metropolitan area (Figure 1.1). For Illinois tourists, "going north" means Wisconsin, although Wisconsinites go north to Canada! "Going north" means going fishing and camping, motor boating, sailing, and sightseeing and staying at one's cottage. Visitors are lured north, in the words of the Wisconsin Division of Tourism, to "Escape to Wisconsin."

> Canoe down lazy winding rivers or test your skills on white water. Row your family across a moon-streaked pond, making silent ripples.

Watch your bobber sink, or see it dance with the nibble of a crappie, or challenge a musky to a one-on-one battle. The variety of your catch will amaze you. Large and smallmouth bass, northern pike, brown, rainbow and brook trout, walleyes and their equally tasty cousins, the perch. Cooked over a crackling campfire, the flavor becomes a memory to lure you back season after season. (Wisconsin Division of Tourism 1982, p. 3)

The large number of rivers and lakes indeed allows residents and visitors to escape to a water wonderland. The state has 14,949 lakes, or nearly 1 million acres (404,700 ha) of water. Wisconsin also has 2,444 cold-water trout streams and another 5,002 warm-water streams. The total mileage of these streams is greater than the distance between Milwaukee and Perth, Australia—fishing in Wisconsin can get you almost halfway around the world without leaving the state! In addition, Wisconsin has 860 mi (1,384 km) of shoreline, including islands, along Lake Superior and Lake Michigan.

Wisconsin has three large distinctive lake districts. About 3,000 lakes are concentrated at the headwaters of the Wisconsin River near Rhinelander. This is a prime resort country, where Milwaukee and Chicago residents are frequent visitors. The second lake district, with about 2,000 lakes, lies between the St. Croix and Chippewa rivers in the area around Hayward. This area has many cottages owned by residents of Minnesota, the Dakotas, and Iowa. The

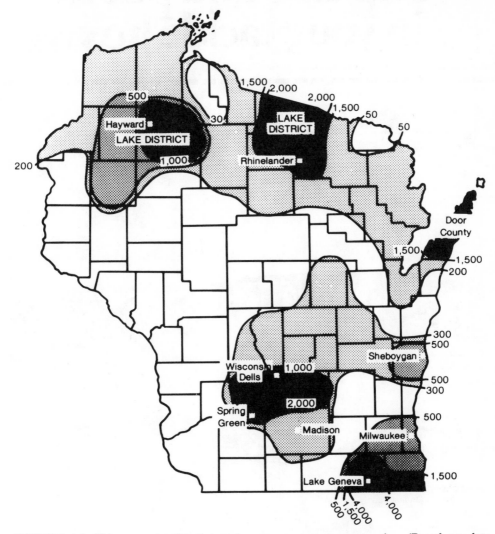

FIGURE 1.1 Chicago recreational travelers per average summer day. (Based on data from the Wisconsin Department of Transportation files, Madison)

concentration of travelers in these two northern districts results from fishing and camping sites in national forests, state parks and forests, and county parks and forests. Indeed, tourist advertisements promote the idea that Wisconsin is one big fishing hole (Figure 1.2). A third, smaller lake district lies in the southeastern corner of the state. Numerous summer camps, expensive resorts, summer homes, and two state parks are located around or near such lakes as Lake Geneva, Lake Koshkonong, Pewaukee Lake, and Lake Mendota. Chicago visitors

predominate here. In addition to these lake districts, two other popular water resort areas are Wisconsin Dells and Door County.

Fishing or water-related festivals are held throughout the state. Fond du Lac on Lake Winnebago holds the national walleye fishing championships in June, including the "world's largest fish fry." Lake Geneva holds the Venetian Festival, including a parade of boats, in August to celebrate the aquatic recreation associated with the Lake Geneva region. Boulder Junction honors the world's most ferocious fish at the city's August

Clip this and put it in your tackle box.

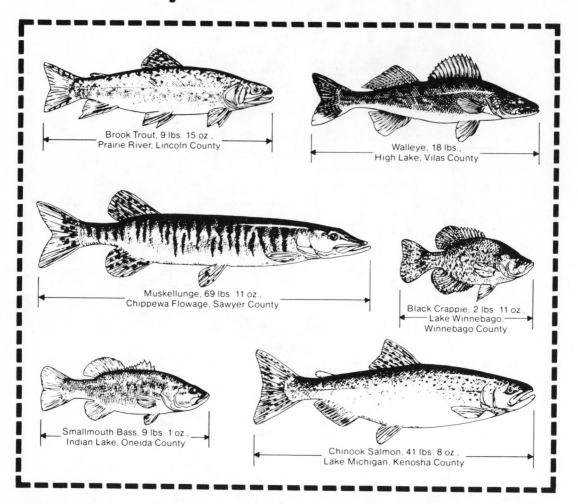

Brook Trout, 9 lbs. 15 oz.,
Prairie River, Lincoln County

Walleye, 18 lbs.,
High Lake, Vilas County

Muskellunge, 69 lbs. 11 oz.,
Chippewa Flowage, Sawyer County

Black Crappie, 2 lbs. 11 oz.,
Lake Winnebago,
Winnebago County

Smallmouth Bass, 9 lbs. 1 oz.,
Indian Lake, Oneida County

Chinook Salmon, 41 lbs. 8 oz.,
Lake Michigan, Kenosha County

Your chance to break a Wisconsin record begins May 5.

Hardly a year goes by that *somebody* doesn't make a record catch in our waters. That's why fishing in Wisconsin generates so much excitement—why, year after year, more non-residents travel to Wisconsin to fish than to any other state.

Remember, the season on most species opens May 5, but be sure to consult 1979 regulations for details and exceptions. Come on up, catch some fish and maybe set a record of your own.

FISH WISCONSIN
Box 7606 SF Madison, Wisconsin 53707
Write for more information on Wisconsin vacations.

Name_____
Address_____
City_____ State_____ Zip_____
Phone_____

WISCONSIN
Get to know us better.
800-356-9508

FIGURE 1.2 Government fishing advertisement. The Wisconsin Division of Tourism lures anglers from other states by means of these magazine ads. (Courtesy of Wisconsin Division of Tourism)

FIGURE 1.3 National Freshwater Fishing Hall of Fame, Hayward. Giant models of several common fish, including a 200-ft (61-m) long muskellunge with open jaws, 60 ft (18 m) above the ground, constitute an angler's Disneyland. (Ingolf Vogeler)

Musky Jamboree, but Hayward is the center for musky "fever." In June the Musky Festival there includes a fishing contest, carnival, and a parade. Hayward is also the site of the National Freshwater Fishing Hall of Fame, where the official world records on freshwater fish are kept and where unsuccessful anglers can see the really big ones that got away (Figure 1.3).

Wisconsin issues the third-largest number of resident fishing licenses in the United States. Every third adult is a licensed angler! The state ranks first in the nation for nonresident fishing licenses, about 400,000 being sold each year. The places where nonresident fishing licenses are sold and usually used and where Chicago recreational travelers stay are more or less the same, but fishing is also concentrated in "remote" counties: Polk in the west and Waupaca in the center. The largest number

of nonresident fishing licenses is sold in the Lake Geneva region, which is closest to the Illinois tourist market.

Door County

Of all the recreational areas in the state, the Door Peninsula and Wisconsin Dells are the most distinctive, and they are very different from each other. Door County appeals to the well-to-do who enjoy—and can afford—sailing, expensive shops and restaurants, rural vegetable and fruit stands, and summer theater. Despite four state parks, many private campgrounds, lodges, motels, and cabins, Door County is rural. For urbanites from Milwaukee, Chicago, and Minneapolis, the Door countryside is appealing for four major reasons. The foremost appeal is probably the seascape (Figure 1.4). The county has sandy beaches, limestone cliffs, rocky and stony shorelines,

FIGURE 1.4 A Door Peninsula scene. Water recreation, small villages, and bold physical landscapes make the coastal areas of Door County very appealing to urbanites.

many islands, numerous bays with villages and hamlets, and more lighthouses per mile of coast than any other county in the United States. Commercial fishing boats and sailboat docks further add to the attractiveness and charm of the county. Almost all harbors and settlements are on the steeper-sloped Green Bay side of the county; the Lake Michigan side is low-lying with many fewer coastline settlements.

A second reason for Door County's appeal is the architecture of the county, which resembles that of New England. Wisconsin writer Mike Link said, "Vermont reminded me of a Door County in the East." White clapboard houses and commercial buildings predominate, but in the countryside log and stovewood buildings are common. Various log notches—dovetail, square, saddle, and V—can be found on barns. Door County has the largest concentration of stovewood buildings in the state. Shingled houses and barns and field-stone walls around cropland further add to the distinctive flavor of the Door Peninsula.

The mark left by many European im-

migrants who settled in Door County also adds to the area's appeal. Washington Island has the largest community of Icelandic people in the United States. The Belgian communities in southern Door are characterized by their brick houses and roadside shrines. The log buildings and the grass-covered roof of Al Johnson's Swedish Restaurant in Sister Bay remind people of yet another ethnic group. Although fish boils are not distinctive to any ethnic group, they have become a tradition in the county and give tourists yet another reason for coming to the peninsula. Cherry orchards, which once covered much of the county, are the fourth major reason for visiting the Door Peninsula. Sufficient numbers of them still remain for visitors to enjoy the spring cherry-blossom season.

Wisconsin Dells

Although much less spectacular than Door County, the physical features of the Wisconsin Dells initially also attracted tourists. But today most tourists spend much less time and money viewing the

Wisconsin River gorge than they do at the adjacent amusements, gift shops, restaurants, and motels. For middle-income families and singles, the Wisconsin Dells are the state's largest commercialized natural wonderland (Figure 1.5).

Tourists are reminded in advertisements to see "First Things First" and to take a boat ride on the Upper or Lower Dells, preferably both. Meltwaters from the last glaciation carved the steep banks of the Wisconsin River, but the geological and topographic significance of the Dells is subordinated to the cultural attractions. Boasting of 55 "family attractions" such as miniature golf, 60 restaurants, 76 motels with 3,700 sleeping rooms that can accommodate 11,000 guests nightly, 12 campgrounds, and 61 retail stores, the area has a resident population of only 3,500. With amusements like Biblical Gardens, Noah's Ark, Storybook Gardens, Fort Dells, Haunted Mansion, Dungeon of Horrors, and OK Corral, as well as minigolf, go-carts, and waterslides, the Wisconsin Dells try to be everything to everybody—Hollywood, Disneyland, and Tombstone, Arizona. Most numerous among the many gift shops in the central business district of Wisconsin Dells are candy shops specializing in freshly made fudge. In 1980, the area received 1.8 million visitors, about 50 percent of whom came from Illinois, particularly from the Chicago metropolitan area.

Although the Wisconsin Dells lack the casinos and nightlife of Las Vegas, the areas share some characteristics: Both display a high concentration of motels, restaurants, and amusements in a downtown pedestrian area and also in a suburban location; the pedestrian landscape of the old central business district (Figure 1.6) and the automobile space of "the Strip" (Figure 1.7) are as striking in Wisconsin Dells as they are in Las Vegas. Along U.S. Highway 12 toward Lake Delton, suburbanized land uses, which are space demanding, are found: go-cart tracks, large amusement parks, and minigolf courses. In contrast, the town of

Wisconsin Dells houses tourist functions in nineteenth-century buildings concentrated along the main street. With all these (dis)attractions, the slogan "First Things First" is sometimes a feeble reminder to tourists to explore the sandstone bluffs along the Wisconsin River gorge—nature's contribution to the distinctive Wisconsin Dells.

BEER

Wisconsin, especially Milwaukee, is synonymous with beer. After all, Schlitz is "the beer that made Milwaukee famous." Wisconsin is the leading beer-producing state in the United States. Although several states have a few more beer companies, Wisconsin outranks other states in the number of employees and in the amount of "value added," which is the value of products when they leave factories minus the value of the raw materials that enter factories (Table 1.1). Wisconsin's contribution makes the United States the largest producer of beer in the world: The United States produces more beer than West Germany and Britain—the second- and third-ranked beer-producing countries—combined. In 1977, only soft-drink production was valued higher ($10 billion) than beer production ($6.7 billion) (the latest available data). Other alcoholic beverages were far less important in the United States than beer: Distilled liquors were valued at $2.3 billion, and wines and brandies at $1.4 billion. U.S. beer production is highly concentrated; about 50 brewing companies own fewer than 100 breweries.

Despite vast production and massive advertising of beer, the United States ranks thirteenth among beer-drinking nations in beer consumption per capita. Nevertheless, the number-one alcoholic beverage in the United States is beer: By volume, beer represented 85 percent of all alcoholic beverages consumed in the United States in 1972. Wisconsin consumed 28.5 gal (108 l) of beer per person, surpassed only by Nevada, the nation's "sin center" for gambling and drinking (Figure 1.8). By com-

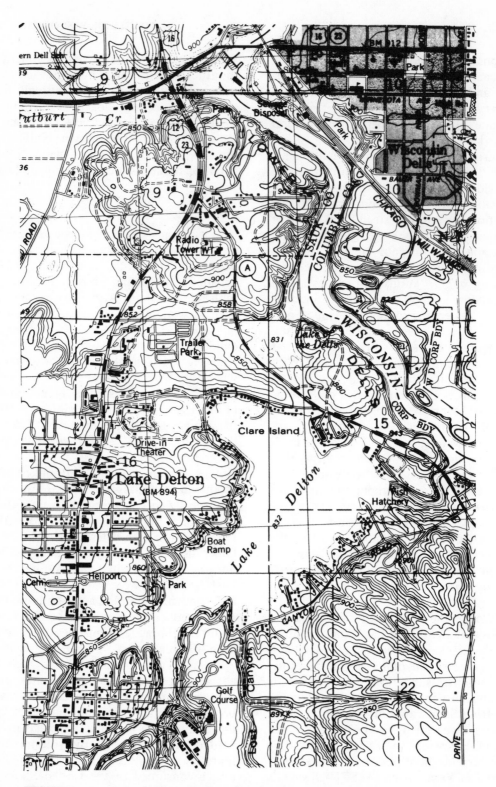

FIGURE 1.5 The Wisconsin Dells recreation area. The topographic map shows the built-up area (solid gray) of Wisconsin Dells and the scattered (and newer) recreational land uses (large black shapes) across the Wisconsin River and along the highway to Lake Delton. (Wisconsin Dells South, 1:24,000)

FIGURE 1.6 (left) Downtown Wisconsin Dells. Gift shops are adjacent to the boat docks for trips on the Upper Dells. (Ingolf Vogeler) FIGURE 1.7 (right) "The Strip," Lake Delton. Motels and large recreational land uses characterize the area between Wisconsin Dells and Lake Delton. (Ingolf Vogeler)

parison, average U.S. beer consumption per person in 1972 was 19.4 gal (73 l). Wisconsin's beer consumption was even more distinctive when its form is considered. The state had the *lowest* ratio of packaged to draft malt beverages consumed (2:1). With 297 legal and illegal drinking bars, taverns, and restaurants per 100,000 adults—the largest proportion in the nation—Wisconsinites enjoyed more of their beer (one-third of it) from taps in neighborhood and crossroads taverns than did other Americans. By contrast, Virginia had only 15 bars, taverns, and restaurants per 100,000 adults. Wisconsin's large German ethnic population, the visibility of six brewing companies in the state, and numerous beer festivals contribute to the high consumption of draft beer.

Breweries

Although the first Wisconsin brewery was started by a Welsh immigrant, the brewing industry was developed by German immigrants in Milwaukee during the 1840s. Pabst was founded in 1844 by Jacob Best, an immigrant from Rheinhessen, Germany. Frederick Pabst, who came from Leipzig, married into the Best family, who also started another brewery that was taken over in 1855 by Frederick Miller. The Schlitz brewing company, under Joseph Schlitz,

grew out of the Krug brewery founded in 1849 by August Krug. The smaller regional breweries in Wisconsin were also started by German immigrants. For example, the original Leinenkugel family arrived from Cologne in 1845 and founded a brewery in Sauk City; their son started the brewery in Chippewa Falls.

A wide distribution of breweries was necessary before the 1870s because beer could not be kept from spoiling after several days (Figure 1.9). After the discoveries of Louis Pasteur led to the development of pasteurization, beer could be safely bottled, and its consumption grew during the 1870s. Thomas Cochran argued that Milwaukee's prominence in brewing came about because of the city's location on the western end of the national beer market. Prior to pasteurization, delivery of a uniform product

TABLE 1.1
Major States Producing Malt Beverages

Major States	No. of Breweries	Employees (1,000)	Value Added ($ Millions)
New York	12	2.9	170.0
Pennsylvania	14	2.6	167.3
Wisconsin	10	7.9	409.4
California	11	2.6	184.5
U.S. total	131	44.0	2,602.5

Source: 1977 Census of Manufactures (Washington, D.C.: U.S. Government Printing Office, 1978, Table 2, p. 20H-9).

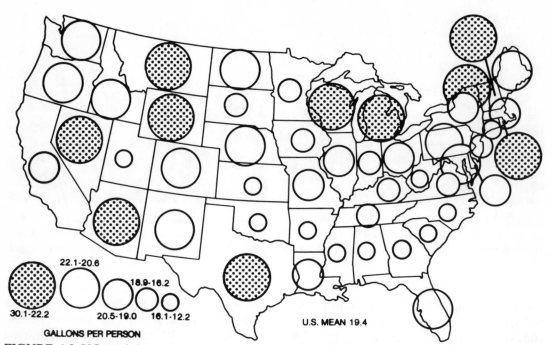

FIGURE 1.8 U.S. malt-beverage consumption by state. (John F. Rooney, Jr., and Paul L. Butt, "Beer, Bourbon, and Boone's Farm: A Geographical Examination of Alcoholic Drink in the United States," *Journal of Popular Culture,* vol. 12 [1978], pp. 832–856. Reprinted by permission of the *Journal of Popular Culture.*)

FIGURE 1.9 Wisconsin breweries, 1850s–1970s. The map shows the total number of breweries each city had during this 120-year period. (Based on data from Wayne L. Kroll, *Badger Breweries: Past and Present* [Jefferson, Wisc.: Wayne L. Kroll, 1976])

to distant markets was difficult. The large breweries in New York, Cleveland, and Chicago did not have to solve distribution problems because they were located in large urban markets, whereas the geographically marginal Milwaukee breweries had the greatest incentive to incorporate pasteurization into their manufacturing processes, in order to break into the large eastern markets. When they did so, they had a decided advantage over breweries in other parts of the United States. During the 1880s and 1890s the three largest Milwaukee breweries—Best (later Pabst), Schlitz, and Blatz—created an elaborate national network for distributing beer. By 1890, malting and brewing was the number one industry in Milwaukee, ranking third in the state, after lumbering and flour milling.

During Prohibition, from 1920 to 1933, beer production officially stopped. Although many of the breweries switched to soft drink production, the financial crisis

FIGURE 1.10 Wisconsin breweries terminated by 1932. With Prohibition many of Wisconsin's breweries ceased production. (Based on data from Wayne L. Kroll, *Badger Breweries: Past and Present* [Jefferson, Wisc.: Wayne L. Kroll, 1976])

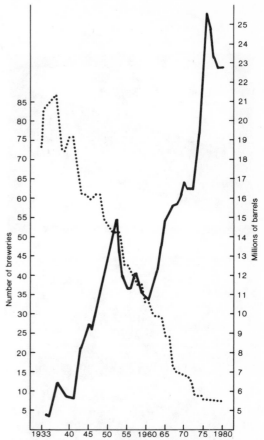

FIGURE 1.11 Wisconsin breweries and production, 1933–1980. Although the number of breweries declined rapidly after the 1930s, total beer production rose dramatically. Production has been concentrated in fewer and fewer breweries. (Based on data from Wayne L. Kroll, *Badger Breweries: Past and Present* [Jefferson, Wisc.: Wayne L. Kroll, 1976])

that ensued accelerated the "rationalization" of the beer industry by destroying many of the smaller-scale breweries (Figure 1.10). Domination of the industry by fewer and fewer companies has continued. In the late nineteenth century, Wisconsin had over 300 breweries; by 1985 only 6 remained (Figure 1.11). The decline in the number of Wisconsin breweries resulted from several factors: (1) Many small breweries were bought up or forced out of business by larger breweries. (2) Large breweries had lower production costs per volume of beer. For example, in the Memphis Schlitz brewery 475 production workers make 6.2 million barrels of beer per year, whereas in the Stevens Point brewery 19 workers make 35,000 barrels. Consequently, a Memphis worker produces seven times more beer than a Stevens Point worker. (3) Beer produced by small breweries, especially in the past, fluctuated in quality. Large breweries have the machinery and professional staff to produce a consistent quality of beer—advertised as a virtue. The decline in the

number of Wisconsin breweries has not meant a decline in beer production. In fact, with the repeal of Prohibition, beer production increased quickly from 4.8 million barrels (676 million l) in 1934 to 22.8 million barrels (3,213 million l) in 1980 (Figure 1.11).

Wisconsin remains the largest producer of beer in the United States. In 1980, 4 of the 10 largest U.S. breweries were located in the state: Joseph Schlitz, Pabst, Miller—all in Milwaukee—and G. Heileman in La Crosse. After a merger in 1981, Schlitz

FIGURE 1.12 Beer labels of Wisconsin's regional breweries. (Reprinted courtesy of Jacob Leinenkugel, Chippewa Falls; Stevens Point, Stevens Point; Hibernia, Eau Claire; and Huber, Monroe)

TABLE 1.2
Production Capacity and Market
Share of Wisconsin Breweries

Brewery	Capacity (Barrels)		Market Share of State (%)
Schlitz	29,000,000		10.0
Miller	20,000,000		6.3
Pabst	18,000,000		44.1
Heileman	6,500,000		15.5
Huber	340,000	(plus beer	
Walter's	150,000	from out	24.1
Leinenkugel	85,000	of state)	
Stevens Point	55,000		
Total	74,130,000		100.0
Concentration: Top 4	99.2%		75.9%

Source: U.S. Federal Trade Commission, The Brewing
Industry. Staff Report of the Bureau of
Economics, December 1978, p. 173.

headquarters were moved to Detroit, and in 1984 the Heileman brewery bought out the Pabst brewery in Milwaukee. Wisconsin also has four smaller regional breweries: Joseph Huber in Monroe, Hibernia (until 1985, Walters) in Eau Claire, Jacob Leinenkugel in Chippewa Falls, and Stevens Point in Stevens Point (Figure 1.12).

Although most of the beer from the small local breweries is sold to Wisconsinites, the state's residents mainly consume beer produced by the nationally known breweries. In 1978, the four largest Wisconsin breweries together sold 76 percent of all beer in the state (Table 1.2). Large breweries dominate beer sales because they have large

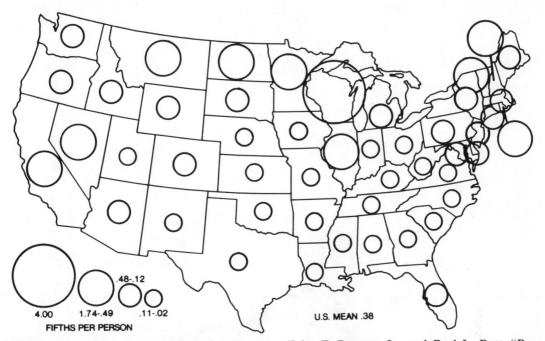

FIGURE 1.13 U.S. brandy consumption by state. (John F. Rooney, Jr., and Paul L. Butt, "Beer, Bourbon, and Boone's Farm: A Geographical Examination of Alcoholic Drink in the United States," *Journal of Popular Culture,* vol. 12 [1978], pp. 832–856. Reprinted by permission of the *Journal of Popular Culture.*)

advertising budgets, which guarantee that their beers are the best known, even though the best-advertised beers do not necessarily mean the best tasting. In Wisconsin, dominant Pabst spent $1.21 per barrel in 1976 to maintain its superior name recognition. Miller, although the second largest brewery in the nation, had the smallest market share of the four big ones in Wisconsin and spent $3 per barrel to capture a greater share of the market.

Brandy

Wisconsin is also distinctive for its high consumption of brandy—over 20 percent of the U.S. intake in 1978. Whereas the U.S. average was 0.38 fifths (1.3 l) per person, Wisconsin's was 4.0 fifths (13.6 l) per person—10.5 times as much. Even Nevada, which had the second highest consumption, averaged only 1.74 fifths (5.9 l) per person. Wisconsin is part of a brandy belt that includes a high concentration of North European ethnic groups (Figure 1.13).

Overall, Wisconsin's consumption of distilled spirits has been larger than the national average.

DAIRYING

The tourist says a cow's face is so fine But I see their back ends most of the time.

—Charlie Maguire,
"Getting in the Cows"

America's Dairyland

Although Wisconsin's auto licenses proclaim that Wisconsin is "America's dairyland," few of the visitors who stop at the many cheese gift shops are attracted to the state primarily for this reason. Yet to the state's farmers and urban workers employed in the dairy industry, this proclamation has a great deal of importance. Situated at the northern edge of the prime U.S. cropland region (Figure 1.14), Wisconsin specializes in dairying, ranking first in the

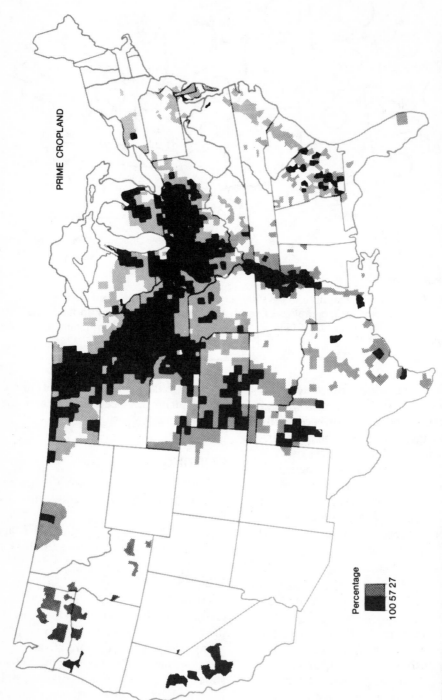

PRIME CROPLAND

Percentage

100 57 27

FIGURE 1.14 Prime cropland as a percentage of total area by county. Only counties with 27 percent or more of their cropland in the U.S. Soil Conservation Service's Class I, II, and III are shown. (Based on U.S., Department of Agriculture, Soil Conservation Service, *Soil and Water Conservation Needs Inventory*, by state, various years)

United States in number of milk cows and in total milk production—in 1982 almost 2 million cows produced 22.7 billion lb (10 billion kg) of milk (Figure 1.15). As the nation's leading cheese-producing state, Wisconsin produced 1.6 billion lb (.7 billion kg) of cheese, or 37 percent of the U.S. total.

The Wisconsin Department of Agriculture promotes dairy-product consumption within and outside the state and makes dairying visible to consumers. Each month a particular agricultural product is promoted. Nine out of the 12 monthly in-state food promotions deal with dairy products— cheese in March, evaporated milk in April, fluid milk in May, all dairy products in June, ice cream in July, butter in August, dry milk in September, cheese in October, and gift cheese in December. The highlight of dairy promotion is the crowning of Alice in Dairyland in June. An employee of the Wisconsin Department of Agriculture for one year, Alice symbolizes Wisconsin's agriculture for millions of people within and outside the state.

Dairy farms are ubiquitous in Wisconsin. The interstate and state highways traverse dairy landscapes accented by the barns and silos of well-kept farmsteads. The crop patterns associated with dairying also add a distinctive motif to Wisconsin's countryside. Cornfields, hay crops, pastures, and woodlots intermingle to provide an ever-changing array of color from spring, through summer, and into the fall.

Barns

Barns are probably the single most visible symbol of the Wisconsin countryside. Their presence helps make the rural landscape interesting and attractive for travelers—a red barn in a wintery scene or a

FIGURE 1.15 Display on a dairy farm. (Ingolf Vogeler)

18

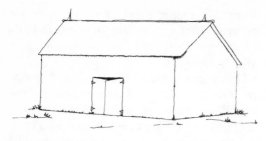

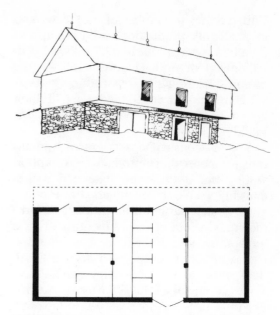

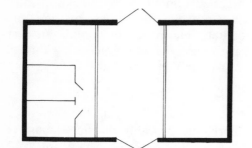

FIGURE 1.16 English barn type.

FIGURE 1.17 German barn type. Notice the forebay projecting over the basement and the bank leading up to the first floor of the barn.

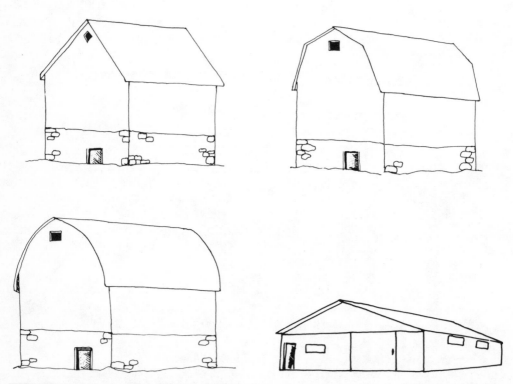

FIGURE 1.18 Barn styles: Gable-roofed (upper left), gambrel-roofed (upper right), gothic-roofed (lower left), and pole (lower right).

set of white barns against the greens of summer is a pleasing sight. The large dairy barns of Wisconsin have been the subjects of paintings and postcards. To visitors from outside the state, barns may have aesthetic value only, but barns are the foremost practical structures reflecting the rural values of hard work, cooperation, and love of the land. Especially on dairy farms, barns are the focus of economic activities and are testimonials to a way of life distinctive to a labor-intensive dairying economy.

Two common barn types, English and Pennsylvania Dutch, are found in Wisconsin. The design for the *English,* or *three-bay,* barns was brought by settlers from New England (Figure 1.16). This barn type has three parts: a central threshing floor and two sides, one side used for livestock and the other for storage of hay and small grains. With the advent of threshing machines, the threshing floor became a drive for hay wagons and was used for storage of machinery during the winter. The *Pennsylvania Dutch*, or more accurately, *German*, barn had its origin in northwestern Europe (Figure 1.17). Germans, who settled first in Pennsylvania and later in Wisconsin, brought the design of this type of barn to the United States. This barn type always has a basement for the dairy cows and a first floor for storing hay and sometimes small grains. The earliest basements were built of local building materials (fieldstones or quarried stones); barns from the 1920s had poured concrete or concrete-block basements. The projection of the first story over the basement results in a *forebay*, which provides shelter for livestock from sun, rain, and snow and allows hay and straw to be thrown into the barnyard without blocking the basement doors. German barns are also *banked*, allowing tractors to pull wagons right into the first story. Banked barns are the most ubiquitous barn type in Wisconsin.

The roofs of Wisconsin barns reflect the ages of the buildings (Figure 1.18). *Gable-roofed* barns are the oldest and were the simplest barns to build. *Gambrel-roofed* barns were built at the beginning of the twentieth century, when dairying became a Wisconsin specialty. *Gothic-roofed* barns became popular during the 1920s; a farmer could store more hay in a gothic-roofed than in a gambrel-roofed barn. Most of the barns built since the 1950s have been *pole* barns. A pole barn consists of a rectangular set of poles covered with colored metal sheets. In the nineteenth and early twentieth centuries, barns were built to last for several generations; pole barns are not expected to last more than 40 years. Barns, like friends, are often taken for granted until they are gone. Now that the labor-intensive wooden hay barns of an earlier agricultural era are being replaced by steel buildings, Wisconsinites are beginning to appreciate the old ones by visiting rural Wisconsin, buying a painting or photo of an old barn, paneling living rooms with barn boards, or eating at Country Kitchens.

Some Wisconsin barns are distinctive because of the murals painted on them. In the past, barns, with their large surfaces and high visibility, were used to advertise flour, tobacco, or beer, but with the advent of free-standing billboards, barns no longer serve as advertising surfaces. Today, barn walls are being used for art. In 1976, 12 barns scattered throughout the state had murals painted on them through the efforts of the Wisconsin Arts Board and its Dairyland Graphics Project. Professional artists supervised, but local people selected the barns and painted the murals. Two of these murals are visible from Interstate 94, one south of Eau Claire and another near Johnston Creek. These two barns catch the eyes of more travelers than do the thousands of "plain" barns in the state!

Converted barns also catch the attention of travelers—reminding us that Wisconsin is indeed a land of barns. Many restaurants and supper clubs are located in former barns. Three of the best known are Rock's Round Barn in Spring Green, the Don Q Inn north of Dodgeville, and Stevenson's III Restaurant in Fontana on the west end of Lake Geneva (Figure 1.19).

FIGURE 1.19 Round Barn Restaurant. This Spring Green restaurant proclaims: "Have a square meal in a round barn." (Ingolf Vogeler)

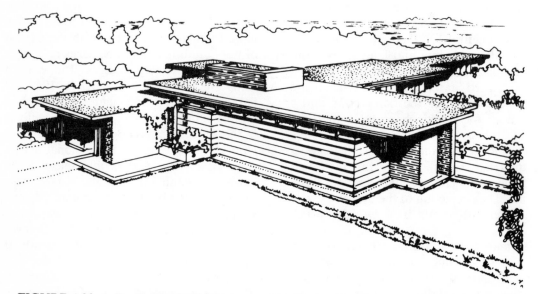

FIGURE 1.20 A Frank Lloyd Wright house. The H. Jacobs house in Madison was built in 1937. Prairie-style houses normally have low-pitched hipped roofs, not flat ones. (D. J. Stith, R. P. Meyer, and J. M. Dean, *Design in Wisconsin Housing: A Guide to Styles* [Madison: University of Wisconsin Extension, 1977, p. 21])

FRANK LLOYD WRIGHT

Although the three words "lakes," "beer," and "cows" reflect the popular images of Wisconsin, a fourth image is equally distinctive and special to those who recognize it. Whereas large dairy barns on farmsteads visually dominate the state's rural vernacular architecture, many of Wisconsin's cities are distinguished by the urban architecture of Frank Lloyd Wright, who is associated with Wisconsin because of his birth, residency, and architectural design. Born in Richland Center in 1869, Wright attended the University of Wisconsin–Madison in civil engineering from 1884–1888. In 1911, Wright, with his mistress, Mamah Borthwick Cheney, moved to Spring Green, Wisconsin, which had been his childhood home, rejecting his wife and six children, his commissions, and the urban setting of Oak Park, a western suburb of Chicago. In Spring Green he built a new home, Taliesin, on his mother's land.

Wright's building designs were part of the Prairie School of architecture, meant to reflect the prairie landscape of the Midwest (Figure 1.20). The emphasis on horizontal lines in the roof styles, the heights of the buildings, and the placement of porches distinguished this style from the late-nineteenth-century, Victorian styles of architecture, which gave a strong vertical appearance. Actually, Wright was influenced by a whole set of traditional architectural styles: by Joseph Lyman Silsbee's midwestern shingle style; by vernacular midwestern house types, especially the common cube-shaped, pyramidal roofed houses; and by traditional Japanese designs that he saw at the Japanese Pavilion in Chicago at the World's Columbia Exposition in 1893.

Outside of Chicago, the largest number of his buildings are in Wisconsin (Figure 1.21). Beginning in 1932 Wright operated a school for architects during the summer months at Taliesin and during the winter

FIGURE 1.21 U.S. distribution of buildings designed by Frank Lloyd Wright, 1887–1953. (Based on data from William Allen Storrer, *The Architecture of Frank Lloyd Wright: A Complete Catalogue* [Cambridge, Mass.: MIT Press, 1974])

months at Paradise Valley in Arizona. Hence, Phoenix has almost as many Wright-designed buildings as Madison. In Wisconsin, Wright's houses are found predominantly in Spring Green, Madison, and metropolitan Milwaukee (Figure 1.22). Taliesin is typical of Wright's prairie style: ground-hugging appearance, overhanging roofs, continuous casement fenestration, walled gardens, terraces, and an extended floor plan.

Wright's reputation became global. When the Tokyo Imperial Hotel, which he designed, withstood the 1923 earthquake, he was hailed as a giant in world architecture. The Johnson Wax Building in Racine, the Unitarian Church in Madison, and Taliesin in Spring Green are among his best works. Wright's creativity put Wisconsin on the architectural map.

Although Wright's personal life-style was not typical of early-twentieth-century midwesterners, his style of architecture was very much appreciated by ordinary people. Geographer Robert Bastian has docu-

mented that in contrast to the clients of other well-known architects of the time, Wright's clients and those of other Prairie School architects were not the social elite (who wanted period revival styles), but rather the middle and lower middle class—professionals, merchants, bookkeepers, and sales personnel—usually in smaller towns. Prairie-style houses appealed to the small-town middle class because they were designed for family living (the central kitchen eliminated the need for servant help) and for easy conversation. Yet the prairie style remained a minor national design because it failed to gain wide acceptance among potential tastemakers in the upper classes of metropolitan Chicago and Minneapolis.

* * *

In this chapter we have seen how popular and individual perceptions and views of Wisconsin make it a distinctive state. In the remaining chapters we will examine systematically various ideas that different groups have had and how their subsequent behaviors created the cultural landscapes of the state. But before doing so, let us consider the major elements of the physical environment with which people had to work.

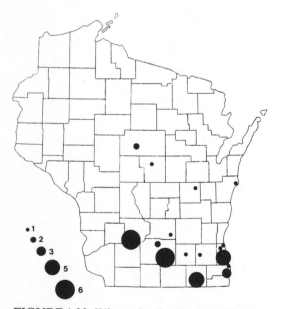

FIGURE 1.22 Wisconsin distribution of houses designed by Frank Lloyd Wright, 1887–1953. (Based on data from William Allen Storrer, *The Architecture of Frank Lloyd Wright: A Complete Catalogue* [Cambridge, Mass.: MIT Press, 1974])

SELECTED REFERENCES

Apps, Jerry, and Allen Strang. *Barns of Wisconsin*. Madison: Tamarack Press, 1977.

Bastian, Robert W. "The Prairie Style House: Spatial Diffusion of a Minor Design." *Journal of Cultural Geography*, vol. 1 (1980), pp. 50–65.

———. "Southeastern Pennsylvania and Central Wisconsin Barns: Examples of Independent Parallel Development." *The Professional Geographer,* vol. 27, no. 2 (May 1975), pp. 200–204.

Cochran, Thomas C. *The Pabst Brewing Company: The History of an American Business.* New York: New York University Press, 1948.

Fitzpatrick, Edward A. *Wisconsin*. Milwaukee: Bruce Publishing, 1931.

Jackson, Michael. *The World Guide to Beer*. Englewood, N.J.: Prentice-Hall, 1977.

Kroll, Wayne L. *Badger Breweries: Past and Present.* Jefferson, Wisc.: Wayne L. Kroll, 1976.

Link, Mike, and Craig Blacklock. *Journey to Door County.* Bloomington, Minn.: Voyageur Press, 1979.

Sergeant, John. *Frank Lloyd Wright's Wisconsin Houses.* New York: Watson-Guptill Publications, 1976.

Storrer, William Allen. *The Architecture of Frank Lloyd Wright: A Complete Catalogue.* Cambridge, Mass.: MIT Press, 1974.

Wisconsin Division of Tourism. *Wisconsin—Summer Escape.* Madison: Department of Development, 1982.

Wright, Frank Lloyd. *The Living City.* New York: Horizon Press, 1958.

_____ . *When Democracy Builds.* Chicago: University of Chicago Press, 1945.

CHAPTER 2

PHYSICAL PROCESSES AND PATTERNS

CLIMATE

Few places on earth experience Wisconsin's variety of weather. Tropical heat and arctic cold, periods of prolonged drought and occasional heavy downpours, ice storms, thunderstorms, and tornadoes—all types of atmospheric disturbances affect the state except hurricanes. What accounts for the variable nature of Wisconsin's weather, and how are human activities influenced by weather features?

Almost daily we hear or read about weather: tornadoes in Oklahoma, droughts in Texas, snow in the Rockies, and heavy rain in coastal New England. *Weather* is the condition of the atmosphere over a short time period, usually less than 24 hours. Over a longer time period, average day-to-day weather conditions form a general pattern of atmospheric conditions that represent an area's *climate*.

Wisconsin's weather and climate are a combination of factors at different scales. At the large scale, Wisconsin's position in the Northern Hemisphere and within the heart of the North American continent is responsible for major seasonal fluctuations. Middle-scale factors largely determine day-to-day weather changes. They include the general westerly circulation of air across the middle latitudes; invasions of warm tropical air masses from the Gulf of Mexico, cold polar air masses from the arctic plains

of Canada, and moderate air masses from the Pacific coast of Washington and Oregon; the fluctuation in the direction and strength of the jet stream; and the alternate patterns of high- and low-pressure systems with their associated cold and warm fronts. Small-scale or local factors, accounting for variations in daily weather conditions, include weather changes related to the presence of water bodies, orientation to the sun, urban versus rural settings, and variations in elevation.

Seasonal Variations

Wisconsin is situated in the middle latitudes, extending from about 42°30′N at the Illinois border to 47° at the Apostle Islands. As a consequence of this position, the intensity of the sun's energy and the length of daylight differ considerably from midsummer to midwinter. In fact the state receives about five times more of the sun's energy in June than in December. At the June solstice (June 21) the earth has revolved to a position around the sun such that the state receives the highest sun angles of the year (68.5° at noon at 45°N). High sun angles and length of daylight (15 hours and 35 minutes) on this first day of summer lead to intense heating and high temperatures. The earth is an effective absorber of solar radiation and in turn radiates back to the atmosphere the energy it absorbs.

However, some objects on the earth's surface, particularly large bodies of water, build up heat in midsummer, and only gradually is the heat radiated to the atmosphere. For this reason the highest temperatures recorded each year in the state are frequently two or three weeks after June 21. Even a slight change in latitude is sufficient to change energy receipt from the sun and consequently to affect temperatures. Average maximum temperatures in July, for example, are about 7°F (2.5°C) lower in the north-central region of the state than in the south-central area.

The earth's position relative to the sun in mid-December is such that Wisconsin receives very low angles of sunlight at noon (22.5°) on December 22, the first day of winter, and the number of daylight hours diminishes to 8 hours and 25 minutes. In fact, for several weeks after December 21, more radiation escapes from the earth at these latitudes than is absorbed, simply because sun angles remain so low. Not until the third week of January does the sun's angle increase sufficiently so that more energy is gained each day by the earth than is lost. For this reason the lowest daily average temperatures each year are in the second week of January—several weeks after the year's shortest daylight period. With the low sun angles in winter and a landscape covered by snow and ice, as much as 90 percent of the sun's energy is reflected back to space on a clear day. The great change in the angle of the sun's energy striking the state accounts for the four distinct seasons each year.

Effects of Bodies of Water

Temperatures change not only because of seasonal variations of absorbed solar energy but also because of the heating and cooling characteristics of land and water. *Specific heat* is the amount of heat (calories) required to raise the temperature of a substance one degree Celsius. Water, which has a higher specific heat than land, responds slowly to heating by the sun and to cooling by energy loss to the atmosphere. Therefore places located along coastal areas generally have cooler summers and warmer winters than places inland. Coastal climates tend to have few great daily or annual temperature changes. Wisconsin lies 900 mi (1,448 km) from the nearest ocean. Its continental climate has much greater temperature variations than does a coastal climate at a similar latitude. For example, the coastal city of Portland, Oregon, which lies at 45.5°N, has a January average temperature of 38°F (3.3°C) and a July average of 67°F (19.4°C). Rhinelander, Wisconsin, at the same latitude, has a January average of 11°F (−11.6°C) and a July average of 68°F (20°C). Portland averages 45 days per year with temperatures below 32°F (0°C); Rhinelander averages 155 days below 32°F (0°C). Similarly, Portland averages 8 days annually over 90°F (32.2°C) and Rhinelander 12 days.

Even large lakes reduce the extremes of temperatures. In Wisconsin, the *lake effect* from Lake Michigan and Lake Superior significantly moderates temperatures. Monthly average temperatures in July increase from Lake Michigan westward and from Lake Superior to the south and west. The average July maximum temperature at Sheboygan on the shore of Lake Michigan is 79°F (26°C), but 150 mi (241 km) west, at La Crosse, the average maximum for July is 83°F (28.3°C). In a similar fashion, the lakes also help to curb extremely low temperatures in winter.

Winds and Air Masses

The general circulation of winds in the atmosphere in the middle latitudes is from west to east. These winds are the *westerlies* and are a feature of middle latitude weather year-round, but they do shift position latitudinally from season to season. During the warmer months the westerlies move farther north. As a result, from late spring until early November, the state has an average wind direction of southwest, whereas in winter the westerlies shift to the south and Wisconsin's winds come mostly from the northwest.

Changes in air pressure cause air to flow from regions of higher pressure to regions of lower pressure. On average, the middle latitudes are a region of low pressure because of the circulation of air in the upper levels of the atmosphere at these latitudes. Average pressures are greater both at higher latitudes and at subtropical latitudes; consequently air flows into the middle latitudes from both polar and subtropical areas. Large volumes of air that move from regions of high pressure around the earth are called *air masses*. Each air mass contains relatively uniform characteristics of temperature and moisture related to surface features of the region in which the air mass originates. A cold, dry air mass, for example, develops over the plains of north-central Canada; a warm, moist air mass forms over the Gulf of Mexico. These air masses travel thousands of miles from their regions of origin. The polar and subtropical air masses that invade Wisconsin bring weather conditions that can vary significantly in temperature and amounts of precipitation. The state typically experiences three types of air masses: the Continental Polar (cP), the Maritime Tropical Gulf (mT), and the Maritime Polar Pacific (mP) (Figure 2.1).

Continental Polar air masses dominate Wisconsin weather in winter. As they plunge across the state from the arctic plains of northern Canada, they generally bring bitterly cold and dry weather and are responsible for occasional record low temperatures. In summer, the cP air mass moves into the state only on rare occasions, and then it brings cool, clear weather.

Maritime Tropical Gulf air masses move northward from the Gulf of Mexico into Wisconsin and dominate summer weather. They are generally heavily laden with moisture and help trigger heavy rains and hot, humid weather. Should these air masses travel through the southwestern Great Plains on their way to the state, they may bring record high temperatures. In winter, mT air masses are generally kept away from Wisconsin by cP air masses. When the mT air masses can push into the southern parts

of the state, they bring mild temperatures and sometimes heavy, wet snow or freezing rain.

Maritime Polar Pacific air masses largely control the weather along the Oregon-Washington coast of North America. They are air masses with moderate temperatures and abundant moisture, but as they head east across the Rocky Mountains and Great Plains much of their moisture is removed before they enter Wisconsin. Hence, these air masses bring moderate temperatures and relatively dry weather in both summer and winter.

Highs, Lows, and Fronts

The different air masses that flow into Wisconsin bring the potential for varying amounts of precipitation depending on the amount of moisture present in the air masses. However, without a mechanism to trigger the condensation process, that is, for converting gaseous water vapor into

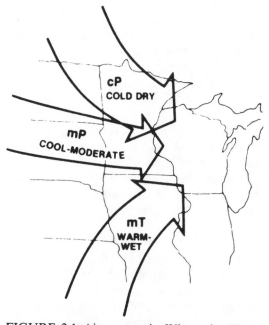

FIGURE 2.1 Air masses in Wisconsin. Three primary air masses influence Wisconsin's weather. (Richard S. Palm and Anthony R. de Souza, *Wisconsin Weather* [Minneapolis: Burgess Publishing, 1983]. Reprinted by permission of the authors.)

either liquid water (rain) or solid water (snow), precipitation would not develop. This is largely the role of low-pressure cells, called *cyclones* (Figure 2.2). Cyclones help generate precipitation when air masses flowing into these systems run together and one air mass rises. When two different air masses collide within a cyclone, the air mass of higher temperature and lower density is forced to rise above the colder, higher-density air mass. Rising air cools and, subsequently, the water vapor in the air begins to condense, forms clouds, and perhaps precipitates. Low-pressure systems therefore bring overcast skies and precipitation. In high-pressure cells, or *anticyclones*, different air masses do not collide, because air flows outward from anticyclones. As a consequence, no air mass is forced to rise, and clear skies result. Pressure cells extend from 500 to 1,500 mi

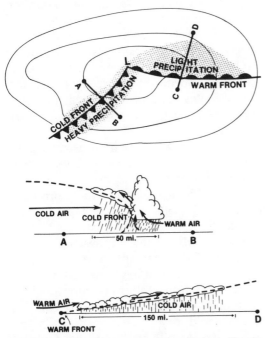

FIGURE 2.2 Cold and warm fronts. Fronts radiate from the cyclone center (top). Profiles of cold front (middle) and warm front (bottom) are also shown. (Richard S. Palm and Anthony R. de Souza, *Wisconsin Weather* [Minneapolis: Burgess Publishing, 1983]. Reprinted by permission of the authors.)

(300–900 km) and influence the weather across several states at one time.

The boundary between two contrasting air masses is called a *front*. Fronts are features of low-pressure systems, where air masses can come together. Fronts extend several hundred or even more than a thousand miles in length. A single cold front in summer, for example, may radiate from the center of a low-pressure cell in upper Michigan into northern Texas, triggering thunderstorms along the entire front. Because warmer air is forced to rise when it collides with cooler air, fronts are major factors for initiating precipitation.

Two major frontal types are common in Wisconsin: cold fronts and warm fronts (Figure 2.2). Cold fronts form where a cold air mass is advancing into a warmer air mass. Weather along a cold front is characterized by thunderstorms and possibly tornadoes in summer, light snow showers in winter, and a decline in temperature. The weather associated with a warm front, in which a warm air mass advances into a cooler air mass, is typically light, steady rain showers in summer, moderate to heavy snowfall in winter, and a rise in temperature.

A glance at an evening television weather map reveals a general pattern of alternating high- and low-pressure cells across North America from west to east (Figure 2.3). These cells travel across Wisconsin and affect any given area for 24 to 48 hours. In winter they can travel from the West coast to the East coast in three to five days, whereas in summer, atmospheric circulation generally is slower and it requires five to seven days for a pressure cell to cross North America. Thus, weather changes more rapidly in winter than in summer, because of the greater frequency with which highs and lows pass over an area.

Storms

Each year Wisconsin experiences several major storms: thunderstorms with heavy rains, lightning, hail, and tornadoes; blizzards; wind storms; and freezing rain. For-

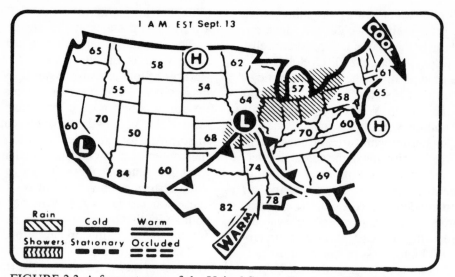

FIGURE 2.3 A forecast map of the United States. Fronts and precipitation are associated with a low-pressure cell and clear weather with highs. Temperatures are average for the areas shown. (From the National Weather Service teletype, National Oceanic and Atmospheric Administration [NOAA])

tunately, very few people die as a result of these storms; however, property damage and loss of crops can total millions of dollars each year.

Wisconsin averages about 35 thunderstorms a year. This rate is similar to that of other states in the Midwest, but much lower than the 70 or more thunderstorms a year common in southeastern states (Figure 2.4). Thunderstorms are primarily features of the warmer months, although they can develop in any month. Cold fronts in low-pressure cells trigger the vast majority of thunderstorms. By midsummer Wisconsin averages two storms per week; the frequency decreases in early and late summer to one per week. These storms usually are responsible for most of the total precipitation in summer and are also the contributors to record daily and monthly amounts. The town of Mellen set the state record for rain in a 24-hour period when it received 11.72 in. (29.77 cm) of rain from a thunderstorm on June 24, 1946. Hail and lightning are often associated with large thunderstorms, although hail is relatively infrequent, falling on an average of only one and one-half to three days per

year across the state. Nonetheless, a farmer can lose an entire year's corn crop in just a few minutes because of hail, and property damage to automobiles, roofs, and windows can be severe. Lightning can be spectacular, beautiful, and deadly. More people in the United States are killed each year by lightning strikes than by any other weather feature.

But no other weather phenomenon strikes as much fear into the people of Wisconsin as do tornadoes. These powerful storms cause considerable destruction of property and even loss of life. On average, 24 tornadoes rip through Wisconsin each year, most frequently in the southwest corner of the state. Tornadoes are formed in thunderstorms along well-developed cold fronts, particularly from mid-May to mid-June, when there is a major temperature contrast between cold, dry cP air from Canada and warm, moist mT air from the Gulf of Mexico. Two-thirds of Wisconsin's tornadoes develop between 3 P.M. and 8 P.M., and travel in a southwest to northeast direction (Figure 2.5); most are about 50 yd (45 m) wide, although some as wide as 1,000 yd (920 m) have occurred; on the

Focus: Wisconsin Thunderstorms

Remembering his boyhood, John Muir described a Wisconsin thunderstorm: The great thunderstorms in particular interested us, so unlike any seen in Scotland, exciting awful, wondering admiration. Gazing awestricken we watched the upbuilding of the sublime cloud-mountains—glowing, sunbeaten pearl and alabaster cumuli, glorious in beauty and majesty and looking so firm and lasting that birds, we thought, might build their nests amid their downy bosses; the black-browed stormclouds marching in awful grandeur across the landscape, trailing broad gray sheets of hail and rain like vast cataracts, and ever and anon flashing down vivid zigzag lightning followed by terrible crashing thunder.

Source: John Muir, *The Story of My Boyhood and Youth* (Boston: Houghton Mifflin Co., 1941).

ground they travel an average distance of 4 mi (6.5 km); and they have wind speeds averaging 100 to 125 mi per hr (160–200 km per hr).

In addition to bitter cold during the winter months, Wisconsin occasionally is blasted by heavy snows accompanied by strong winds and rapidly falling temperatures—the prime ingredients for a blizzard (Figure 2.6). Snowfalls in excess of 4 in. (10 cm) in 24 hours are classified as heavy. When high-velocity winds combine with heavy snow, visibility can be cut to nearly zero, making travel impossible. Deep drifts on roadways can be extremely expensive to remove and usually have a major impact on the budgets of cities and towns.

The Jet Stream

Forecasting weather in Wisconsin and other places in the country would be greatly simplified if meteorologists only needed to know whether a high-pressure or low-pressure system was approaching and what type of air mass, or air masses, was associated with the oncoming system. But highs and lows do not follow a set path across the continent, and the direction they follow varies significantly from week to week. Therefore, forecasters must continually monitor the movement of pressure systems in order to accurately predict the location of air masses and the fronts associated with them. Because the direction in which a pressure system travels can change in less than 24 hours, the weather is difficult to predict for more than one day ahead.

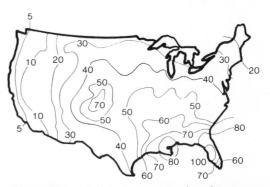

FIGURE 2.4 Annual average thunderstorms across the United States. (Data are from NOAA)

FIGURE 2.5 Major tornado tracks in Wisconsin. They display a primary southwest to northeast pattern. (Richard S. Palm and Anthony R. de Souza, *Wisconsin Weather* [Minneapolis: Burgess Publishing, 1983]. Reprinted by permission of the authors.)

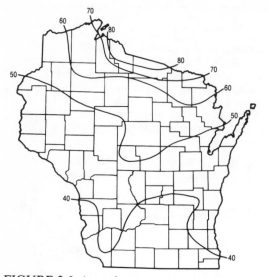

FIGURE 2.6 Annual average snowfall (inches). (Based on a map by the U.S. Department of Agriculture)

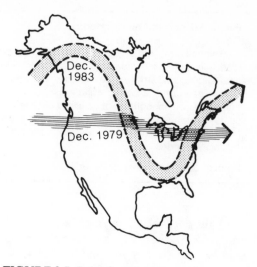

FIGURE 2.7 Polar front jet stream. Large north-south waves usually result in significant departures from normal temperatures and precipitation (December 1983). A nearly direct west-to-east pattern is typified by moderate weather conditions (December 1979). (Richard S. Palm and Anthony R. de Souza, *Wisconsin Weather* [Minneapolis: Burgess Publishing, 1983]. Reprinted by permission of the authors.)

What causes pressure systems to change direction so markedly? In the middle latitudes in the upper atmosphere at elevations of about 18,000 ft (5,500 m) to 40,000 ft (12,000 m) winds flow from west to east at velocities of 75 to 180 mi per hr (120–290 km per hr). These high-velocity winds, called the *jet stream,* meander back and forth in a snakelike pattern across the middle latitudes (Figure 2.7). The jet stream dictates the path that high- and low-pressure cells will follow near the earth's surface. The greatest single problem in forecasting weather is that the jet stream frequently changes its path in an unpredictable way; meteorologists do not know exactly when it will change and in what new direction it will head. Without such knowledge, detailed weather forecasts beyond 48 hours in advance are largely educated guesses.

Climate of Selected Cities

The data on day-to-day and season-to-season weather, accumulated over many years, provide an "averaged" weather, or climate, for the state. Based upon the combined elements of weather, Wisconsin's climate may be described as humid with four distinct seasons. Table 2.1 provides the monthly and annual average weather conditions for six cities across Wisconsin.

LANDFORMS

Wisconsin has some of the most beautiful scenery on earth: steep erosional hills and valleys, glacial deposits, about 15,000 lakes in addition to two of the Great Lakes, large rivers, a mixture of natural vegetation types, and diversified soils. To understand these variations requires a brief glimpse of the geologic past.

Geologic History

Unlike many western states, or those east of the Appalachians, Wisconsin has not undergone massive movements of the underlying rock structure to create mountains or valleys. Generally, Wisconsin has had a relatively stable geologic history. The oldest bedrock underlying the state is ancient Precambrian crystalline rock, such as

TABLE 2.1
Temperature and Precipitation for Six Wisconsin Cities

Milwaukee

Month	Temperatures (°F)				Melted Precipitation (in.)		Snow (in.)	
	Average		Record					
	Max.	Min.	Max.	Min.	Average	Record	Average	Record
Jan	27	12	62	−26	1.57	4.04	12.1	33.6
Feb	30	16	65	−19	1.24	3.10	8.6	34.0
Mar	39	24	77	−10	2.31	6.93	10.5	26.7
Apr	53	35	91	12	3.06	7.31	2.1	15.8
May	64	44	90	21	2.58	4.55	0	0.4
June	75	55	99	36	3.55	8.28	0	0
July	79	60	100	44	2.77	7.07	0	0
Aug	80	61	105	40	3.64	7.66	0	0
Sept	71	52	98	30	2.83	9.41	0	0
Oct	60	42	89	18	2.18	6.42	0	0.8
Nov	44	29	78	−8	1.97	3.91	2.1	13.0
Dec	32	18	64	−21	2.01	4.34	10.6	27.9
Total					29.71		46.0	

Madison

Month	Temperatures (°F)				Melted Precipitation (in.)		Snow (in.)	
	Average		Record					
	Max.	Min.	Max.	Min.	Average	Record	Average	Record
Jan	25	7	56	−37	1.17	3.31	8.8	31.8
Feb	30	11	63	−28	1.04	3.90	6.2	17.9
Mar	40	21	82	−29	2.05	5.04	10.0	28.4
Apr	57	34	94	0	2.90	7.19	1.7	17.4
May	69	44	101	20	3.29	9.35	0	5.0
June	79	54	100	31	3.99	9.95	0	0
July	83	58	101	35	4.04	7.56	0	0
Aug	79	61	107	36	3.28	10.93	0	0
Sept	71	53	99	25	3.74	10.69	0	0
Oct	59	42	90	13	2.29	5.95	0.3	5.2
Nov	43	29	77	−11	2.03	7.86	3.1	14.9
Dec	29	17	62	−23	1.37	3.65	7.3	24.6
Total					31.19		37.4	

32

TABLE 2.1 (Cont.)

Green Bay

Month	Temperatures (°F) Average		Record		Melted Precipitation (in.)		Snow (in.)	
	Max.	Min.	Max.	Min.	Average	Record	Average	Record
Jan	23	6	50	-31	1.18	2.64	9.6	28.0
Feb	27	9	55	-26	1.07	3.56	8.1	21.7
Mar	36	19	73	-29	1.78	4.68	8.9	32.1
Apr	53	33	89	7	2.73	5.52	2.0	11.8
May	66	43	91	21	3.03	9.70	.1	3.5
June	76	53	97	32	3.15	8.47	0	0
July	80	58	104	40	3.40	6.50	0	0
Aug	78	56	100	38	2.66	7.31	0	0
Sept	70	48	95	24	3.23	7.80	0	0
Oct	59	38	88	15	2.11	5.00	0.1	2.5
Nov	42	26	72	-7	1.75	4.99	3.7	14.1
Dec	28	13	62	-21	1.45	3.15	9.5	27.0
Total					27.54		42.0	

Eau Claire

Month	Temperatures (°F) Average		Record		Melted Precipitation (in.)		Snow (in.)	
	Max.	Min.	Max.	Min.	Average	Record	Average	Record
Jan	20	0	55	-45	.93	3.47	10.2	35.3
Feb	26	4	61	-34	.71	3.10	7.2	28.2
Mar	37	17	82	-35	1.48	4.82	9.1	36.9
Apr	55	32	92	0	2.77	7.07	2.2	31.1
May	68	44	107	20	3.88	10.54	0	3.0
June	77	54	105	30	4.09	9.85	0	0
July	81	58	111	42	3.89	8.78	0	0
Aug	79	56	104	36	3.81	11.64	0	0
Sept	69	47	101	23	3.37	9.82	0	0
Oct	59	37	89	7	2.28	10.35	0.1	5.9
Nov	40	23	79	-18	1.27	5.42	4.1	16.3
Dec	26	8	63	-30	1.08	3.05	9.9	31.4
Total					29.56		42.8	

TABLE 2.1 (Cont.)

Rhinelander

Month	Temperatures (°F) Average		Record		Melted Precipitation (in.)		Snow (in.)	
	Max.	Min.	Max.	Min.	Average	Record	Average	Record
Jan	21	1	53	−40	1.05	3.54	11.6	31.5
Feb	26	3	60	−41	.82	2.82	9.7	39.5
Mar	36	14	74	−36	1.47	4.09	9.8	27.4
Apr	53	30	92	−4	2.22	4.79	2.8	13.7
May	66	41	99	20	3.53	6.86	.5	11.0
June	75	51	104	30	4.01	10.22	0	0
July	79	55	108	31	3.84	8.62	0	0
Aug	77	54	97	33	4.02	8.89	0	0
Sept	67	46	95	24	3.84	8.38	0	0.5
Oct	57	37	86	9	2.29	5.90	0	6.0
Nov	38	23	79	−11	1.76	4.09	6.5	21.5
Dec	25	9	61	−31	1.28	3.32	13.2	46.0
Total					30.13		54.1	

Superior

Month	Temperatures (°F) Average		Record		Melted Precipitation (in.)		Snow (in.)	
	Max.	Min.	Max.	Min.	Average	Record	Average	Record
Jan	20	0	53	−37	.95	3.79	9.6	28.8
Feb	25	3	60	−38	.75	2.20	9.4	22.0
Mar	35	14	70	−38	1.34	8.38	9.6	29.0
Apr	50	28	92	−2	2.18	6.37	3.6	16.9
May	61	36	94	11	3.61	6.96	.4	5.0
June	71	45	96	25	3.36	6.83	0	0
July	78	52	99	34	4.23	9.99	0	0
Aug	76	52	99	31	4.07	8.63	0	0
Sept	67	45	93	19	2.86	7.00	0	0
Oct	57	36	89	10	2.25	5.91	0.2	4.0
Nov	39	23	74	−15	1.59	3.43	5.6	20.0
Dec	26	8	60	−29	1.01	2.82	10.9	35.5
Total					28.20		49.3	

Source: Data supplied by NOAA.

granites, quartzites, and slates, formed by volcanic activity more than 1 billion years ago. Most of these ancient rocks are deeply buried by more recent geologic deposits, although they are near the surface in the northern part of the state (Figure 2.8). Several major landform features such as the Baraboo Range, Rib Mountain, Tim's Hill, and the Penokee-Gogebic Range are visible reminders of this Precambrian period (see Table 2.2).

The majority of the bedrock in the state is derived from sediments deposited in ancient seas during the Paleozoic era (1 billion to 200 million years ago). The sedimentary rocks—the limestone, dolomite, shale, sandstone, and conglomerate that cover all the Precambrian rocks except those of the north—are Wisconsin's principal aquifers, containing the state's groundwater supply. Many of these rocks are utilized as building stone such as Lannon Stone and Fond du Lac Sandstones. Agricultural lime, extensively used to reduce soil acidity, is derived from limestone.

No bedrock in the state is younger than Mississippian age (260 million years ago), a period late in the Paleozoic. Since then, glacial and stream erosion have altered land surface features. Until 900,000 years ago, during the Mesozoic and early Cenozoic eras, erosion and some deposition modified

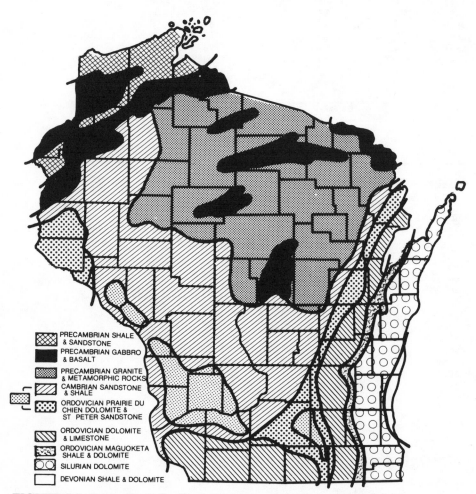

PRECAMBRIAN SHALE & SANDSTONE
PRECAMBRIAN GABBRO & BASALT
PRECAMBRIAN GRANITE & METAMORPHIC ROCKS
CAMBRIAN SANDSTONE & SHALE
ORDOVICIAN PRAIRIE DU CHIEN DOLOMITE & ST PETER SANDSTONE
ORDOVICIAN DOLOMITE & LIMESTONE
ORDOVICIAN MAGUOKETA SHALE & DOLOMITE
SILURIAN DOLOMITE
DEVONIAN SHALE & DOLOMITE

FIGURE 2.8 Generalized distribution of bedrock in Wisconsin. (Based on a map by the Wisconsin Geological and Natural History Survey, Madison)

TABLE 2.2
Generalized Geologic History of Wisconsin

Era	Period	Years Before Present	Present Characteristics & Features
Cenozoic	Quaternary (includes Pleistocene and Recent)	9,000	Recent epoch. Post-glacial period. Development of modern-day landscapes by erosion. Present stream patterns, Wisconsin Dells, soils and vegetation; Great Lakes adjust to current levels.
		900,000	Pleistocene epoch. Advance and retreat of glaciers. Deposited materials for present glacial features, inland lakes and wetlands, and formed basins for the Great Lakes.
	Tertiary		A period of uplifts and erosion. Northern Wisconsin lifted higher and sedimentary rocks eroded away exposing Precambrian in north.
Mesozoic	Cretaceous		Only partially eroded in south. Development of present distribution of bedrock. Major features today are the cliffs along Lake Winnebago, Door Peninsula, Blue Mounds, and other bluffs, such as Camp Douglas, Roche a Cri; hill country in southwest, Mississippi River valley, and Devils Lake gorge.
	Jurassic		
	Triassic		
	Permian		
	Pennsylvanian	260,000,000	
Paleozoic	Mississippian		A period of submergence beneath ancient seas and deposition of muds, sands, and gravels that hardened into rock: limestone, dolomite, shale, sandstone. These rocks covered all the ancient Precambrian rocks. Today's exposed sedimentary rocks are derived from this time. Includes building stones such as Lannon Stone, Fond du Lac Sandstone, agricultural lime; and principal aquifers. Zinc and lead deposits laid in southwestern Wisconsin.
	Devonian		
	Silurian		
	Ordovician		
	Cambrian	475,000,000	
Precambrian		600,000,000	A period of erosion. Most ancient rocks eroded to form a nearly flat plain except for some resistant features such as the Baraboo Range, Rib Mountain, Tim's Hill, and the Penokee-Gogebic Range.
		1,100,000,000?	Development of ancient crystalline rocks such as granites, quartzite, slates, and basalt. Some volcanic activity formed rocks for the Baraboo Range, Rib Mountain and iron ores of northern Wisconsin.

Source: Based on Robert Finley, Geography of Wisconsin (Madison: University of Wisconsin, 1976, p. 6).

the land. Also during this period the bedrock underlying northern Wisconsin was gradually forced upward, resulting in the lifting of the land surface into a dome. At the same time erosion stripped away much of the sedimentary rocks in the north, but only partially eroded those in the south. Running water shaped the land into hills and valleys, and several of today's prominent land features owe their formation to this time: the high ridge east of Lake Winnebago; the Blue Mounds and Platte Mounds; the bluffs of Camp Douglas, Roche a Cri, Friendship Mound, and Ship Rock; the steep hill country of southwestern Wisconsin; the coulee country along the Mississippi River; the Dells of the Wisconsin River; and the Devils Lake gorge.

Glaciation

In the Pleistocene period, glaciers advanced and melted away four separate times. Glaciation helped to modify the existing landforms by carving away rock in some places, completely covering the bedrock with deposited glacial debris in others, and altering the drainage pattern of rivers and streams. Continental glaciers, or ice sheets more than several hundred feet thick, advanced into the state from Canada for the first time about 900,000 years ago. This stage of glaciation, called the Nebraskan, is thought to have lasted several tens of thousands of years before the ice sheets melted to a position north of Hudson Bay. About 200,000 years passed before the second, or Kansan, stage advanced into the state. As with the previous stage, the ice melted only to reappear during the Illinoian stage 300,000 years later (200,000 years ago). The Wisconsin stage, which marks the last glacial advance, began about 70,000 years ago and ended about 9,000 years ago, and it has had the most effect on today's land surface because it covered the deposits of the previous stages (Figure 2.9).

One area in the state was completely surrounded by glacial ice, but was itself never covered by any glacial advances. This unglaciated region, shown in Figure 2.10,

FIGURE 2.9 A glacial landscape. Glacial deposits often leave very stony soils. (Ingolf Vogeler)

is referred to as the Driftless Area because no drift (glacially deposited sand, rocks, and boulders) was deposited there. The failure of glaciers to cover this area was due to the inability of the advancing ice to override the high elevations in the north-central region of the state. Instead, the ice flowed more easily to the east through the Lake Michigan basin and to the west down the lowland occupied today by the Minnesota and Des Moines rivers. The glacier joined together again in Illinois just south of the Wisconsin border.

Glaciers during the Wisconsin stage progressed through three periods of advance and retreat within the state's borders. After the earliest period, a layer of glacial drift remained free of glacial ice for more than 12,000 years before later advances occurred. As a result, these older drift regions (Figure 2.11) were exposed to weathering and erosion long enough to remove much of their

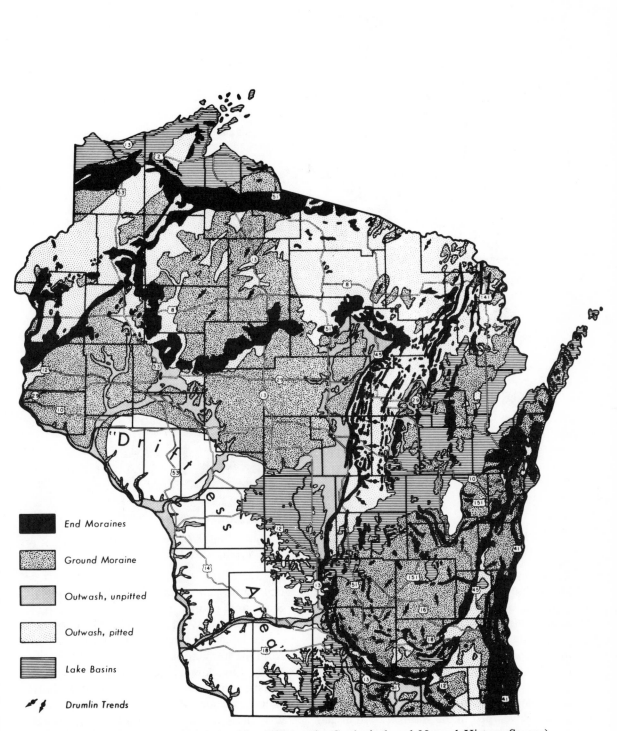

End Moraines

Ground Moraine

Outwash, unpitted

Outwash, pitted

Lake Basins

Drumlin Trends

FIGURE 2.10 Wisconsin glacial deposits. (Wisconsin Geological and Natural History Survey)

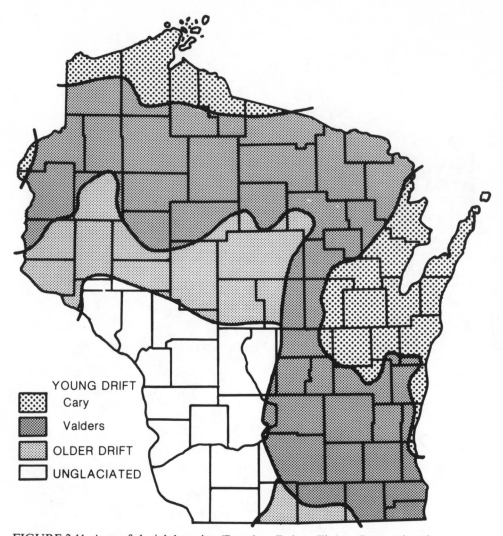

FIGURE 2.11 Ages of glacial deposits. (Based on Robert Finley, *Geography of Wisconsin: A Content Outline* [Madison: College Printing and Typing Co., 1965], p. 50)

glacial landforms, smooth the major irregularities of the land, and establish well-defined stream systems.

During the past 30,000 years the latest advances of ice penetrated the region. These deposits provide much of the character of the land surface in the northern one-third and eastern half of the state. Drainage is poorly developed in the younger drift areas; lakes and swamps are numerous; and landforms are highly irregular, with rolling hills and a generally rugged countryside. Youthful-appearing glacial landforms dot the young drift regions: moraines, eskers, ket-

tles, kames, crevasse fillings, and drumlins. State and county parks have been established on many of these glacial deposits.

As the glaciers melted, large lakes formed from the tremendous volume of runoff meltwater. One large lake, Glacial Lake Wisconsin, covered much of Juneau, Adam, Wood, Jackson, Monroe, and Sauk counties. Originally the lake drained down the Black River, but as the ice melted further east it cut through glacial deposits near Wisconsin Dells and drained down the Wisconsin River. The great volume of meltwater cut deeply into the underlying sandstone that is known today as the Dells of the Wisconsin River. Much of the present landform in these counties reflects its origin as a former lake bottom: It is relatively flat and poorly drained, and its peat bogs support a major cranberry industry. As the ice continued to melt, the Lake Michigan and Lake Superior basins, which had been carved by advancing glaciers, were filled with meltwater.

In summary, although in some places glaciers stripped away the loose preglacial materials, exposing the bedrock beneath, most glacial action in the state was depositional and in this way changed the surface features of much of the state. To the south of ice margins, many areas were made flat by outwash and lake plains (Figure 2.10). Where ice had stood, a surface of remarkable irregularity was created by deposits ranging from tens of feet to hundreds of feet thick. Some preglacial features could not be destroyed or buried by glacial action, and these features retained much of their preglacial character. Drainage patterns established during preglacial periods were totally obliterated by glacial action. Meltwaters sought the easiest paths downslope, often to be impounded in deep drift, creating lakes and swamps connected by numerous small streams. These lakes are a vital part of Wisconsin's tourist and recreation attractions. The major rivers in Wisconsin flow in channels carved by meltwater from receding glaciers.

Glacial deposits in the state are the parent material from which postglacial soils are derived. In northern sections this material is largely composed of ground-up crystalline Precambrian rocks that yield generally coarse, granular, highly acidic soils abundant in sand—soils that are not as conducive to agriculture as are soils in the eastern and southern regions of Wisconsin. When acid rain, created when rain absorbs atmospheric pollution, falls on these soils, the water that infiltrates the soil and penetrates to the groundwater, as well as that which runs off the land surface into lakes and streams, remains especially acidic (Fig-

ure 2.12). If acid levels in water are too high, the flora and fauna of the region are likely to be adversely affected. In the eastern region, the glacial materials are derived largely from disintegrated dolomitic rocks that yield soils abundant in soluble carbonates and have a considerable volume of silt and clay. These soils are generally fertile and counteract acid rain by neutralizing the acid as water filters through the soil.

The depth and character of the glacial deposits also affect water supplies, soils, and building resources. In northern sections of the state, the Precambrian bedrock lacks the porosity to trap water. But glacial deposits, which are porous, are capable of trapping moisture as it seeps into the ground and thus serve as the source of well water. In many areas, running water sorted glacial deposits into large accumulations of sand, pebbles, and gravel. These separated deposits are valuable sources of road-building materials.

Physiographic Regions

Wisconsin's varied geologic history has resulted in the physical structure of the state's landforms or physiography. Wisconsin is structurally an upwarped dome that slopes downward to the east, west, and south from its highest point in the north-central region. For descriptive convenience, the state can be divided into five regions, each possessing distinctive landform characteristics: Lake Superior Lowland, Northern Highland, Central Plain, Western Upland, and the Eastern Ridges and Lowlands (Figure 2.13).

Lake Superior Lowland. At Wisconsin's northern extreme is a narrow plain, 10 to 20 mi (16–32 km) wide bordering Lake Superior. This plain is a *graben*, or fallen piece of earth's crust, formed by faulting. Bordering the plain on the south is a steep ridge, or escarpment, that rises 300 to 400 ft (91–122 m). The Black, Amnicon, and Brule rivers have cut deep valleys into the escarpment, and they continue to erode

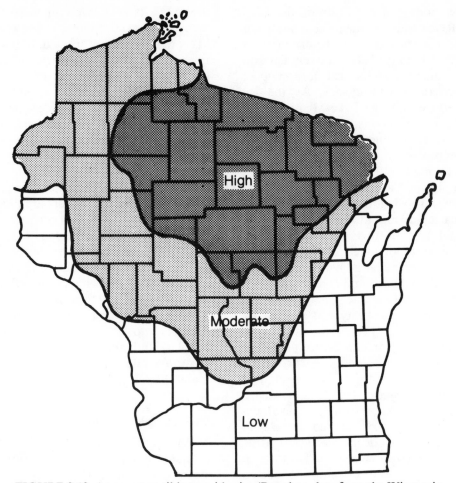

FIGURE 2.12 Areas susceptible to acid rain. (Based on data from the Wisconsin Department of Natural Resources)

channels, tumbling over waterfalls and rapids as they flow to Lake Superior. The Black River at Manitou Falls in Pattison State Park cascades 160 ft (49 m) over the escarpment.

Forest dominates the landscape in this region and, in combination with Lake Superior, makes this an important region for tourism. The Apostle Islands National Park and Madeline Island are extremely popular. Tourism, however, has not always been the primary economic activity in this area. Superior and Ashland were established as major shipping points in the 1800s. Iron mines operated in the Penokee-Gogebic Range near Hurley from the 1830s until the mid-1960s, and the ore was shipped from Ashland. Shipbuilding was also a major activity at these ports but has decreased in importance substantially since the 1940s. Agriculture was never a primary activity because of the heavy clay soils and short growing season, although small dairy farms serving local urban markets are scattered across the region.

Northern Highland. A high, gently rolling plain with isolated hills characterizes this region. Because of the arching of northern Wisconsin into a dome during the late Paleozoic period, the Northern Highland has the greatest average elevation in the state; from an average high of 1,708 ft (521 m) above sea level at Land O' Lakes, elevations decrease gradually in all directions. Nearly the entire region has been covered by glacial deposits of varying

FIGURE 2.13 Physiographic regions of Wisconsin. (Loyal Durand, Jr., "Physiographic Diagram of Wisconsin." Copyright Permission: Hammond Incorporated, Maplewood, New Jersey.)

depths. Although the general landform originated in preglacial times, the glacial deposits greatly modified drainage, resulting in numerous lakes, swamps, waterfalls, rapids, and irregular stream patterns, as well as making the soils stoney and sandy. Hills in the Northern Highland are either resistant Precambrian monadnocks, sandstone outliers, or moraine deposits. Resistant monadnocks include the Gogebic Range in Iron and Ashland counties, the Barron Hills (Blue Hills), Flambeau Ridge, McCaslen Mountain, Thunder Mountain, and Rib

Mountain; sandstone outliers are sparsely scattered throughout Portage, Wood, and Clark counties, and moraine hills are a feature of the terminal moraines formed by ice of the Wisconsin age. Most dramatic in terms of elevation are Tim's Hill, the highest point in Wisconsin (1,953 ft or 595 m), and Pearson Hill (1,944 ft or 593 m), both in Price County; Rib Mountain in Marathon County rises 1,941 ft (592 m) above sea level.

In the older drift areas of the Northern Highland, south of the terminal moraines, the landforms are best described as midway between nonglaciated erosional landforms and newly glaciated landforms. In these areas, most of the lakes and swamps are gone, streams have evolved to include their own tributaries, and landforms are generally more erosional than depositional. Glacial deposits behind the terminal moraines are youthful, covering bedrock to depths of about 75 to 100 ft (23–30 m). Features of glacial deposition of all types are a part of the variety of landforms in this region. And only a very few places on earth have as many lakes per square mile as those formed on the glacial deposits in Vilas, Oneida, and Iron counties.

The Northern Highland has never been a prime agricultural region because of poor soils and abundant wetlands; a limited growing season further restricts most agricultural activities. The cool summer season, however, does favor the growth of potatoes, and cranberries are grown on the wetland soils. Small dairy farms also dot the landscape, although agriculture remains a secondary activity. The many forests of the region were used by early settlers for lumber; the virgin forests were virtually extinct by World War I, but second-growth forests in the region are today the source for an extensive pulpwood industry. Pulp mills are numerous along the Wisconsin River and are very important economically to such cities as Rhinelander, Tomahawk, Merrill, and Wausau. The landscape of forests and numerous lakes formed by the glaciers is the basis for tourism, the leading economic activity in the region. The "Northwoods" attract people not only from throughout Wisconsin but also from neighboring states and beyond. Many towns in the region double or even triple their populations during the summer months as people come to enjoy pleasant temperatures, lakes, and forests. Communities such as Eagle River, Monocqua-Woodruff, Rhinelander, Three Lakes, Hayward, and Spooner rely on tourist dollars from June through August to provide most of their annual income.

Central Plain. Bordering on the southern edge of the Northern Highland is the Central Plain (also called the Central Sand Plain)—a lowland formed mostly on sandstone. Generally, the local relief is less than 100 ft (30 m). The lowland is covered in parts by river deposits, glacial lake deposits, glacial drift, and large marshes and swamps. In some of the unglaciated sections, resistant sandstone buttes and mesas project vertically above the surrounding plains. Many of these rock features have been eroded into shapes resembling castlelike turrets and spires.

Two regions of young glacial deposits exist in the Central Plain: (1) the northwest corner of the region behind the southern extent of glacial deposits and (2) areas east of the western margins of glacial deposits (see Figure 2.10). Landforms in these areas are typically irregular and undulating with a poorly defined drainage network, swamps, kettle lakes, and numerous glacial deposition features. Older glacial drift deposited during the earliest part of the Wisconsin stage covers portions of Eau Claire, Dunn, Barron, Clark, Wood, and Chippewa counties (see Figure 2.11). These areas display more mature erosional landforms with better-defined stream networks, fewer lakes and swamps, and bedrock hills, with their upper slopes unglaciated, projecting through the glacial drift.

In the unglaciated sections of the region, the lowland is a gently rolling plain interrupted by highly scattered buttes and mesas (Figure 2.14). One area in which these irregularly carved buttes are easily seen is along Interstate 94 between Tomah and Mauston. Mill Bluff at Camp Douglas, Roche a Cri and Friendship Mound in Adams County, and Sheep Pasture Mound in Juneau County are other spectacular examples of these erosional features.

A large section of the unglaciated Central Plain was covered during the Wisconsin stage by Glacial Lake Wisconsin. This lake, at its greatest extent, covered 1,825 sq mi (4,730 sq km) of Adams, Juneau, Jackson, Monroe, and Wood counties to a depth of

FIGURE 2.14 Castle Rock at Camp Douglas. This sandstone erosional butte rises over 100 ft (30 m) above the surrounding plain. (Ingolf Vogeler)

75 to 150 ft (23–46 m). Initially it drained west down the Black River but at a later stage was diverted into the Wisconsin River. The area today is a very flat plain dotted by large swamps with highly porous sandy soils covering impervious clay.

The Dells of the Wisconsin River, the most unusual feature of the Central Plain, were formed as the river eroded a channel through sandstone bedrock of varying resistance. For about 7 mi (11 km) the river flows in a narrow gorge with nearly vertical walls up to 100 ft (30 km) high; side canyons gouged by the river and small tributaries add to the unusual appearance of the landform. The Dells of the Wisconsin River are the focal point for one of the most intensive tourist-related industries in the Midwest. The cities of Wisconsin Dells and Lake Delton contain many motels, amusement parks, theme parks, restaurants, and river trips, and the area explodes in population from the end of the school year in June to Labor Day, although nearly all tourist activities close during the winter season.

The Central Plain is among the least-populated regions in the state because of its sandy soils, directly attributed to glacial deposits, that limit agriculture. As in the Northern Highland, potatoes and cranberries are the two leading crops in the region. Second-growth pine forest provides raw material for the pulp and paper industries, which are concentrated at Stevens Point and Wisconsin Rapids on the Wisconsin River.

Western Upland. Of all the landform regions in the state, the Western Upland has the most rugged terrain. Lying 200 to 300 ft (60–90 m) above the Central Plain, this dissected upland has four sections: St. Croix River to Chippewa River; Chippewa River to La Crosse River; La Crosse River to Military Ridge; and Military Ridge to the Illinois border (see Figure 2.13).

The St. Croix–Chippewa section is mostly a plateau with steep hills and deeply cut valleys. Tributaries to the Mississippi erode significantly into the upland. Where glacial deposits are young, they are thick and not greatly weathered. However, most of the section is covered by older drift, highly weathered; lakes and swamps are absent, and moraines are generally not major features.

Wide, flat valleys with narrow ridges typify the landforms in the Chippewa–La Crosse section. Valleys are usually more than 1 mi (1.6 km) wide, and ridges sit 300 to 400 ft (91–122 m) above the valley floors. Along the eastern margin of this section where it meets the Central Plain, lies a steep slope or escarpment that rises 150 to 300 ft (46–91 m) above the plain. This escarpment extends northwest-southeast from Eau Claire to Tomah.

The La Crosse–Military Ridge section is a strongly dissected upland with ridges and valleys dividing the land equally. Most ridges are capped with resistant dolomite, whereas valleys are cut into sandstone. The French name *coulee* is commonly applied to the deeply cut valleys of this region. The Baraboo Range, which rises 500 to 800 ft (150–245 m) above the surrounding region, reaches a maximum elevation of 1,620 ft (494 m) above sea level. Several streams have cut gaps into the range. One large gap, cut by the ancestor of the Wisconsin River, contains Devils Lake State Park. An escarpment extends along the eastern edge of this section from Tomah to Baraboo, where it turns westward and forms an irregular zigzag wall to the Mississippi River at La Crosse.

The Military Ridge–Illinois border section lies south of the coulee region. The Military Ridge runs east-west, parallel to the south bank of the Wisconsin River for roughly 60 mi (97 km), varying in width from 1 to 12 mi (1.6–19 km) and rising about 500 ft (152 m) above the Wisconsin River. Asymmetrical in shape, it has a short, steep north-facing slope and a long, gradual south slope. Streams on the north slope are only 1 to 4 mi (1.6–6.4 km) long and join the Wisconsin River. Near the eastern edge of Military Ridge are the Blue Mounds, hills capped by resistant dolomite or shale. West Blue Mound is the highest point in southern Wisconsin (1,716 ft or 523 m). Underground water has eroded more than a dozen caves in these dolomite hills; Cave of the Mounds—the largest cave in the state—is a tourist attraction. This entire section slopes gradually south at the rate of 6 to 8 ft per mi (1.8 to 2.4 m per km). Because of the resistant dolomite and sandstone caps on the ridges, stream valleys in this section are very narrow and increase in depth and width to the south. Most of this section was unglaciated except for eastern Dane, Green, and Rock counties. Landforms here have gentler slopes and broader valleys, and few glacial features are noticeable because the older drift is greatly weathered.

Flowing along the entire western edge of this region is the Mississippi River. The river flows in a gorge over 200 mi (322 km) long from Prescott to Dubuque. The valley bottom is from 1 to 6.5 mi (1.6–10.4 km) wide, and valley walls rise 200 to 650 ft (61–198 m) above the river. For picturesque scenery, a trip along Wisconsin Highway 35 is highly recommended.

The Western Upland is generally an agricultural region. Dairy farms dominate the rural scene, but mixed farms with dairy cows, beef cattle, and crops of alfalfa, corn, and soybeans are nearly as abundant. Tobacco is also an important crop in several western counties. Lead and zinc mines operated in Iowa, Grant, and La Fayette counties beginning in the 1840s, but by the late 1960s mining activity had ceased because of low world prices and high production costs. Limestone from this region is used mostly for agricultural lime, but some varieties are suitable as building stone.

Eastern Ridges and Lowlands. Glacial deposition has had a marked effect upon the landforms of this region. In nearly all sections glacial deposits have obscured the preglacial topography so that low relief and a highly irregular, rough landscape are common. Three preglacial cuestas cross the region, although glacial deposits and erosion have modified them. The Niagara cuesta forms Washington Island and Door Peninsula and extends south into Washington County and south of Milwaukee. The major upland between Lake Michigan and the Green Bay–Lake Winnebago–Rock River Lowlands, the Niagara escarpment is most pronounced just east of Lake Winnebago, where it is called High Cliff. At Stockbridge, the escarpment rises 230 ft (70 m) in a horizontal distance of only 700 ft (210 m). The Galena-Platteville cuesta forms a low ridge on the west side of Green Bay and extends southwest. Between the Galena and Niagara escarpments, the Fox River Valley and Lake Winnebago occupy the lowland. The Prairie du Chien cuesta extends from Marinette County to south of the Baraboo Range. The steep face of the cuesta is 300 ft (91 m) high between Dane and Lodi, but generally it is much lower in relief because of glacial deposition and erosion.

Glacial depositional features are especially notable in the Eastern Ridges and Lowlands. The Wisconsin terminal moraine and the Kettle interlobate moraine contain outstanding glacial depositional features such as eskers, kames, crevasse fillings, kettle lakes, and ground moraines (Figure 2.15). The landscape in these moraine areas is highly irregular and dotted by numerous small lakes. The Kettle Moraine is unusually high because it sits atop the Niagara cuesta. The highest elevations in this region of the state are associated with this moraine; for example, Holy Hill in Washington County is 1,361 ft (415 m) above sea level, and Lapham Peak in Waukesha County rises 1,233 ft (375 m).

Drumlins are another feature of this region. Fond du Lac, Dodge, Dane, Jefferson, and northern Rock counties contain one of the three largest drumlin fields in North America (see Figure 2.10). These

FIGURE 2.15 An esker in the glaciated Eastern Ridges and Lowlands. (Adam Cahow)

hills of glacial drift are shaped like overturned teaspoons and rise up to 150 ft (45 m) above the surrounding countryside. Interstate 94 between Madison and Milwaukee dissects several drumlins, and others can be seen from highways in eastern Dane and Jefferson counties.

Other prominent features in the region include the large flat outwash plains near Janesville and Beloit, which formed in front of the terminal moraine to the north, and the huge Horicon Marsh in Dodge and southern Fond du Lac counties, a filled lake, formed in a basin created by glaciation. Horicon Marsh covers about 50 sq mi (80 sq km) and is a favored stopping point for Canada geese and other waterfowl as they migrate between winter and summer habitats.

Like many areas in the Western Upland, the Eastern Ridges and Lowlands has thick loam soils and a long growing season that support agriculture, which has flourished in this region since the first European farmers entered the state. Corn, soybeans, and dairying are the primary types of farming; in addition, peas, beans, and other vegetables are raised commercially throughout much of the area, and cherries are grown in Door County. The region's state forests are important recreation areas. The ports on Lake Michigan in Milwaukee, Sheboygan, Manitowoc, and Green Bay provide an important economic link to international markets.

VEGETATION

Alterations in climate over many centuries have contributed to changes and adjustments in vegetation patterns. Even when general climate conditions are similar, vegetation may vary from one area to another because of differences in soils, the steepness of slopes, and the orientation of slopes to the sun. For these reasons vegetation is a dynamic feature of the landscape, subject to a progression of adjustments.

The Evolution of Wisconsin's Vegetation

Pollen analysis is a research technique by which the vegetation that occupied an area in the past can be determined. All plants have unique pollen configurations, just as each human has a different fingerprint. Pollen falls into water and settles to the bottom of a lake or pond. Over many years accumulations of pollen-rich sediment are piled one layer atop the other. A cross-section taken through such sediment reveals the dominant vegetation in the region of the pond or lake and any changes that may have occurred. Once the age of the sediment is determined, a history of changing vegetation patterns is revealed. Based upon several such investigations scientists know what the vegetation was like at different periods of Wisconsin's history, back to the last major glacial period about 9,000 years ago.

Immediately following glacial retreat, the vegetation in Wisconsin was much like that of present-day northern Canada: tundra and scattered coniferous forest dominated by balsam fir and white spruce, interspersed with smaller clusters of tamarack and black spruce. A warming climate led to an invasion of deciduous trees from the southern sections of the Midwest and to the demise of tundra vegetation and most conifers. Shortly thereafter, a progressively dryer climate restricted the deciduous forest to the northern and eastern sections of the state, whereas prairie grass dominated the west-central and southern areas south of a line from about Minneapolis to Milwaukee.

Increasing moisture and continued warmth marked the next major climate change, and these conditions favored the spread of deciduous forest across the entire state. During this period Wisconsin's climate was much like the present climate of southern Illinois and Indiana. Sugar maple, basswood, red oak, and some beech were the major hardwoods. In the far north deciduous trees dominated but were interspersed with conifers in a mixed forest.

A second major dry period followed the deciduous period. Prairie grass again replaced the deciduous forests in southern and southwestern sections of Wisconsin. Fires, triggered by lightning, assisted in the removal of most deciduous trees, and only fire-resistant burr oak remained. Historians also believe that the early Indian groups in this region deliberately set grass fires as a method of flushing game and to make travel across the grasslands easier. In the east and southeast, deciduous trees from the previous climate period persisted in isolated clumps. To the north, the forest was largely a mixture of deciduous and coniferous species.

The dry period was followed by a gradual cooling period with greater amounts of moisture. The grasslands in the southern sections were not totally replaced, but oak forests increased in size at the expense of the grasslands. The isolated deciduous forests of the east and southeast expanded, and in the far north near Lake Superior, the boreal forest of spruce and fir returned. A mixed forest composed of varieties of pine and hardwoods flourished over most of the north and west. This was the vegetation pattern in the 1850s, when white settlement of Wisconsin began. Because present climate conditions are similar to those of the 1850s, the vegetation distribution shown in Figure 2.16 would, for the most part, probably be duplicated today if the land were allowed to revert to its natural state. This map shows the major species of natural vegetation in the state.

Forests

When white settlers first came to Wisconsin, forests covered over 22 million acres (8.9 million ha), roughly 63 percent of the total land surface. In the north, hardwood forest characterized by sugar maple, yellow birch, and hemlock dominated the land. White pine took over the dominant role in drier areas, whereas in wetter areas black spruce, black ash, and tamarack prevailed. In the northernmost corner of Wisconsin and at the tip of Door Peninsula, a small band of boreal forest, mainly white spruce and balsam fir, both typical of the vast forests of present-day Canada, fringed the cool shores of Lakes Superior and Michigan.

Hardwood forests also dominated in the south, but there the sugar maple stood among basswood, slippery elm, and ironwood. Dry areas supported a variety of oak species, whereas wet lowland areas of river valleys and lakeshores supported silver maple and American elm. Grasslands surrounding these southern woodlands were maintained by both natural fires and fires started by Indians. Without these fires, most of the land would have been covered by forest. The combination of forest and grasslands benefited wildlife by creating a forest edge. In northern areas where few grasslands occurred, openings caused by fallen trees or natural burns were likewise beneficial to wildlife.

White settlement brought drastic changes to Wisconsin's forests. Southern forests were the first cut, and the land was cleared for farming. Much of the oak forest of southern and western Wisconsin was used to construct plank roads from the port of Milwaukee to the farming region in the south

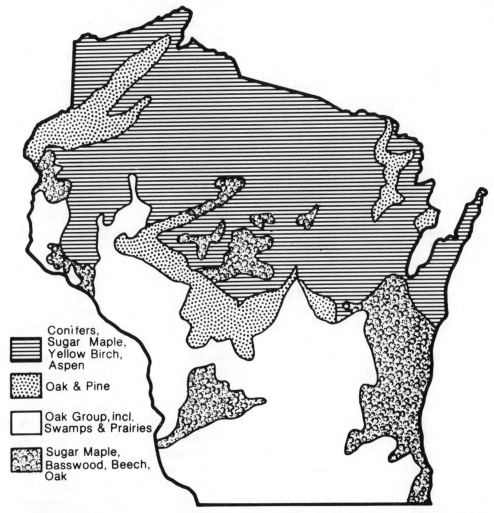

Conifers, Sugar Maple, Yellow Birch, Aspen

Oak & Pine

Oak Group, incl. Swamps & Prairies

Sugar Maple, Basswood, Beech, Oak

FIGURE 2.16 Vegetation types of Wisconsin about 1850. (Based on Robert Finley, *Geography of Wisconsin: A Content Outline* [Madison: College Printing and Typing Co., 1965], p. 67)

between 1830 and 1870. Wagons traveled these plank roads, bringing wheat to the grain elevators from which it could be loaded onto ships. Because trees were considered obstacles to farming, forests were cleared as quickly as possible, and logs not used for local building materials were used for fuel.

In the north, forests were viewed as a resource to be harvested. Logging began around 1840 and reached its peak by the turn of the century, at which time Wisconsin was the leading lumber-producing state in the nation. High market demand and competition for the lumber led to frenzied cutting, which took a heavy toll on the land. Fires swept through cutover areas. The worst forest fire in the United States happened in Peshtigo, Wisconsin, on October 8, 1871; about 1,000 people died out of a total population of 1,700. (On the same night, another fire destroyed much of the city of Chicago. Five times as many people died in the Peshtigo fire as died in Chicago; yet the Chicago fire received more attention in the nation's newspapers.) Such fires denuded the land and damaged the soil, and large areas became wastelands sparsely covered by weeds and grasses. Later, aspen and other pioneer species sprang up under conditions not suited to the original forest components, setting the forest back to its earliest stages of development.

Today, trees again cover much of Wisconsin, but the landscape does not look like the original forests of 150 years ago. Oaks dominate in the south with young maples and basswood just beginning to come in. In the north, aspen, birch, balsam fir, pine, and maple are found, most of them young stands. Pockets of the original forests are found relatively undisturbed in a few areas of the state and are extremely valuable reservoirs for a host of rare plants. Many are protected in state scientific areas, but others are jeopardized by development.

In addition to their importance as sources of lumber and pulpwood today's forests also have important recreational uses. The attraction of the Northwoods to tourists is extremely vital to the state's economy. National, state, county, and community forest lands are utilized for many activities: camping, hiking, skiing, snowmobiling, and fishing. The high number of resident deer-hunting licenses sold reflects not only the human population concentrations in the state, but also the abundance of deer in Wisconsin. Hunting of white-tail deer, black bear, and a variety of game birds would be impossible without forest habitat for their protection.

Grasslands

Early white explorers encountered grasslands in several sections of southern Wisconsin. These grasslands were largely woodless landscapes with trees completely absent or occurring in widely separated clumps. The term *prairie* is used to describe treeless areas; the term *savanna* refers to grasslands interspersed with trees. Prior to European settlement, Wisconsin grasslands are estimated to have covered more than 11 million acres (4.5 million ha), about 30 percent of the total land area, mostly in a triangle cornered by what are now Racine, Grant, and Polk counties. As the distance from the prairie region increased, the density of trees increased, and grasslands merged into savannas and eventually into forests. Although there were no true prairies in the north, pine savannas were scattered amidst the vast forests.

The blooming of prairie plants colored the landscape from early spring to late fall, with low-growing spring wildflowers giving way to towering grasses by summer's end. Plants found in a particular piece of prairie varied with the soil and moisture conditions present there. In the savannas, oaks were the typical tree species in the south, and jack pine in the north. However, prairie grasses and wildflowers clearly remained the dominant savanna vegetation.

Today, Wisconsin's grasslands are largely gone, occurring only in remnants along railroad corridors, on bluffs too steep to cultivate, or in specially managed areas. In their place are the corn and alfalfa fields so characteristic of Wisconsin's dairy industry. Savannas have been converted to woodlots. Through natural succession in the absence of fire, the giant trees that grew in the open of the old grasslands are now engulfed by new-growth forests. Today's most productive farmland is former prairie, with upland prairies converted to cropland and lowland areas used for pasture. In both cases, prairie plants were replaced by domesticated plants.

WATER

Wetlands

In the early 1800s, Wisconsin wetlands covered 10 million acres (4 million ha), roughly 25 percent of the state's total surface area. Wetlands were so extensive in central Wisconsin that the area came to be known as the "great swamp." Except for the steeply drained hillsides of the southwest, wetlands were scattered throughout the state, often covering huge areas. Whether they were called swamps, marshes, sloughs, bottomlands, or bogs, these wetlands had one thing in common: standing water. If they were not covered by water, they were soggy. In most cases, poorly drained soils or exposed groundwater accounted for the wetness, but the water was not deep enough or permanent enough to form a lake. Partly water and partly land, wetlands support plant communities that indicate that soil is not far below the water's surface.

The Indian inhabitants of Wisconsin and the first European explorers viewed the wetlands as a valuable source of food and fur. Wild rice, blueberries, and cranberries grew abundantly, and waterfowl, fish, and fur-bearing mammals occurred in great numbers. Indian settlements were located near wetlands to take advantage of this richness. Wild rice was so important to the Indian diet that wars were fought over harvest rights. Early settlers used the drier lands to harvest hay and graze livestock, and a few pioneering individuals made the first attempts to grow cranberries commercially.

But this harmony between people and wetlands did not last. As Wisconsin's population grew larger and needed more agricultural land, wetlands were viewed as wasteland because they could not be cultivated and as a public menace because they were thought to breed disease. As early as the late nineteenth century, when land was no longer available on the frontier, wetlands were drained and filled: Over 3 million acres (1.2 million ha) have been drained for agricultural use, most of them for corn and vegetable crops, and many other wetlands have been converted to pasture. Some of the most ambitious wetland drainage schemes failed when fires swept the exposed peaty soils or early frost killed crops, and many of these lands were simply abandoned, but some were reclaimed as fish and wildlife habitats. Such wetland reclamation marked the return to a recognition that wetlands are best left in their natural state.

Today, an estimated 2.5 million acres (1 million ha) of wetlands remain in Wisconsin. Public attitudes have come full circle, and wetlands are again looked upon as a valuable resource. Besides providing some of the last open spaces in urban areas, wetlands serve important biological functions. Acting as natural sponges, they absorb floodwaters and nutrients that would otherwise erode the land and pollute lakes and streams. Farmers continue to manage and harvest natural crops of berries, hay, wild rice, and sphagnum moss. Wetlands also provide habitats for other plants and for animals.

Lakes and Streams

Closely related to wetlands are lakes and streams. In fact, most wetlands are either lakes that have grown old and shallow, oxbows of rivers cut off from the main channel, or seasonally flooded river shorelands. Wisconsin's inland lakes cover almost 1 million surface acres (404,700 ha), and Wisconsin's streams, if placed end to end, would measure 30,000 mi (48,270 km) long. In addition, Wisconsin is bordered by water on all but its southern edge, with two Great Lakes and the Mississippi River boundary adding huge acreages of water to the state's total. The number of lakes and streams has actually increased through the years by impoundments constructed for recreation and industry.

Wisconsin's lakes and streams have always been exploited, first for their fish and as transportation, later as "highways" to bring logged timber to market, and more recently for their hydroelectric power. They also are used as dumping grounds for garbage, sewage, and industrial wastes. Many lakes and streams are being altered biologically by pollution, dams, and shoreline development, and for the plants and animals living there, the effect is often devastating. Dams cut off migrating fish from their spawning grounds, pollution chokes off life-essential oxygen, and shoreline development destroys feeding and nursery areas for wildlife and growing room for plants.

SELECTED REFERENCES

Adams, D. N., and J. D. Brodie. *Wisconsin's Forest Resources: Present and Potential Uses.* Madison: College of Agricultural and Life Science, University of Wisconsin, Research Bulletin R2044, 1976.

Benjamin, D. M., and D. W. Renlund. "A Phenological Survey of Red Pine in Wisconsin." *Wisconsin Academy Review*, vol. 8 (1963), pp. 26–28.

Collins, Charles. "The Influence of Drumlin Topography on Field Patterns in Dodge County, Wisconsin." *Transactions of the Wisconsin Academy*, vol. 59 (1971), pp. 56–66.

Curtis, John. *Vegetation of Wisconsin.* Madison: University of Wisconsin, 1959.

Dorman, R. G. *Preliminary Map Showing Thickness of Glacial Deposits in Wisconsin.* Madison: Geological and Natural History Survey, 1971.

Dutton, Carl E. *Mineral and Water Resources of Wisconsin.* Washington, D.C.: U.S. Government Printing Office, 1976.

Finley, Robert. *Geography of Wisconsin.* Madison: University of Wisconsin, 1976.

Hole, Francis. *Soils of Wisconsin.* Madison: University of Wisconsin, 1976.

Leopold, Aldo. *A Sand County Almanac.* New York: Oxford University Press, 1970.

Martin, Lawrence. *Physical Geography of Wisconsin.* Madison: University of Wisconsin, 1974.

Ostrom, M. E.; R. A. David, Jr.; and L. M. Cline. *Field Trip Guide Book for Cambrian-Ordovician Geology of Western Wisconsin.* Madison: Geological and Natural History Survey, 1970.

Palm, Richard S., and Anthony R. de Souza. *Wisconsin Weather.* Minneapolis: Burgess Publishing, 1983.

Paull, Rachel, and Richard Paull. *Geology of Wisconsin and Upper Michigan.* Dubuque, Iowa: Kendall/Hunt Publishing, 1977.

Reuss, Henry; Gilbert Tanner; Phillip Kinsmoor; and Robert Hellman. *On the Trail of the Ice Age.* Milwaukee: Milwaukee Public Museum, 1976.

Yanggen, Douglas A., et al. *Wisconsin Wetland.* Madison: University of Wisconsin Extension, Bulletin G2818, 1976.

Zakrzewska-Borowiecki, Barbara. "Land Forms in Southeastern Wisconsin." In *Landscapes of Wisconsin—A Field Guide*, edited by Barbara Zakrzewska-Borowiecki. Washington, D.C.: Association of American Geographers, 1975.

CHAPTER 3

HISTORICAL LANDSCAPES

In the fifteenth century, European explorers and traders sought out "new" lands. During this Age of Discovery, in the words of historical geographer Donald Meinig, "Europeans of whatever origin, impelled by whatever motivations, imposed themselves by whatever means upon the political lives of other people" (1969, p. 213). "Western imperialism," according to Meinig, took many forms in different places depending on the European powers involved. In North America, the French, British, and Spanish established their respective empires. In the territory that was to become Wisconsin, three distinctive empires developed: the boreal riverine empire, the settler empire, and the nationalistic empire. (Throughout this chapter, "Wisconsin" refers to the area that was to become the present state of Wisconsin.) During each type of empire the dominant institutions changed, new immigrants arrived, and the look of the land was transformed; hence each type of empire had its own historical landscape.

THE BOREAL RIVERINE EMPIRE: INDIAN CULTURE AREAS AND EUROPEAN FUR TRADING

The first Europeans who came to Wisconsin were fur traders. During the sixteenth and seventeenth centuries a growing and prosperous class of Europeans was seeking luxuries: silks and spices from Asia, ivory and jewels from Africa, furs from North America. Fur hats and coats provided warmth and status for European aristocrats, kings, and the wealthy. When many fur-bearing animals in northern Europe became extinct, fur traders went to the New World to find more furs. The type of northern wooded, or boreal, landscape found in Eurasia was spread across North America as well. The rivers of the boreal landscape provided the habitat of fur-bearing animals and the transportation routes for fur traders.

Both the French and the British fur-trading empires expanded across the boreal lands of North America. There the fur trade was dominated by the French from 1634 to 1763, by the British from 1763 to 1814, and by the Americans from 1814 to 1834. The St. Lawrence River, with Montreal at its mouth and with its access to the Great Lakes, allowed the French to reach far into the interior of the continent, including Wisconsin. The Hudson's Bay Company, a private British commercial trading company, worked out of northern Canada. As the British expanded southward and the French westward, they came in conflict. In Wisconsin, the French and then the British controlled the political affairs of thousands of Indians for economic, religious, and empire-building reasons and accomplished their goals by means of trade, conversion, wars, and divide-and-conquer strategies.

The westward expansion of European domination was motivated primarily by the search for profits, in the form of furs obtained by trade from Native American people. In their appearance, form, and function, the American boreal riverine systems of each empire were identical: a network of summer camps, stockaded and clustered log-structured winter outposts, and regional and systemwide headquarters. These were tied together by continental waterways. This far-flung commercial system depended heavily on the indigenous population to extract the furs that relatively few Europeans could afford. The Indians' knowledge of the terrain and their mastery of water routes were invaluable to first the French and later the British and settlers from the eastern United States. The merchants exploited the labor of the tribes, trading goods of much less value than the pelts they received in return. The Indians did nearly all of the trapping; Europeans were clerks, boat handlers, and traders, not hunters or trappers.

All the lands that the British and French explorers and traders traversed were claimed and annexed to their native countries, regardless of whether or not these lands were valuable for furs, and the local Indian tribes were brought under European control. In what was to be Wisconsin, the French established only fur-trading centers, but later the U.S. government built forts at Fort Howard (Green Bay), Fort Crawford (Prairie du Chien), and Fort Winnebago (Portage) (Figure 3.1). Most of the fur traders who came were sojourners in search of profits, not settlers in search of land, yet wherever fur posts were situated in fertile areas, these sites eventually became nuclei for European colonization.

Impact of the Fur Trade on the Indians

The interaction of Indians and whites, however, was tragic for the Indians. In the fur-trade economy, Indians received trinkets for their furs; ultimately they were a cheap labor pool for European nations. After the fur-bearing animals had been depleted, Anglo settlers took Indian land as well.

With essentially a Stone Age technology, Indian people had relied on other members

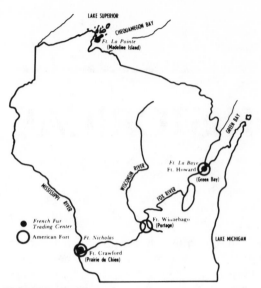

FIGURE 3.1 Boreal riverine empire in Wisconsin.

of the tribe to survive. They had organized themselves collectively, working together and sharing their gathered wealth. Contact with Europeans taught the Indians to compete with each other to secure the most and best furs. Europeans had an industrial technology, which allowed them to dominate the Indians through brute force. These trade relations resulted in the rapid depletion of the fur-bearing animals and the gradual destruction of Indian cultures. European dominance was thus a result of technological, rather than cultural, superiority.

Wisconsin Indians hunted for subsistence and for the fur trade—the Indians' primary introduction to European material culture and economy. Although historians have tried to explain Native American hunting activities in terms of Western marketplace theory, Jeanne Kay argued that evidence from the Wisconsin fur trade shows that Indians placed higher values on the social and religious aspects of their existence than on economic profit. Indians hunted for furs in order to achieve a satisfactory, rather than a maximum, income level. As one Wisconsin fur trader reported: "The Savages attained their necessities for a few peltries and would not hunt afterwards." Nevertheless, the Indians of the upper Great Lakes shared a non-Indian material culture shortly after European contact: Nearly all the tools used in their daily lives were manufactured in Europe.

Prior to European contact, Indians had trapped for survival only. But white traders, whose wealth depended on obtaining as many furs as possible, regarded the Indians' lack of desire for material possessions as laziness. Traders used liquor and especially the Indian's addiction to it to force the Indians to collect more furs than they preferred, in order to pay off their debts and to receive more liquor. Frequently, Indian leaders protested against the deliberate pushing of liquor among their people. Indians engaged in the fur trade were caught in a vicious cycle: Resources of fur-bearing animals diminished as the Indians' dependence on European trade goods grew.

Hunting Grounds

The quality of hunting grounds depended on the character of wildlife habitats. Northern Wisconsin forests were mediocre game habitats; the Fox River Valley and southeastern Wisconsin were good; and the oak savanna ecotones, especially in the upper Mississippi Valley, were excellent hunting grounds. White-tailed deer and beaver—two of the fur trade's most important species—were especially concentrated along the forest-savanna interface. Fur-collecting records kept by the American Fur Company for Lac du Flambeau, Green Bay, and Milwaukee from 1819–1821 indicated the spatial variation in wildlife species traded. At Lac du Flambeau, in northern Wisconsin, far greater numbers of muskrat and marten were hunted than any other species; more bear were hunted here than at the other two trading centers as well. Hunters at Green Bay also exploited muskrat and marten, but deer—a species of the savanna-forest ecological niche—were of major importance to the local trade in animal hides and fur. Milwaukee's deciduous forest and open grassland and marshes yielded high percentages of muskrat, raccoon, and deer. Throughout the nineteenth century the muskrat, which had many suitable natural habitats, was economically the most important fur-bearing animal in Wisconsin.

French Space, 1634–1763

Jean Nicolet's visit to Green Bay in 1634 marked the beginning of the French phase of the fur trade. Through explorers, traders, and missionaries, France extended control over the new fur lands. Daniel Greysolon Duluth, Pierre Le Seur, Nicholas Perrot, Louis Joliet, and Jacques Marquette explored a great deal of Wisconsin north and west of the Fox and Wisconsin rivers.

The French government in Montreal could only loosely control the fur trade at the periphery of its empire. Ideally, the French crown sold trading licenses each year to *bourgeois*, who hired the *voyageurs* and provided the trading goods, canoes, and provisions. The voyageurs were usually recruited from the peasant class living along the St. Lawrence River. They were a vital part of the fur trade, because they did the hard work of paddling the canoes and carrying the cargoes over portages. Trips from Montreal to the western ports, such as the one at La Baye (Green Bay), and back commonly were as much as 2,500 mi (4,023 km) long. Because the fur trade was conducted far away from the seat of French authority at Montreal, many *coureurs de bois* (or rangers of the wood), young men from Upper Canada, pushed into the wilderness, including Wisconsin, without first receiving fur-trading licenses from the crown.

French missionaries also played an important role in changing the continental interior. They introduced Christianity to the Indians and established missions, some of which became forts. The first missionary to work in Wisconsin was Rene Menard, who established a mission in 1661 at La Pointe on Madeline Island in Chequamegon Bay. Claude Allouez established many Indian missions between 1665 and 1676, including those at La Baye, Oshkosh, and

De Pere. Often, missionary activities and fur trading were carried out in the same places. The French government erected Fort La Baye (1717) and Fort La Pointe (1718) (Figure 3.1).

French control ended when the Treaty of Paris, signed in 1763, passed sovereignty over all the lands east of the Mississippi River to the British crown. Even before that time the French population in Wisconsin was very small. About 15,000 French Canadian fur traders from Upper Canada went west between 1670 and 1760, but few had settled at the French forts in Wisconsin. After the departure of the French garrison, perhaps 200 to 300 persons lived at La Baye, and only a few families lived at Portage and Prairie du Chien, although Prairie du Chien was a major fur-trading center. Nevertheless, the French occupied the territory for 130 years, leaving a legacy of names of rivers, cities, and counties; the long-lot survey system remains at Green Bay and Prairie du Chien (see Figure 3.3).

British Space, 1763–1814

Wisconsin was part of the vast North American hinterland of European metropolitan centers, focused first on Paris and then on London. This *mercantilist* system concentrated wealth in Europe and extracted valuable resources from the hinterland, disrupting and destroying, in the process, the Indian way of life. Mercantilism was a dynamic force, shaping and transforming the New World.

In the mid-eighteenth century competition within the international trading system intensified. French and British merchants scrambled to gain control of one another's New World colonies. After the military defeat of France in 1759 at Quebec City in Upper Canada (presently the Canadian province of Quebec), the British crown expanded its empire into the former French fur-trading areas, which included Wisconsin; in 1763 the Treaty of Paris made the British occupation official.

For the British, Wisconsin was even more peripheral than it had been for the French. The French had maintained one permanent settlement at Green Bay, but apart from renaming a few forts—Fort La Baye to Fort Edward Augustus (after the brother of George III) and Fort Nicholas to Fort McKay—the British never maintained any official settlements in Wisconsin. The British crown did not control the fur trade directly as the French had done. Instead, private commercial trading companies, such as the Hudson's Bay Company and, in Wisconsin, the Northwest Company, paid the crown for the privilege of doing business.

Essentially, the British adopted the same western policy as had the French, and so the everyday life of the Indians and voyageurs was unaffected by the change in colonial rule. In the spring, the Indians planted crops of corn, watermelons, potatoes, and squashes. Summer was a time for rest. In the fall they collected wild rice, harvested the crops, and readied for the hunting season. Before going off to the hunting grounds, they bought goods, such as blankets, coarse cloth, kettles, hatchets, guns, powder, tobacco, and liquor on credit from the white traders. Indian hunters were given credits worth $40 to $50, upon which traders could expect a gain of almost 100 percent, or an annual value of furs from $80 to $100. This credit system assured the dependence of the Indians on foreign traders for their supplies, status, and often their survival. Throughout the British colonial period, and until the late 1810s, semi-independent French entrepreneurs continued to trade with Wisconsin Indians for Montreal firms.

In the aftermath of the War of 1812, in which Britain invaded its former colony, the United States, Britain lost control of the Northwest and the fur trade. In the negotiations at Ghent, Belgium, the British commissioners asserted the sovereignty and independence of the Indians over the Northwest Territory as a barrier between Canada to the north and the United States to the south and east. This territory, the British argued, should be free to the traffic

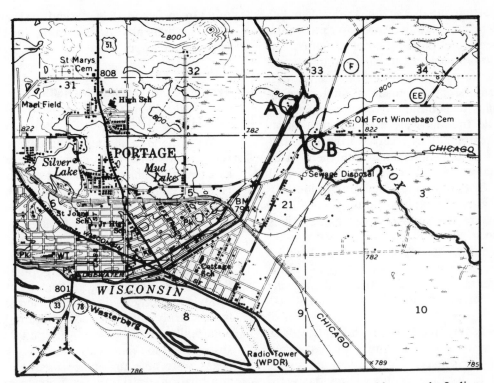

FIGURE 3.2 Fur-trading settlements at Portage. On this topographic map, the Indian Agency is located at *A;* the remnants of Fort Winnebago are at *B* with the military cemetery close by. This strategic site was used in 1851 to connect the Wisconsin and Fox rivers by a canal. (Portage, 1:24,000)

of both nations, but not open to purchase by either. This proposition would have excluded the Northwest Territory from the sovereignty of the United States and effectively given it over to the British fur traders. The United States rejected the proposal and took possession of the Northwest, including Wisconsin. The Treaty of Ghent in 1814 officially transferred Wisconsin to the United States, although the territory had been effectively under U.S. control since the 1780s.

U.S. Space, 1814–1834

The U.S. government did not establish garrisons in Wisconsin until 1816, when Fort Howard and Fort Crawford were built; Fort Winnebago was built in 1826 (Figure 3.2). These forts, each having 100 to 200 soldiers, were part of the network that guarded the 1,500-mi (2,414-km) national

frontier of the United States. President George Washington and others held the view that the fur trade was such an integral part of the federal government's Indian policy that the government should participate directly and undertake the role of trader. Consequently, from 1796 to 1822, Congress financed a system of federally owned and operated trading posts.

U.S. traders initiated a cash system: Furs fetched full market value, and supplies were sold at cost. But the Indian tribes disliked this method of selling furs. They were dependent upon the system of the private traders, who had provided unsecured credit for supplies in return for pledges to deliver furs at the end of the season. High prices for supplies and low prices for furs had been the consequences of the credit system under the French and British; nevertheless, this lending system had allowed the Indians to participate in the fur trade. The U.S. traders, on the other hand, were unwilling to lend the Indians supplies (guns, ammunition, blankets, traps, food) in advance of the fur-trapping season; hence the cash system essentially made it impossible for Indians to continue in the fur trade.

The Indians were also unhappy about the treatment they received from U.S. traders, who only interacted with them in essentially economic ways. During the French and British periods, traders periodically gave gifts of weapons, clothing, and liquor to assure the good will of Indian tribes. Personal ties were also maintained through interracial marriages. The U.S. "factory system," as it was called, stripped white-Indian relations of their personal character and substituted instead an impersonal cash system.

Generally, the U.S. government trading-post system was a failure. Ora Peake gave several reasons: (1) Government posts were fixed in location, whereas previously the private traders went to the Indian hunting grounds; (2) the government traders did not give credit; private traders did; (3) no whiskey was sold at government posts; only private traders sold it; and (4) government traders were often unfamiliar with the Indians; private traders were usually related to the Indians through marriage, lived with them, and knew their ways.

Lead-mining activities gradually replaced fur trading in the southwestern part of the state. Miners began arriving in 1822, and by 1829 the southwestern lead-mining district had been taken from the Indians. By 1826, 432 miners were working in the area; two years later, 10,000 miners worked the lead-mining district, including parts of Illinois. Nevertheless, fur trading continued in other parts of the territory. Milwaukee was a fur-trading center until 1833 and Green Bay until 1845. Fur trading continued in northwestern Wisconsin until 1860, but by then the boreal riverine empire had been replaced by the settler empire in the southern half of the state. With the establishment of land offices at Mineral Point and Green Bay in 1834, agricultural settlers were permanently transforming the Wisconsin landscape.

THE SETTLER EMPIRE: MINERS, AGRICULTURALISTS, AND LOGGERS ON THE NATIONAL FRONTIER

With the gradual encroachment by, and final triumph of, European settler expansion over the ephemeral fur trade, the boreal riverine empire was transformed into a settler empire, first by miners, then by agriculturalists, and finally by loggers. The early fur-trading posts became centers of expanding colonization by farmers, who began displacing the Indian populations. Because the Indians were semi-nomadic, thinly and loosely distributed across the land, sharply differentiated culturally, technologically in the Stone Age, and highly susceptible to European diseases, Europeans were able to replace them through annihilation, drastic diminution, or expulsion. Transatlantic migration of permanent settlers to the lower St. Lawrence valley in Upper Canada and similar colonization in New England, Pennsylvania, Virginia, and Georgia established the settler empires in North America. The expansion of these settler empires into the interior of the continent destroyed the indigenous Indian population and transformed settlement patterns.

Fur-trading posts were the first settlements in the upper Midwest with the potential of developing into permanent settlements. Both Prairie du Chien and Green Bay were such settlements in Wisconsin. In 1800, these two settlements had only 65 and 50 people, respectively. But by 1830, their combined population was 1,500, and another 1,500 people were settled in the mining region of southwestern Wisconsin. As the southern part of the territory became part of the settler empire, the region north of the Wisconsin and Fox rivers remained Indian territory, and fur trading was still the primary industry there until the late 1830s.

French fur traders who became farmers influenced the earliest land survey systems in Wisconsin. Wherever the French settled the land, they left their unique land survey system behind: long-lots such as those along the St. Lawrence River in the province of Quebec, Canada, along the Wabash River at Vincennes, Indiana, and along the Mississippi at New Orleans. The French monarchy granted *seigneurs* (nobility) landed estates in the New World in lieu of payment for military service and other services to the crown. The seigneurs, in turn, subdivided their lands: peasants, or *censitaires,* each received a *roture*—a long, narrow strip of land that ran more or less at right angles to a river. Farmers built their farmsteads beside the river and cleared the land as far back as they needed. Although French settlements never developed as extensively and thoroughly in Wisconsin as in Quebec and Louisiana, the long-lot survey system and resulting settlement morphology have persisted to the present. Long-lots are found in the two oldest settled parts of Wisconsin: at the mouth of the Wisconsin River on the Mississippi River at Prairie du Chien and at the mouth of the Fox River in Green Bay (Figure 3.3). Elsewhere in the state, French place names are the only geographical evidence of the French legacy in the state.

Indian Land Treaties

The Indians had played a crucial role in providing furs to European traders. But after the late 1830s, when the furs were depleted and the fur trade had moved north of Wisconsin, Indians had no useful role to play for Europeans—indeed, in the eyes of white settlers, Indians prevented the expansion of the settler empire. Consequently, Indian nations were made to cede their lands, most of which was taken between 1829 and 1848 (Figure 3.4), although two small parcels had already been transferred at Fort Crawford (Prairie du Chien) in 1815 and 1816.

The pattern of land-stealing by Europeans corresponded to the land needs of

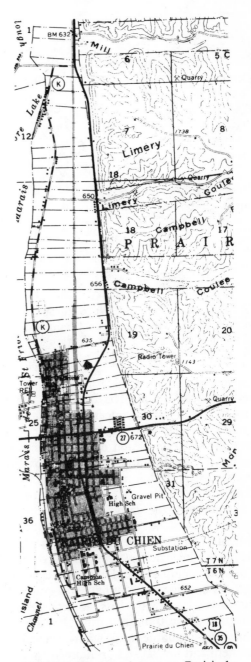

FIGURE 3.3 Long-lot survey, Prairie du Chien. The narrow parcels are located in the Mississippi River flood plain. On the uplands, the more common township and range survey is found. (Prairie du Chien, 1:24,000)

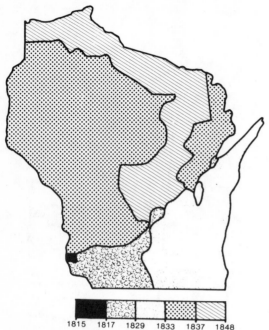

FIGURE 3.4 Indian land lost to European expansion, 1815–1848. (Based on "Indians Lose Lands in Wisconsin," *Badger History*, vol. 29, no. 4 [March 1976], p. 46)

European settlement. The first land taken was in the oldest European settled areas: around Fort Howard (Green Bay) and in the southwestern section of the region, including the lead-mining area. The Fox Indians were moved from the Fox River to Tama, Iowa, where the reservation bears their name; in the early 1830s the southeastern section was taken for agricultural settlement; and by the late 1830s most of the remaining state had been removed from the Indian nations, as European agriculturalists and logging companies spread up the Mississippi Valley, its adjacent river valleys, and west and south of Green Bay. The least-valuable and least-accessible northern and central areas remained Indian territory until the Europeans took them in the 1840s.

The retreat of Indian lands was the reciprocal of white frontier expansion. Once the hopelessness of military resistance was apparent, the objectives of Indians and whites became almost parallel: The Native Americans wanted to remain free from intruders; the U.S. government wanted the Indians isolated from the settlers. Thus, the Indians ceded much of their territory in return for the promise that they would be able to live in peace on reservations. Although reservation boundaries have fluctuated tremendously, and reservation land is still being lost to whites, the existing reservations remain vital cultural enclaves that serve as the last points of resistance to Occidental influences.

The earliest ceded lands were quickly settled by European agriculturalists. This farm population supported Wisconsin's earliest towns. In 1845 all towns lay south of a line from La Crosse to Portage to Green Bay. In northern Wisconsin the initial pressure to take Indian lands came from lumber interests, and sometimes treaties protected the Indians against the land claims of logging companies. But as soon as treaties were signed, lumbering began in earnest. For example, small-scale lumbering operations were begun at Chippewa Falls and Menomonie shortly after this territory was ceded by the Indians. Wisconsin became a state in 1848, the same year that the last Indian lands were taken in central and northern Wisconsin. In 1848 the state legislature authorized the building of a road from Prairie du Chien to Hudson via Sparta, Black River Falls, and Eau Claire. The scattered logging and agricultural towns of the north-central interior were being linked to the rest of the state, thereby consolidating the settler empire. Thus, statehood and the cession of Indian lands permanently established the settler empire.

Township and Range Survey

The Ordinance of 1785 authorized the federal government to survey the public domain ahead of settlement into 36-sq-mi (58-sq-km) townships and 1-sq-mi (1.6-sq-km) sections of 640 acres (259 ha). This survey characterizes 69 percent of the land in the 48 states. In Wisconsin this township and range survey consists of a *base line* along the Wisconsin-Illinois state line and a *principal meridian* running perpendicular to the base line along the Grant-Lafayette county line. *Township lines* run east and west of the principal meridian; *ranges* are tiers of townships, which in Wisconsin run north of the base line. The term *township*, or town, as it is called in Wisconsin, represents an area usually 6 by 6 mi (9.6 by 9.6 km), or 36 sections. Although there are some exceptions, most of the townships' boundaries correspond in shape and direction to the congressional survey lines (Figure 3.5).

The township and range survey is generally taken for granted, yet it shaped the U.S. and Wisconsin landscapes. It is important for several reasons:

1. To Thomas Jefferson and other like-minded eighteenth-century intellectuals, a nation of small-scale farmers would provide political freedom, independence, self-reliance, and the ability to resist political oppression. The Ordinance of 1785, although only authorizing a national land survey, reflected the philosophy of the U.S. Declaration of Independence—that all people possessed the rights to life, liberty, and the pursuit of happiness. By surveying the public domain into equal parts, land ownership could also be equal.

2. To assure that the ideals of agrarian democracy were achieved, government surveyors, not private companies, were used to lay out the land into sections and townships. The very basis of Wisconsin's human landscapes resulted from one of the earliest socialistic governmental acts.

3. The township and range system determined the morphology of rural and urban areas alike. The shape and location of townships, sections, fields, farms, farm buildings, and rural roads and city streets are the direct result of this survey. The placement of city buildings conforms to the gridiron plan of the city streets, which are only subdivisions of the original rural

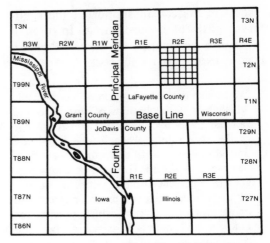

Township and Range Survey

FIGURE 3.5 The township and range survey in southwestern Wisconsin.

section roads. Truly, we live in the land of the squares!

Surveying the land and initiating settlement was done entirely by the federal government. By the 1830s this procedure followed a routine pattern: extinction of Indian land titles, survey, establishment of land offices, advertisement, sale of land at auction, and after the auction, sale of remaining land at minimum prices. By 1849 about 15 million acres (6 million ha), or three-sevenths of the state, had been surveyed. In 1865 the Wisconsin survey was completed.

The settling of the surveyed land usually resulted in sections (640 acres, or 259 ha) being divided into four 160-acre (65-ha), or quarter-section, farms, which reflected the Homestead Act of 1862 (see Figure 3.5). The Homestead Act granted settlers equal amounts of land from the public domain, land that had been divided equally by the Ordinance of 1785. Political and economic leaders in Wisconsin supported the egalitarian goals of homesteading. In 1854 a Wisconsin newspaper, the *Green Bay Advocate,* expressed its support.

> We believe that the adoption of the principle which lies at the bottom of this wise and popular measure . . . would constitute one of the most salutary, beneficient, important and glorious reforms that our Government has ever sanctioned. It would be a practical acknowledgement of the maxim that the soil of the country belongs to the people, and break away the barriers which prevent the landless and homeless from making for themselves an estate and a home. . . . Such a good law would operate with a democratic equality that would furnish one of the most beautiful and glorious results which flow from the existence of democratic institutions. (Hibbard, 1965, p. 371)

Today, town roads and often county trunk roads throughout the state, except in the topographically rougher Driftless Area, tend to follow section lines, though in places they give way to unyielding surface features—rough terrain, lakes, and swamps. As seen from the air, the general pattern is one of squares, interspersed here and there with irregular patches in which the checkerboard is discontinuous or entirely absent. Farmsteads are dispersed along or very near town roads; few are far from section margins; fewer still are sited on natural lakes or streams. The farmsteads repeat the basic square-in-square motif of their surroundings, and because they are widely spaced, emphasize the relatively unconstricted or open nature of land occupance. In the northern parts of the state little visible evidence from the air indicates how the land below is divided. Fields are more irregular in both size and shape. Farmsteads are fewer in number, wider spaced, and tend to be strung along the major highways that cross through the region. Even in places where agriculture was tried and found lacking, however, downed fences and abandoned fields maintain the cardinal orientation.

Cities and villages in Wisconsin closely follow the regularity set by the surrounding surveyed countryside. Most are either linear or crossroads in pattern. Streets, tracts, blocks, and lots in town match town roads, sections, quarter sections, and forties (sixteenth sections) in the country. No abrupt change in the grid nor appreciable discontinuity between urban and rural settlement patterns is characteristic; only the density of settlement. However, unlike farmsteads, which were sited with market accessibility foremost in mind, cities and villages— themselves inherently capable of attracting lines of communication—were less restricted in location. Other factors of location were more influential. Great significance was attached to lakeshore and streamside sites for their transportation and energy potential. Practically all incorporated places are located on significant surface waters. Many are along streams at rapids or waterfalls; others are on large natural lakes, especially lakes in chains; a few are on or between small lakes. But in each case, despite the initial direction of settlement set by the natural features and the angle at which major routes of transportation, such as railroads, eventually cut through these places, local streets and roads virtually without exception were quick to realign themselves with the universal grid.

Lead Mining in Southwestern Wisconsin, 1822–1860s

The miners who arrived in Wisconsin in the 1820s created the beginnings of a settler empire (Figure 3.6). By 1822 the news of rich lead deposits in southwestern Wisconsin attracted miners from Missouri and would-be miners from southern Illinois, Kentucky, and Tennessee, who came up the Mississippi River. In 1825 six melting furnaces were operating at Gratiot's Grove, and three teams made regular every-other-day trips to Galena, Illinois. From Galena, the lead was shipped south along the Mississippi River to St. Louis and New Orleans—critical points in the transfer of lead to eastern markets. When the lead-mining

FIGURE 3.6 The Wisconsin lead-mining district. (Reproduced from R. W. Chandler's 1829 map of Galena in files of the State Historical Society of Wisconsin)

district was ceded to the U.S. government in 1829, an army officer was appointed superintendent of mines. He enforced government leases and tax regulations and settled claim disputes. Permits allowed individuals to stake off a 200-yd-sq (183-m-sq) plot. If a $5,000 bond was given, however, 320 acres (130 ha) could be worked.

Lead was used for a variety of purposes: pewter, printer's type, weights, and shot. But much of it was made into white lead, the basis for paint. The custom of painting houses started in New England about 1734, and the tradition of white-painted towns and villages, associated with New England settlements and depicted on Christmas cards and travel posters, dates from the middle of the eighteenth century. Paint had become so popular that the British government levied a duty on it under the Townsend Act of 1767. The duty on paint was later removed, but the duty remained in effect on tea. How easily the American Revolution could have been sparked by paint! By 1840 Wisconsin, Illinois, and Missouri produced 93 percent of U.S. lead; Wisconsin alone accounted for about 50 percent. But frontier communities of the lead-mining district could not afford such a decorative luxury, and instead, unpainted log houses were the rule in Wisconsin.

Although a few miners made as much as $30 a day digging ore, common laborers made 50 cents to $1 a day. Skilled carpenters and masons earned $3 to $4 for a long workday. The cost of living was much lower than today, but still relatively high for these workers. A night's lodging cost 12.5 cents; meals were 37.5 cents; to bed a horse cost 50 cents, and to feed it, 25 cents. Yet lead mining was lucrative for the operators of smelters. In about 10 years one smelting company, the Gratiots, paid $60,000 worth of lead, which was 10 percent of its total production, to the U.S. government in taxes. By treaty, the Winnebago Indians were to receive $540,000 in cash over 30 years for the lead-mining region, yet *one* company earned $600,000 in 10 years!

In 1829 the price of lead fell to less than 1 cent a pound (2.2 cents per kg); in the 1810s it had sold for 5 cents a pound (11 cents per kg). With low prices for lead ore and high prices for food—in a region that had always imported its food—unemployed miners lobbied the U.S. government to allow them to farm their mining claims. Transient miners became homesteaders, displacing the Sauk and Fox Indians. A U.S. land office in Mineral Point officially opened the area to agriculturalists in 1834, although legally land containing lead could not be sold.

By 1840 the character of lead mining had changed substantially. The surface ore had been taken and below-the-surface deposits presented problems of shafting and draining. Experienced miner immigrants from Cornwall, England, brought technological solutions, arriving in this region during the 1830s. The Americans were ready to abandon the mines, but hundreds of skilled, unemployed miners from southwestern England found their earnings from the diggings to be good; in 1845 half of Mineral Point's population of 1,500 was Cornish. Tourists today associate southwestern Wisconsin with these Cornish miners.

By 1860 zinc was discovered in the deeper lead mines. From 1872 to 1882, zinc production more than doubled lead production; in 1880, it was three times as much. Zinc was mined differently than was lead, at or near the water table, not near the surface. Only a few large firms, rather than many small companies and farmer-miners, had the capital necessary to reach these ores, which were mined almost exclusively (70 percent) at Mineral Point, rather than throughout the southwestern area. Consequently, after 1860, many small-scale lead miners were using their lands for agriculture.

The lead region of Wisconsin was unusual compared to other mining areas in the United States because it had both productive agricultural land and rich mineral deposits. It also had the advantage of being able to ship lead to markets by way of the

Mississippi and Rock rivers. Mining farmers or farming miners were able to produce lead at a lower cost than in other mining districts, such as the one in Missouri, which imported all food supplies. When lead prices fell by a half in 1827, Wisconsin production figures were not yet affected, although Missouri's production fell markedly.

The population of the mining district was distinctive compared to the rest of the state. The southwestern section had a larger percentage of U.S.-born settlers and English-speaking foreigners (English, Irish, Welsh) than did other parts of Wisconsin. The U.S.-born population derived largely from southern states, such as Missouri, Kentucky, Tennessee, North Carolina, Virginia, and the southern part of Illinois. The foreign-born population consisted of two groups: natives of England; and Irish, Welsh, and Germans. The English were smelters and mine bosses from Yorkshire, but the miners were primarily from Cornwall.

The southeastern counties were settled by Yankees from the eastern United States; the upper lakeshore counties, on the other hand, were home to a mixture of Yankees and Germans. Beginning in the 1830s, foreign immigrants followed the Erie Canal and the Great Lakes to the Northwest Territory, which included Wisconsin. Settlement grew along the lakeshore to such an extent that the size of its population challenged that of the lead-mining district, which had been settled earlier. When Wisconsin became a state in 1848, the lead-mining area had been overshadowed by the more-populated areas of the eastern part of the state.

The location of the state capitol reflects this shift in the population and in political power. When the mining region was the most populated section of the state, politicians from this part of the state controlled state politics, and the first state capitol was located in Belmont, La Fayette County, reflecting the economic and political strength of the southwestern section. After immigrants settled the farmland along Lake Michigan, the state capitol was moved to Madison, Dane County. This change reflected a geographical compromise between the Republicans and the Democrats, the political parties representing the two oldest settled areas—the lead-mining and agricultural lakeshore regions.

Agricultural Settlement in the South, 1830s–1880s

At the time of agricultural settlement in Wisconsin, economic and political unrest in Europe was strong. This unrest gave people the impetus to emigrate to the United States. In addition, Wisconsin received and generated considerable publicity for its fertility and beauty, which attracted both Yankee and European settlers. The content and feeling of this publicity was captured in a 1931 report, which Joseph Schafer, a historian of Wisconsin agriculture, cited:

> It is not presuming too much to say at least two thirds of it is fit for cultivation and offers attractions to the agriculturalists rarely to be found in any county. The soil presents every indication of great fertility. . . . The whole county is bountifully supplied with water . . . ; it is covered with a heavy growth of oak, hickory, maple, cherry. . . . I cannot refrain from again calling your attention to the dazzling attractions offered by this county to an industrious and enterprising population. (1927, pp. 50–51)

The southeastern counties were first settled by whites in about 1835; just four years later the region was thickly settled. The principal settlements were near the lakeshore, from the southeastern corner of Kenosha County north to Milwaukee County; along the Fox River in Kenosha and Racine counties; along the Rock River, near Beloit and Janesville; and in Walworth County, including villages such as Lake Geneva, Troy Lake, Whitewater, and Delavan.

Studies of land purchase records, survey descriptions, and topographic maps indicate that pioneers selected land parcels in the southern part of the state that included three different ecosystems: high prairie for cultivation, low prairie for hay and pasture,

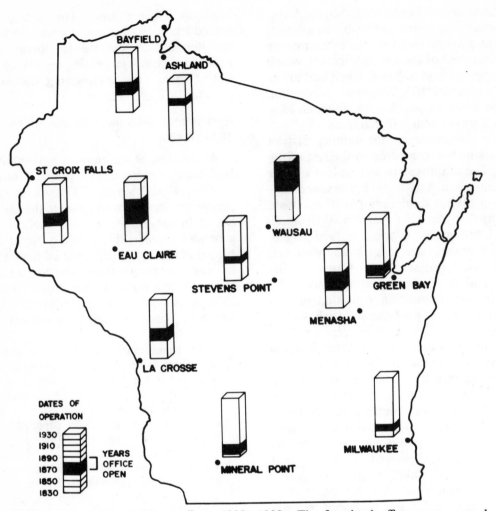

FIGURE 3.7 Wisconsin land offices, 1830s–1900s. The first land offices were opened in 1834 at Mineral Point and Green Bay. The Wausau office was the last to close in 1928. (Based on data from Randall D. Sale and Edwin D. Karn, *American Expansion* [Homewood, Ill.: Dorsey Press, 1962])

and forest for building supplies and fuel. Although European immigrants and Yankees both preferred the same kind of land, settlers from New York and New England tended to settle in more-open lands, whereas foreign-born settlers (mainly Germans) occupied more-wooded lands. Why did many Germans, in the words of one immigrant, spend "murderous toil" to clear such farms? Joseph Schafer explained that "it is at bottom a question of economic ability, not personal or racial tastes. . . . They took what was at hand, the heavily wooded lands

avoided by persons who were in a position to pick and choose" (Schafer, 1922, p. 39). Much of the fertile land in the eastern Midwest had already been sold or was being held for high prices, so European immigrants—the Germans being the first large group—settled on the frontier, which in 1850 had reached the Wisconsin and Fox rivers (Figure 3.7).

By 1850, two years after statehood, Wisconsin's population of 300,752 consisted of three groups. The U.S.-born accounted for about 64 percent, English-speaking foreign-born for 16 percent, and non-English-speaking foreign-born for 20 percent of the population. Over half the U.S.-born settlers came from northeastern states, mostly from the northern and western parts of New York and western Vermont, where wheat farming was changing to livestock and dairy farming, as canal construction opened new markets. Livestock farming required larger acreage, and so the bigger farmers had bought out the smaller ones. According to local historians of Chenango and Chantauque counties, New York, "the latter class emigrated to the west [Wisconsin] where land was cheap" (Schafer, 1922, p. 49). Other U.S.-born settlers came from the Old Northwestern Territory, from Ohio to Illinois; only a few settlers came from southern and southwestern states.

Among English-speaking foreigners, the Irish were more common in Wisconsin than were the English. The Germans far outnumbered all other non-English-speaking immigrants (Table 3.1); about half of them lived in Milwaukee. Scandinavians were the next largest group, consisting essentially of Norwegians. By the mid-nineteenth century Wisconsin still had a sizeable French Canadian population, one that equaled the Norwegian population. Former fur traders in the French boreal riverine empire, they had become agriculturalists in the settler empire.

Joseph Schafer vividly described the early southern Wisconsin settlements:

They were the crude beginnings of agriculture on the part of those who, devoid of financial means, relied almost solely on their personal strength and fortitude to make a living from timber and soil. Suited to this class was the rough cabin of unhewn logs, covered with "shakes," chinked, and daubed with mud, floored with "puncheons," and fitted with a few awkward homemade stools and benches, a board across the flour barrel and the pork barrel for a table, with beds of leaves or of straw. Those, however, who were accustomed to good homes in the East, or in Europe, and who had the means to do so, promptly

erected more pretentious houses. These might be made of dressed logs, neatly pointed up with mortar, and fitted with sawed-board floors and doors, glass windows, and decent furniture. If lumber in quantity was procurable, such settlers delayed scarcely a year or two, or at most a few years, before building comfortable frame houses or, in some cases, houses of brick or of stone. (1922, p. 31)

In a detailed study of wealthholding in 1860, Lee Soltow found that Wisconsin settlers who were born in England, Wales, and Scotland had twice the wealth of those born in Germany and Ireland, who in turn had one-fourth larger average wealth than those born in Scandinavia. The class origins of settlers (such as landed gentry, large-scale farmer, peasant, day laborer) and their lengths of residence in the state accounted for these differences in wealth.

TABLE 3.1
Wisconsin's Population in 1850

Population Group	Number
U.S.-Born Settlers	
Northeastern	103,371
Wisconsin-born	63,015
Northwestern	21,367
Southern	5,425
	193,178
English-Speaking Immigrants	
Irish	21,043
English	18,952
Welsh	4,319
Scotch	3,527
	47,841
Non-English-Speaking Immigrants	
Germans	38,054
Norwegians	8,600
Swedes	1,244
Danes	1,157
Swiss	1,244
Dutch	1,157
French Canadians	8,277
	59,733
Grand Total	300,752

Source: Partially based on Edward A. Fitzpatrick, Wisconsin (Milwaukee: Bruce Publishing Co., 1931), p. 246.

In 1860, few women owned property, and 30 percent of all men owned none; 2 percent of the population held 31 percent of the state's wealth. Put another way, the 86 richest individuals had as much wealth as the 200,000 poorest ones in Wisconsin. The highest average wealth was concentrated in the southeastern part of the state, including Kenosha, Milwaukee, Beloit, Janesville, and Madison. Already in this decade, Duluth-Superior represented an outlier of high wealth in northern Wisconsin. The counties with above-average wealth were in general those with below-average wages. These areas of greatest inequality of wealth became the sites of labor unrest in the 1880s.

Old and New Immigration

Two nineteenth-century immigrants are talking. "Wisconsin is so cold and has so many Norwegians." A Norwegian overhears the complaint and says: "Why don't you go to hell. It's warm and has no Norwegians."

Wisconsin, similar to other states, experienced two distinctive periods of European immigration: the Old Immigration (before 1880) and the New Immigration (after 1880). During the Old Immigration, most European settlers came from northwestern Europe, particularly Britain, Ireland, and Germany. They sought farmland, business opportunities, and religious and/or political freedom. During the 1850s the government of Wisconsin had actively recruited settlers from Europe, offering voting rights to new immigrants after only one year of residency in the state, even if the Europeans did not understand English. This wave of immigrants—especially the Germans—settled the southern and eastern parts of Wisconsin, which in 1860 was on the northern edge of the national frontier.

Although other northwestern Europeans, such as the Scandinavians, arrived in large numbers after 1880, a marked increase occurred in the number of immigrants from eastern European countries, such as Russia and Poland, and from southern European countries, such as Italy. This pattern was typical of the New Immigration. In the late nineteenth century the northern parts of the state were settled by Scandinavians, particularly the later-arriving Finns. Because other immigrants had already been settling Wisconsin for almost 50 years, these far-northern counties contained the only lands still available. The eastern Europeans, arriving even later, tended to locate in the industrial cities, such as Milwaukee, because the last agricultural land had already been taken by Germans and Scandinavians. The German and Norwegian immigrations illustrate the settling process of the state during the settler empire.

Germans. Representing the single largest group of Europeans to settle in the United States and in Wisconsin, by 1900 people of German background numbered 710,000 or 34 percent of the state's population. They emigrated in three distinctive periods from three different regions of Germany. From 1845 to 1860 they came from southwestern Germany, where small, mortgaged farms, repeated crop failures, and the potato blight characterized the farmers' lot. In the second period, 1865 to 1875, immigrants came from northwestern Germany, an area of prosperous middle-sized grain farms. Cheap wheat from the United States depressed world wheat prices and threatened to bankrupt these German grain farmers. Many sold their farms while they still could to get enough cash to acquire farmland in the New World. The third period of German outmigration lasted from 1880 to 1893 and coincided with the New Immigration of eastern and southern Europeans. These Germans came from northeastern Germany—Prussia, Pomerania, and Mecklenburg—where the Prussian aristocracy, or Junker class, had consolidated their estates and had in the process displaced 21,000 peasants. This landless rural population sought relief in the New World.

Wisconsin actively sought to attract Germans. In 1852, the state legislature established a Commission of Immigration with

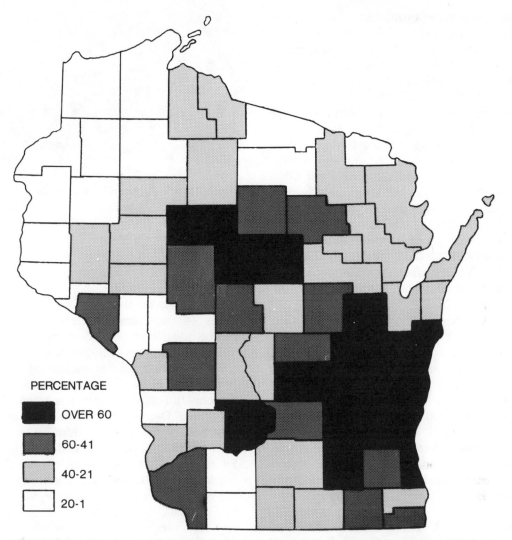

FIGURE 3.8 Percentage of German-born population by county, 1890. (Based on Richard H. Zeitlin, *Germans in Wisconsin* [Madison: State Historical Society of Wisconsin, 1977])

a resident commissioner in New York City. Leaflets praising Wisconsin were distributed in East Coast ports and in coastal areas of Germany. Recently arrived settlers also fostered additional German settlement when they wrote back to their relatives, friends, and neighbors in the Old World.

Intolerance of religious sects, as well as economic conditions, in Germany contributed to bringing settlers to Wisconsin. Farming abounded on the edge of the national frontier, but religious nonconformists also sought refuge in Jefferson, Dodge, and Ozaukee counties. In addition, communal

religious Germans settled at St. Nazianz in Manitowoc County. Germans tended to settle in specific townships according to their religious and regional origins (Figure 3.8). This selective process of migration is termed *chain migration;* the social and familial bonds in the homeland often determined where the newcomers would settle in Wisconsin.

German communities were able to maintain their cultural distinctiveness until 1914 through numerous musical, athletic (*Turnverein*), and horticultural (*Gartenverein*) societies; free-thinking (*Freie Gemeinden*)

and socialist organizations; and the Ger-
man-language press. The ubiquitous tavern
or beer hall was an integral part of German
social life; U.S. taverns were much more
for serious drinking than they were social
meeting places. Buildings made of half-
timbered construction, or *Fachwerk*, were
also a distinguishing ethnic trait of the
earliest German settlements (Figure 3.9).
But in actuality, the Germans were a large
and varied group with many different, often
conflicting, views. For example, German
radicals, Protestant liberals, and free think-
ers supported the antislavery cause, and
thus the pro-union, pro-Republican, and
pro-Lincoln position. Yet many German
Catholics of the nineteenth century actively
opposed reforms and supported the Democratic party.

Many Europeans, including the Germans, had emigrated to escape political
and religious persecution, but in the United
States they found ethnic persecution. The
U.S. economic and political elite saw the
retention of ethnic languages as retarding
Americanization. With the industrialization of the U.S. economy, people as well
as machines had to be interchangeable.
"Foreign" languages allowed ethnic groups
to maintain their culture and local liveli-
hoods, but prevented industrialists from
easily replacing one immigrant labor pool
with another. Common skills (reading and
writing in English and arithmetic) and
upper-class white-Anglo-Saxon-Protestant-
biased history assured that immigrant children would become assimilated. Wisconsin's Bennett Law (1889), which banned
the use of foreign languages in public and
private schools, legalized and institution-
alized this Americanization process.

The Bennett Law aroused the most bitter
ethnic and religious antagonisms in the
state's history. Germans in particular,
whether Catholics or Protestants, and to
some degree Scandinavian Lutherans, opposed the law because it would extinguish
foreign languages and cultures in Wisconsin
and destroy the system of parochial education. Ethnic and religious freedoms were

FIGURE 3.9 *Fachwerk* barn. Barns with this
construction continue to be common in northern
Germany. Old World Wisconsin displays this
and other ethnic buildings. (Wisconsin Division
of Tourism)

being curtailed in the very country to which
many of these immigrants had come to
escape social and legal discrimination. In
1890, with strong anti–Bennett Law sen-
timent, German and Scandinavian voters
swung the state election to the Democrats—
for only the second time since the Civil
War. The Democratic party captured 41
counties; in the entire eastern half of the
state only 6 counties remained Republican.
Except for 4 counties along the southern
border that were populated heavily by Brit-
ish-born settlers, the Republicans remained
the majority in 1890 in only the western
and northwestern counties, where native-
born Americans and generally nonthreat-
ened Scandinavians predominated.

Although German-born settlers were the
largest foreign-born ethnic group in Wisconsin, they continued to face extreme forms
of discrimination, especially during World
War I, when the United States was at war
with Germany. President Woodrow Wilson
and the U.S. Congress passed the Espionage
Act, which outlawed "disloyal" conduct.
Wisconsin had a disproportionate number
of prosecutions under this law, with western
and small-town Wisconsin tending to have
more prosecutions than other parts of the
state. Indictments were handed down for
such acts as criticizing U.S. foreign policy,
praising Germany, insulting the U.S. flag,

and saying that it was "a rich man's war and the poor man's fight." Most of these statements were made in private conversations, often over a beer; nevertheless, people were subject to heavy fines and even prison terms. Not only German-Americans but also unionists and socialists were persecuted by self-appointed patriots such as the American Protective League. Many German-Americans changed or anglicized their last names and the German names of their towns and villages.

Norwegians. No other country, except Ireland, contributed as large a proportion of its population to the United States as did Norway. From 1825 to 1915 about 750,000 Norwegians emigrated to the United States. From 1838 to 1865 Wisconsin was their principal place of settlement, and by 1900 Norwegians were the second largest foreign-born nationality in the state.

The earliest Norwegian settlements were on the Rock Prairie in Rock County, in southeastern Waukesha County near Lake Muskego, and in southeastern Dane and western Jefferson counties, all established in the 1840s. By 1850 most of the fertile land in southern and eastern Wisconsin had been settled. Colonies were later established in northeastern Wisconsin in Manitowoc County and in north-central Wisconsin in Winnebago, Portage, and Waupaca counties, but these Norwegian settlements were small and scattered compared with the large and compact colonies in southeastern Wisconsin. In the 1850s, under the Homestead Act, government land could still be bought for $1.25 an acre in these northern counties. In 1857 a rail line from Milwaukee to the Mississippi River facilitated Norwegian settlement in western Wisconsin. By 1870, Norwegian pioneers had spread over a 17-county region in western Wisconsin, stretching from Crawford to Polk and Chippewa counties (Figure 3.10).

At first, Norwegian immigrants worked as farm laborers for prosperous native-born farmers. They learned English, and learned about local crops and agricultural methods.

Tobacco, initially a Yankee cash crop, was quickly taken over by Norwegian farmers. The association between tobacco cultivation and Norwegians remains strong in Wisconsin today.

Norwegians brought their own ethnic culture, including food, religion, and politics. *Lefse*, unleavened potato bread, symbolizes Norwegian culture to Norwegians and to other ethnic groups as well. In 1982 Eau Claire had a shop selling only lefse! Although most Norwegians were Lutherans, they were also attracted to the Methodist and Episcopal churches. A Norwegian religious experiment was attempted in the Moravian communistic community in Ephraim on the Door Peninsula. The Norwegian-American newspapers supported progressive causes but were never as radical as the Finnish-American papers. Yet the *Emigranten* (the Emigrant), for example, published in the late nineteenth century, was against slavery, favored a liberal public land policy, and was hostile toward frontier land speculators.

Wisconsin's Ethnic Diversity. Several patterns resulting from Wisconsin's early ethnic settlement persist today. No large areas of the state are occupied by a single ethnic group; rather many small, relatively internally homogeneous communities are scattered throughout Wisconsin, although the German population is more heavily concentrated in the east and north-central portions, whereas Norwegians are more concentrated to the west and in the south-central regions. Norwegians represent majorities, for example, in Vernon County, southeastern Dane County, and in New Hope Township in Portage County. Similarly, German Lutherans are the majority in northern Jefferson County, Schleswig and Liberty townships, Manitowoc County, and in northeastern Dane County. Other ethnic groups, although not widely found in the state, are also highly localized. Poles form the majority in 11 out of 14 townships in Portage County and are major pockets in Marathon County and near Green Bay in Brown County; Belgians are concentrated

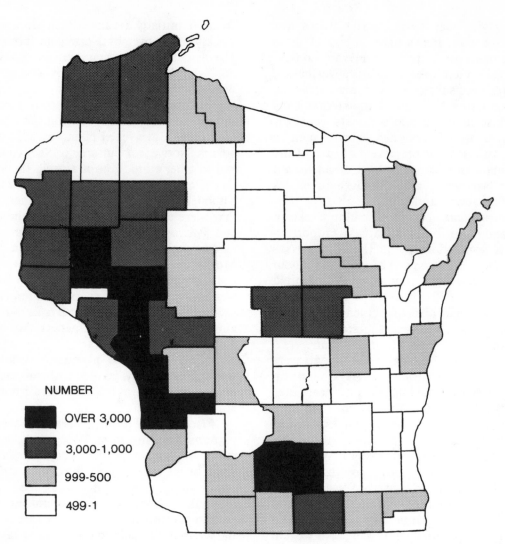

FIGURE 3.10 Number of Norwegian-born persons by county, 1890. (Based on Richard J. Fapso, *Norwegians in Wisconsin* [Madison: State Historical Society of Wisconsin, 1977])

in and east of Green Bay; Swiss are primarily found in Green County (Figure 3.11). In the great majority of rural townships a single ethnic group represents more than 50 percent of the population.

In addition to settlement location, cultural identification remains distinctive. In Vernon and Dane counties, tobacco growers are almost exclusively Norwegians. Polish settlers in the Stevens Point area specialize in potatoes. Swiss settlers in Green County produce Swiss cheese. Certain towns are known by locals and tourists as ethnic places: Wesby for Norwegian Lutherans,

Polonia for Catholic Poles, New Glarus and Monroe for Swiss, and Milwaukee for Germans. Numerous ethnic festivals in these and other towns keep the European ethnic heritage of Wisconsinites alive. Mount Horeb has its Little Norway, Song of Norway Pageant, and Nobrsk Golf Bowl. A Holland Festival is held in Cedar Grove. New Glarus has the Edelweiss Stars (Swiss singers), Heidi Festival, the William Tell Pageant, and the Swiss Volkfest. A city of Monroe brochure advertises "Swiss storefronts, a Swiss-style parking ramp and modern-Swiss style municipal building, the only

FIGURE 3.11 Alpine yodelers. Green County was the center for the New Glarus Swiss colony. In 1850 the Swiss represented 20 percent of the total county population; by 1890 they accounted for 33 percent. (Courtesy of the State Historical Society of Wisconsin, Madison)

Focus: Ethnic Festivals in Wisconsin

The many European ethnic groups who settled Wisconsin have maintained some of their cultural traditions, which are celebrated in ethnic festivals. The ethnic geography of Wisconsin is most visible to tourists in these festivals. For tourists and local residents alike these ethnic events make the people and places of the state special. A sample of these festivals indicates that ethnic pride is very much alive and that the sale of culture is profitable.

Syttende Mai, Stoughton. In May residents honor their rich Norwegian heritage with a parade, displays of Norse arts, crafts, and foods.

International Picnic, Green Bay. During June, Belgian, Czech, German, Greek, and Polish clubs sponsor outdoor picnics, including a folk fair, dancing, and ethnic bands.

Fyr Bal Festival, Ephraim. A Scandinavian celebration announcing the arrival of the summer season. Festivities include a fish boil, art exhibit, bonfires along the bay, and the blessing of the fleet of sailboats and motorboats.

Heidi Festival, New Glarus. Residents perform all the roles in the traditional Swiss story of Heidi. The Little Switzerland Festival includes yodeling, flag throwing, and a craft and food fair.

Holland Festival, Cedar Grove. This July Dutch event features dancers with *klompen* (wooden shoes), *woostebroodjes* (flavored sausages baked in a bun), an ethnic parade, folk fair, garden show, and operetta.

Festa Italiana, Milwaukee. One of the largest Italian festivals in the United States celebrates this ethnic group's food, entertainment, and heritage each July.

Volksfest, New Glarus. This August event honors Switzerland's independence day with authentic folk dancing, foods, native costumes, and yodeling. Each Labor Day weekend, the Wilhelm Tell Festival recounts one of Switzerland's national heroes.

Oktoberfest, Milwaukee and La Crosse. In September, folk dancers, German brass bands, yodeling, sing-alongs, and Bavarian foods, including *spanferkel* (roast pig), are featured in Glendale at the Old Heidelberg Park in Milwaukee. The Mississippi River city of La Crosse also celebrates Oktoberfest, turning the city into "a miniature Bavaria."

Swiss-type bandshell and outdoor theater in the nation, and a Swiss-motif water department building."

William Millard, a rural settlement geographer, studied the "sale of culture" in New Glarus, by which he means that a community sets out overtly to sell its cultural background to tourists (Figure 3.12). The sale of Swiss culture includes bits of its settlement history, language, religion, clothing, architecture, and diet. Millard found that towns selling culture share several characteristics: (1) saleable cultural items—festivals, foods, clothing, and souvenirs; (2) authentic cultural/ethnic relics (historic sites, pioneer buildings, museums); (3) economic stagnation; (4) strong local leadership; and (5) a physical site that is attractive or at least within a day's drive of a major metropolitan area. The tourist catchment basin for New Glarus, defined by a one-way, three-hour drive, reaches to Chicago, Eau Claire, Green Bay, and Cedar Rapids.

Religion and ethnicity are closely related. Southern and central Germans, who settled the western part of the state, were Catholics. Immigrants from northern Germany and parts of Switzerland were Lutherans, as were Scandinavians, who generally settled the western parts of the state. The later-arriving eastern European settlers were predominantly Catholic.

Settlement in the North, 1830s–1920s

Lumbering. Until late in the nineteenth century the westward movement of agricultural settlement had virtually bypassed the densely timbered regions of northern Wisconsin. After a series of treaties with the Winnebago, Menomonee, Sioux, and Chippewa Indian tribes were signed, loggers invaded the *pineries*, or white-pine forests. Within a few years, sawmill towns developed on the southern fringes of the white-pine belt. The buoyant pine logs, cut in the valleys upstream, were floated to sawmill centers located at strategic points on the rivers flowing out of the pineries.

The expansion of lumbering along the northern reaches of the Wisconsin, Chip-

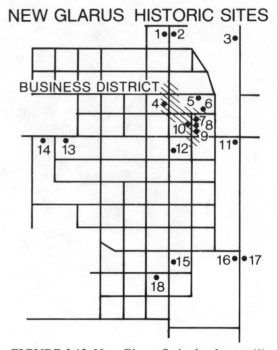

FIGURE 3.12 New Glarus Swiss land uses: (1) New Glarus Theater, (2) Wilhelm Tell Supper Club, (3) State historical marker, (4) Strickler's supermarket, (5) Swiss United Church of Christ, (6) Settlers Monument (commemorating the colonization of New Glarus in 1845), (7) Alpine Cafe, (8) Glarnor Stube (cafe), (9) New Glarus Bakery, (10) New Glarus Hotel, (11) Floral Clock, (12) Chalet of the Golden Fleece Historical Museum, (13) Historical Village Museum, (14) Swiss Reformed Cemetery, (15) Upright Swiss Embroideries (factory), (16) Swiss Miss Textile Mart, (17) Swiss Maid (cheese and sausage shop), and (18) E. Thierstein's Swiss Chalet (not open to public). (From William Millard, "The Sale of Culture: New Glarus, Nauvoo, and Galena" [Ph.D. dissertation, University of Minnesota, Minneapolis, 1969])

pewa, Red, Cedar, Black, St. Croix, and Wolf rivers and north of Green Bay contributed greatly to the state's frontier economy. In 1840 the value of lumber produced in this northern region was greater than the value of Wisconsin wheat. Although wheat production had again become far more important than lumbering by 1860, the value of lumber again overtook wheat in the 1870s and peaked in 1890 at $61 million.

By the early 1870s, as railroads reached the major sawmill centers and replaced rivers as supply lines, agricultural settlements developed along the southern fringes of the pineries. The Wisconsin Central pushed northward from Stevens Point through the heart of the pine belt to Ashland on Lake Superior, and during the next two decades railroads began to crisscross northern Wisconsin, opening up new territory. Before the 1870s only softwoods were marketable, and consequently the presence of white pine gave land value. Once the pine was removed, the land became virtually worthless. But railroads made hardwood lumbering possible. Suddenly, hardwood timber became valuable, and even land from which pines had been stripped had value because of the remaining hardwoods. Mills were erected at almost every railroad siding. Moreover, railroad companies (especially those that received land grants from the state to build railroads) and speculators began to promote agricultural settlements along the railroads, and the land as well as the timber acquired value.

In the nineteenth century, westward-moving farmers had remained south of the northern forest region and had traveled west across the prairies. When the 1890 census reported that the national frontier had virtually closed in the west, the Cutover region, which had previously been logged for timber, remained a reservoir of cheap land, a new frontier for U.S. agriculture.

Farming. As lumbering declined in the 1890s, agricultural colonization of northern Wisconsin began in earnest. The evolution of three distinctive agricultural and settlement regions—southern Wisconsin, the Old North, and the New North (Cutover region)—indicates the spread of farming northward (Figure 3.13). In Joseph Schafer's (1922) regionalization, the 16 counties of the Old North had 6 percent of the state's population (122,000) in 1860, whereas the New North—representing more than half of the state's land surface—had only 31,000 inhabitants. Lumbering was practiced in the New North, farming in the Old North.

Farming had replaced lumbering in the Old North. By 1869, 8 of these counties were among the top 14 wheat-producing counties in the state. But U.S.-born settlers tended to avoid these counties and settled in the fertile prairie lands of Minnesota, Iowa, and the Dakotas. Farming opportunities there were so attractive that nearly 250,000 Wisconsinites had migrated out of the state by 1890. Nevertheless, immigrants were being lured to the New North. In 1895 the state legislature created a State Board of Immigration, whose office was in Rhinelander, and appropriated money to conduct a study of northern agriculture. The research, done by William Henry, dean of the College of Agriculture, was published in 1895 in *Northern Wisconsin: A Handbook for the Homeseeker*. It was distributed by the State Board of Immigration and by 39 northern counties that had immigration bureaus.

Within 30 years the New North had gained 340,000 people; the total population in 1920 was 703,000. Although growth occurred in both urban and rural places, rural population increases were especially noteworthy; indeed, from 1900 to 1920 northern Wisconsin was the only section of the state to show an increase in rural population. Land was still available and foreign-born immigrants settled the area. In 1920 Scandinavians, especially Norwegians (19,000) and Swedes (16,000), predominated, followed by Germans (32,000) and a much smaller number of Poles (14,000). Of all the European immigrants, the Finns made the most distinctive contribution to the historical geography and cultural landscape of the Cutover region.

Finns. From 1874 to 1893 almost 70,000 emigrants left Finland for overseas countries; close to 2,000 of these settled in Wisconsin. Most left northwestern Finland, and they were the sons and daughters of landlords or the children of especially large families. The majority hoped to purchase farms in the United States or to save enough money to return to Finland and buy farms there. Many of these settlers had little formal education and their individual goals

FIGURE 3.13 The Old North and New North in Wisconsin in the 1860s. (Based on information from Joseph Schafer, *A History of Agriculture in Wisconsin* [Madison: State Historical Society of Wisconsin, 1922])

and political views tended to be conservative.

By the 1890s a second wave of emigration left southern and eastern Finland. These Finnish emigrants differed from the rest of the northwestern European settlers in that over 85 percent of them were landless laborers (both agricultural and industrial)—one of the highest percentages among all immigrant groups. They were fleeing harsh working conditions, severe unemployment (75 percent in Helsinki in 1892), and widespread famines. In addition, because southern Finland was the center of

socialist organizing and anti-tsarist agitation, the emigrants of the 1890s had been exposed to the Finnish Labor party's radical demands for universal suffrage, for an eight-hour day, and for the improvement of conditions for town workers and for landless agricultural laborers.

Al Gedicks, a sociologist, demonstrated that the socialist Finns had "proletarianized" backgrounds, whereas other immigrant groups who arrived in the upper Midwest (Minnesota, Wisconsin, and Michigan) around the same time did *not* share this same socioeconomic background.

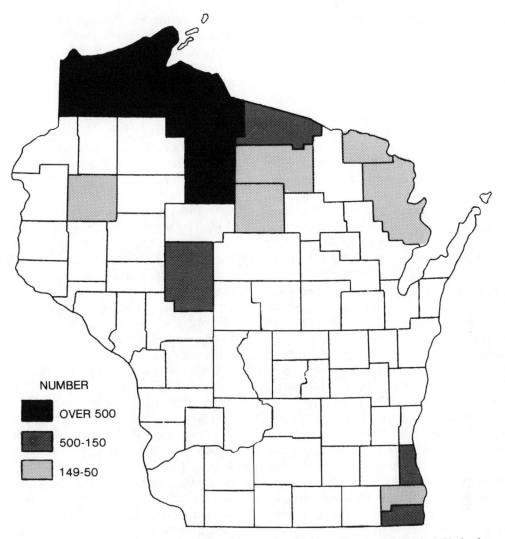

FIGURE 3.14 Number of Finnish-born persons by county, 1920. (Based on Mark Knipping, *Finns in Wisconsin* [Madison: State Historical Society of Wisconsin, 1977])

The most relevant comparison is with the Swedes who arrived at about the same time as the second wave of Finnish immigrants, but who were not involved in the early Upper Great Lakes labor-management disputes so characteristic of the late nineteenth century. Indeed, employers in the iron and copper mines frequently contrasted the "disruptive" Finns with the "cooperative" Swedes. Whereas the Finnish immigrants were primarily landless agrarian and urban workers, small farmers predominated in the influx from Sweden. Finnish immigrants had already been exposed to socialist ideas;

the majority of Swedish immigrants arrived in the United States before socialism became important in Sweden. Finnish immigrants possessed a collective consciousness, whereas Swedish settlers were more individualistic.

That Finns would settle in northern Wisconsin was inevitable, not because the land resembled their homeland, but because of the possibilities for mining and farming employment (Figure 3.14), although Michigan and Minnesota had many more iron and copper mines than did Wisconsin and therefore attracted most of the Finns. In

Wisconsin, dazzling advertisements by land promoters helped lure Finns to northern counties. Douglas, Iron, Bayfield, Price, and Ashland counties had two-thirds of the state's total Finnish population in 1910; by 1920 foreign-born Finns in the United States attained their peak population of 149,824— 44 percent of which was concentrated in the three Upper Great Lakes states.

In the north, Finns worked in iron-ore mines and lumber camps, on railroad construction and docks, and in Racine and Kenosha they toiled in tanneries. Working and living conditions were frequently not much better in Wisconsin than they had been in Finland. In the 1890s a Finnish worker could earn 75 cents for a 10-hour working day loading ore boats in Ashland and Superior. In 1899 a shoveler had to shovel nearly 50 tn (2.3 mt) to earn five dollars!

Many Finnish workers became active in the U.S. labor movement as socialists, communists, and members of the Industrial Workers of the World (IWW) and the Finnish Socialist Federation. The radical, political activism of the Finns was a most distinctive characteristic of this immigrant group. Several influential Finnish-language newspapers were published in Superior; one remains: the *Tyomies,* a socialist working-class newspaper. Finns also organized consumer cooperatives, which were operated on a nonprofit basis on the principle of one vote per member. In 1941 the Central Cooperative Exchange at Superior had sales of $5 million and 126 local affiliates, 29 of them in Wisconsin. The Finnish and Scandinavian cooperative tradition has helped make Wisconsin and Minnesota the leading states for all kinds of cooperatives in the United States. Indeed, the Wisconsin Department of Public Instruction requires a university course in cooperative economics for teacher certification.

The Finns, like other ethnic groups, brought with them their own cultural traditions. One of the most well known features of their material culture was, and still is, the sauna. In 1937, about 80 percent of the farms in Finland had their own sauna (6.5 persons per sauna). In the Swedish-speaking southwestern part of Finland, however, saunas were much less common (20.8 persons per sauna). Rural geographers Cotton Mather and Matti Kaups conducted several field traverses through Finnish settlements in the Upper Great Lakes states to see if saunas were associated with U.S. Finns. They found that over 9 out of 10 Finnish farmsteads had saunas and that this Finnish settlement index correlated with other Finnish landscape features as well. The features Mather and Kaups also found were the *lato,* or field barn, the connecting barn constructed in different stages, log structures with squared timbers, the presence of ladders along the sides and on the roofs of buildings, a larger percentage of unpainted buildings, often with flower-filled window boxes, and covered stoops on houses.

Finns built their farm buildings of hewn logs in the Scandinavian tradition. Exterior walls were of logs, right up into the gable. Germanic settlers, concentrated in the southern part of the state, used log construction also, but the gable peak was closed with vertical board and batten siding. Scandinavians shaped their logs for a closer fit, whereas the Germans tended to hew only the inner and outer surfaces leaving the tops and bottoms of the natural log. The Finns settled the northern coniferous forests of Wisconsin, and the Germans settled the southern deciduous forests. Both groups initially used wooden shingles and thatched roofs of rye straw, but the Finns also used forest materials traditionally used in Scandinavia, maintaining their traditional building techniques and folkways much longer than other immigrant groups. Three reasons explain their relative tenacity:

1. Finns arrived 60 years after the arrival of the Germans and Norwegians, who had already been assimilated into U.S. society for over two generations.
2. Finns had low-paying jobs and suffered economic hardship much longer than

other groups. Their poverty assured the survival of their culture.

3. Finns clustered in rural, relatively isolated, northern settlements and could therefore maintain their language and cultural traditions better than those groups concentrated in thickly settled, heterogeneous southern agricultural counties and cities.

Certainly, some Finnish cultural features have changed. Personal names such as Maki have been changed to Mackey, Kasi to Casey, and Lassi to Lassey. Yet many aspects of this ethnic culture remain visible in the rural landscape of northern Wisconsin.

Conclusion

The settler empire was not completely established in northern Wisconsin until the early twentieth century, whereas in southern Wisconsin it had existed since the 1830s. Indeed, 50 years of agricultural settlement in the southern counties were never matched by 90 years of development in the northern region. Officially, Wisconsin's agricultural frontier closed in 1928, when the last land office closed its doors at Wausau; yet the U.S. government had considered the agricultural frontier already closed by 1890.

THE NATIONALIST EMPIRE: RAILROADS AND FACTORIES

The generation between 1865 and 1895 was already mortgaged to the railroads, and no one knew it better than the generation itself.
—Henry Adams

In the late nineteenth century, Wisconsin's economy and landscapes were again transformed—this time from an agricultural settler empire, which at first had relied heavily on Britain and western Europe for markets and manufactured goods and later more on the U.S. economy, to an industrializing nationalistic empire, controlled completely by the United States. During the 1880s the vigorous expansion of an industrial economy, with its constant demands for raw materials, its need for expanding markets, and its development of ever-more efficient ways of overcoming distance, resulted in a mature industrial urban-based economy.

The building of railroads in the 1850s represented the first phase of industrialization, although the freight consisted largely of agricultural products. In the second phase, factories were built to process the state's natural resources, such as logs, grain, and hides. With the concentration of employment in factories and cities and of wealth among the upper classes, workers organized to improve their working and living conditions. Labor protests characterized Wisconsin in the late nineteenth century. Unionizing efforts and strikes culminated in radical politics that lasted until World War I.

Railroads, 1850s–1910s

Logging and railroad investors were the first major industrial entrepreneurs in Wisconsin. Investments in both industries were large and at high risk; consequently, consolidated companies were common. Private railroad investors, unlike lumber barons, based their investments and fortunes on congressional land grants, which were distributed by the Wisconsin government between 1850 and 1872. Wisconsin railroads were given 2.9 million acres (1.2 million ha), or nearly 8 percent of the state, to finance their ventures. Over half of this land was in the northwest where the La Crosse and Milwaukee Railroad was building a line across the state.

The first railroads, however, were built with local capital without the aid of land grants. These first trains ran between Milwaukee and Waukesha in 1851. In 1860 Wisconsin's railroads covered 891 mi (1,434 km), crisscrossing the state from the southern end of Lake Winnebago to Prairie du Chien (Figure 3.15); only one line ran outside this densely settled area to La Crosse. Southern Wisconsin was a major wheat-

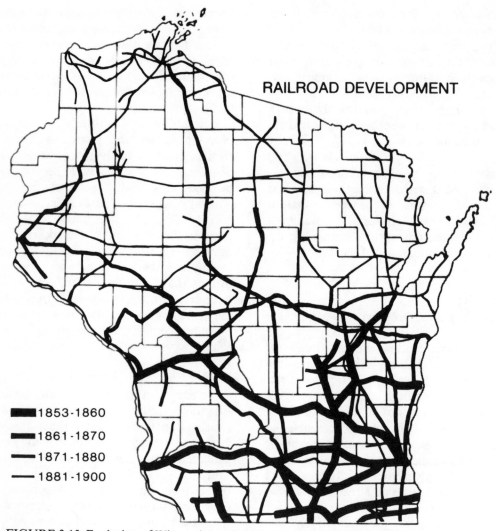

RAILROAD DEVELOPMENT

1853-1860
1861-1870
1871-1880
1881-1900

FIGURE 3.15 Evolution of Wisconsin's railroad network, 1853–1900. (Based on Wisconsin Regional Planning Committee, December 1934)

producing area at this time, and railroads hauled grain to storage facilities at Milwaukee and Racine. Throughout the 1860s agricultural produce, mainly wheat, accounted for 75 percent of all freight carried on Wisconsin's railroads. In 1867, 1,030 grain mills had been constructed, and by 1873 rail trackage amounted to 2,060 mi (3,315 km). By 1916 railroads covered 7,693 mi (12,380 km).

By the 1860s the state's railroads were linked to the national transportation system and to the national economy. Better ac-

cessibility attracted eastern investors to build even more railroads—for example, the Wisconsin Central Railroad in 1871. The line from Menasha to Stevens Point to Ashland was completed in 1877, and its construction preceded settlement, so no communities were there to invest in or lose money on the line. Instead, eastern investors risked about $9 million, and their company received 837,000 acres (338,734 ha) of government land.

Wisconsin had an extensive rail network long before most roads were even gravel-covered. In 1900, when every city and agricultural and natural resource region was connected by a railroad, only 17 percent of the state's rural roads had gravel surfaces, and not until 1916 did the state take direct responsibility for roads. Railroads, not roads, formed the transportation basis for industrialization in the late nineteenth and early twentieth centuries.

Manufacturing, 1860s–1920s

Twenty-five years after the first white agricultural settlement, the state government actively fostered industrialization by lowering interest rates and introducing tax rebates and credit regulations. The earliest attempts at manufacturing were aimed at the state's self-sufficiency; producing for regional and national markets was neither promoted nor important.

Prior to the Civil War, Wisconsin industries were a mixture of household manufacturing, craft shops, mills, and factories manufacturing mainly processed raw materials (grain, logs, and hides). In 1850 about 40 percent of the total value added by manufacturing came from the milling of flour and lumber. In 1860 flour milling alone represented 40 percent of the total volume of the state's manufacturing, but wheat farming collapsed rapidly thereafter, and by 1870 flour milling accounted for only 25 percent of the state's value of processed products.

The kind and location of manufacturing in the 1860s were tied to local natural resources and to the distribution of population for both labor and markets. Counties south of a line from Green Bay to Grant County contained 93 percent of the state's population (305,391) and 92 percent of the state's value added in manufacturing ($3.8 million) in 1850. A decade later, as the north began to be more populated, these southern counties slipped to 83 percent of the state's population and 84 percent of the value added.

Throughout the 1850s and 1860s one, two, or three types of manufacturing dominated most county economies. Generally,

the more rural the county, the fewer kinds of industries; the more urban the county, the more diversified the industrial base. In Milwaukee and elsewhere in the agricultural southern part of the state, factories processed farm products and produced agriculturally related machinery. Meat packing, tanning, and malt-liquor brewing were important enterprises. Flour milling was the most common way of processing grain, and the E. P. Allis Company in Milwaukee produced much of this flour-milling machinery. The J. I. Case works at Racine became a major U.S. farm-machinery manufacturer during the 1860s, selling 1,500 10-horse threshers annually. Other Wisconsin factories were important producers of seeders.

Lumbering involved the largest manufacturing investment and payroll after 1860. At its peak from 1888 to 1893, lumbering accounted for 25 percent of all wages in the state, and the value of lumber products represented more than the combined value of grain-milling, malting and brewing, leather, and foundry and machine-shop products. By 1890 Wisconsin had over 1,100 sawmills, and this industry produced $61 million in manufactured products (Table 3.2). The E. P. Allis Company specialized in sawmill machinery and later supplied steam engines to the nation's industries. Lumbering and flour milling continued to be the dominant industries in the state until 1900. Providing machinery for both flour mills and sawmills, Allis became Milwaukee's largest industry by the late 1880s, with an average of 1,500 employees. Dairy farming and the manufacturing of dairy products grew rapidly from 1880 to 1890, as wheat farming declined. Butter, cheese, and condensed milk climbed within a decade from sixteenth place to eighth place in the value of manufactured products (Table 3.2).

By the turn of the century, the timber industry was becoming more diversified as the paper and pulp industries reached eighth place among Wisconsin's industries (Table 3.2). The paper and pulp industries were

TABLE 3.2
Ten Leading Industries by Value of Manufactured Products, 1880-1920

Industry	1880	1890	1900	1910	1920
	Millions of Dollars				
Flour & grist milling	27.6	24.2	26.3	31.6	58.3
Lumber & timber	18.4	60.9	57.6	57.9	88.8
Leather	8.8	11.1	20.0	44.6	94.7
Liquors, distilled & malt	6.6	14.1	19.3	32.1	
Iron & steel	6.5	6.5	8.9		
Slaughtering & meat packing	6.5	8.3	13.6	27.2	104.2
Clothing	4.8	8.0			
Carriages & wagons	4.7				
Foundry & machine shop parts	3.9	8.4	22.2	54.1	198.6
Agricultural implements	3.7				
Planing & milling		6.2			
Butter, cheese, & condensed milk		6.9	20.1	53.8	221.4
Paper & wood pulp			10.8	25.9	80.3
Furniture & refrigerators			8.7	18.6	
Car & general construction				14.3	
Engines & waterwheels					90.9
Knit goods & textiles					51.7
Motor vehicles					119.3

Source: J.H.H. Alexander, "A Short Industrial History of Wisconsin," The
Wisconsin Blue Book, 1929 (Madison: Democrat Printing Co.,
1929, pp. 31-49).

concentrated on the lower Fox River at Neenah and Menasha, where flour milling had been their predecessors, and on the upper Wisconsin River, where they had been built with lumbering profits. Elsewhere in the state, specific places often became associated with specific industries. Manitowoc was identified with kitchen pots and pans; Beloit with the largest paper-making machines; Sheboygan with plumbing fixtures, chairs, and bratwurst; and Chippewa Falls with shoes and boots.

By 1910 Wisconsin ranked eighth in industrial production in the United States. The industrial economy of the state had grown rapidly and had shifted its emphasis. The total value of manufactured products was $590.3 million, with lumber and timber, foundry and machine-shop parts, dairy products, leather goods, and liquors the major industries. By 1920, manufactured dairy products, and foundry and machine-shop parts led all industrial types (Table 3.2).

SELECTED REFERENCES

Alvord, Clarence W. The Mississippi Valley in British Politics. 2 vols. New York: Russell and Russell, 1959.

American Fur Company. "American Fur Company Invoices, 1821–22." Collections of the State Historical Society of Wisconsin, vol. 11 (1888), pp. 370–379.

Askin, John. "Fur Trade on the Upper Lakes, 1778–1815." Collections of the State Historical Society of Wisconsin, vol. 19 (1910), pp. 234–374.

Bennett, Sari J., and Carville V. Earle. Labor

and Its Power in the Gilded Age: The Northeastern United States, 1881–1894. Baltimore: Occasional Papers in Geography, University of Maryland Baltimore County, 1981.

———. Labor Power Lost, and Regained: The Geography of Strikes in the Northeastern United States, 1881–1894. Baltimore: Occasional Papers in Geography, University of Maryland Baltimore County, 1981.

———. The Failure of Socialism in the United States: A Geographical Interpretation. Baltimore: Occasional Papers in Geography, University of Maryland Baltimore County, 1980.

———. The Geography of American Labor and Industrialization, 1865–1908: An Atlas. Baltimore: Occasional Papers in Geography, University of Maryland Baltimore County, 1980.

Blair, Emma H., ed. The Indian Tribes of the Upper Mississippi Valley and Great Lakes Region. 2 vols. Cleveland: The Arthur Clark Co., 1911.

Bolus, Malvina, ed. People and Pelts: Selected Papers of the Second North American Fur Trade Conference. Winnipeg, Manitoba: Peguis Publishers, 1972.

Bolz, J. Arnold. Portage into the Past. Minneapolis: University of Minnesota Press, 1960.

Bridgewater, William R. "The American Fur Company." Ph.D. dissertation, Yale University, 1935.

Campbell, M. W. The North West Company. Toronto: The Macmillan Co. of Canada, 1973.

Cass, L. B. "Considerations on the Present State of the Indians and Their Removal to the West of the Mississippi." North American Review, no. 66 (1980), pp. 1–15.

Chittenden, Hiram M. The American Fur Trade of the Far West. 3 vols. New York: Francis P. Harper, 1902.

Clark, James I. Wisconsin Meets the Great Depression. Madison: State Historical Society of Wisconsin, 1956.

———. Wisconsin Women Fight for Suffrage. Madison: State Historical Society of Wisconsin, 1956.

———. The British Leave Wisconsin. Madison: State Historical Society of Wisconsin, 1955.

———. The Civil War of Private Colonies. Madison: State Historical Society of Wisconsin, 1955.

———. Wisconsin Grows to Statehood. Madison: State Historical Society of Wisconsin, 1955.

———. Wisconsin: Land of Frenchmen, Indians, and the Beaver. Madison: State Historical Society of Wisconsin, 1955.

———. The Wisconsin Lead Region. Madison: State Historical Society of Wisconsin, 1955.

Clayton, James L. "The Impact of Traders' Claims on the American Fur Trade." In The Frontier in American Development: Essays in Honor of Paul Wallace Gates, edited by David M. Ellis. Ithaca, N.Y.: Cornell University Press, 1969.

———. "The Growth and Economic Significance of the American Fur Trade, 1790–1890." In Aspects of the Fur Trade: Selected Papers of the 1965 North American Fur Trade Conference, pp. 62–72. St. Paul: Minnesota Historical Society, 1967.

———. "The American Fur Company: The Final Years." Ph.D. dissertation, Cornell University, 1964.

Corcoran, Charles. "The Location of La Pointe." Wisconsin Magazine of History, vol. 30, no. 1 (1946), pp. 78–84.

Curot, Michael. "A Wisconsin Fur-Trader's Journal, 1803–1804." Collections of the State Historical Society of Wisconsin, vol. 20 (1911), pp. 396–472.

Davidson, John N. "Missions on Chequamegon Bay." Collections of the State Historical Society of Wisconsin, vol. 12 (1892), pp. 434–452.

Douglass, John M. "Cultural Changes Among the Wisconsin Indian Tribes During the French Contact Period." The Wisconsin Archeologist, vol. 30, no. 1 (1949), pp. 1–21.

Dunham, Douglas. "The French Element in the American Fur Trade, 1760–1816." Ph.D. dissertation, University of Michigan, 1950.

Fapso, Richard J. Norwegians in Wisconsin. Madison: State Historical Society of Wisconsin, 1977.

Fitzpatrick, Edward A. Wisconsin. Milwaukee: Bruce Publishing Co., 1931.

Folsom, William H. C. Fifty Years in the Northwest. St. Paul: Pioneer Press, 1888.

Gara, Larry. A Short History of Wisconsin. Madison: Kingsport Press for the State Historical Society of Wisconsin, 1962.

Gates, Charles M., ed. Five Fur Traders of the Northwest. St. Paul: Minnesota Historical Society, 1965.

Gedicks, Al. "The Social Origins of Radicalism Among Finnish Immigrants in Midwest Mining Counties." The Review of Radical Political Economics, vol. 8, no. 3 (Fall 1976), pp. 1–31.

Gilman, Rhoda R. "The Fur Trade in the Upper Mississippi Valley." *Wisconsin Magazine of History*, vol. 58 (Autumn 1974), pp. 3–18.

Glaab, Charles N., and Lawrence Larsen. "Neenah-Menasha in the 1870's: The Development of Flour Milling and Paper Making." *Wisconsin Magazine of History*, vol. 52 (Autumn 1968), pp. 19–34.

Hamilton, Raphael N. *Marquette's Explorations: The Narratives Reexamined.* Madison: University of Wisconsin Press, 1970.

Hastenrath, Sharon. "The Influence of the Climate of the 1820's and 1830's on the Collapse of the Menomini Fur Trade." *The Wisconsin Archeologist*, vol. 53, no. 1 (1972), pp. 20–39.

Hibbard, Benjamin Horace. *History of the Public Land Policies.* Madison: University of Wisconsin Press, 1965.

Hill, George. *Wisconsin's Changing Population.* Madison: University of Wisconsin, Science Inquiry Publication, Bulletin IX, 1942.

Holley, John M. "Waterways and Lumber Interests of Western Wisconsin." In *Proceedings of the State Historical Society of Wisconsin*, 1906, pp. 208–215.

Hunt, George T. *The Wars of the Iroquois.* Madison: University of Wisconsin Press, 1940.

Hurst, James W. *Law and Economic Growth: The Legal History of the Lumber Industry in Wisconsin, 1836–1915.* Cambridge: Harvard University Press, 1954.

"Indians Lose Lands in Wisconsin." *Badger History*, vol. 29, no. 4 (March 1976), pp. 46–49.

Innis, Harold A. *The Fur Trade in Canada.* Toronto: University of Toronto Press, 1956.

———. "The North West Company." *Canadian Historical Review*, vol. 8 (1927), pp. 308–321.

Irwins, Matthew. "Fur Trade and Factory System at Green Bay." *Collections of the State Historical Society of Wisconsin*, vol. 7 (1908), pp. 269–288.

Jaenen, Cornelius. "French Colonial Attitudes and the Explorations of Jolliet and Marquette." *Wisconsin Magazine of History*, vol. 56, no. 4 (1973), pp. 300–310.

Johnson, Hidegard Binder. *Order Upon the Land.* New York: Oxford University Press, 1976.

Kay, Jeanne. "Wisconsin Indian Hunting Patterns, 1634–1836." *Annals of the Association of American Geographers*, vol. 69, no. 3 (September 1979), pp. 402–418.

———. "The Land of La Baye: The Ecological Impact of the Green Bay Fur Trade, 1634–1836." Ph.D. dissertation, University of Wisconsin–Madison, 1977.

Kellogg, Louise P. *The British Regime in Wisconsin and the Northwest.* Madison: State Historical Society of Wisconsin, 1935.

———. "The Americanization of a French Settlement." *Green Bay Historical Bulletin*, vol. 5, no. 3 (1929), pp. 1–5.

———. "The Fur Trade in Wisconsin." *The Wisconsin Archeologist*, vol. 17, no. 3 (1918), pp. 55–60.

Knipping, Mark. *Finns in Wisconsin.* Madison: State Historical Society of Wisconsin, 1977.

Levathes, Louise. "Milwaukee: More Than Beer." *National Geographic*, vol. 158, no. 2 (August 1980), pp. 180–201.

Lewis, Herbert S. "European Ethnicity in Wisconsin: An Exploratory Formulation." *Ethnicity*, vol. 5, no. 2 (June 1978), pp. 174–188.

Mather, Cotton, and Matti Kaups. "The Finnish Sauna: A Cultural Index to Settlement." *Annals of the Association of American Geographers*, vol. 53, no. 4 (December 1963), pp. 494–504.

Meinig, Donald. "A Macrogeography of Western Imperialism: Some Morphologies of Moving Frontiers of Political Control." In *Settlement and Encounter,* edited by Fay Gale and Graham H. Lawton, pp. 213–240. Melbourne: Oxford University Press, 1969.

Millard, William. "The Sale of Culture: New Glarus, Nauvoo, and Galena." Ph.D. dissertation, University of Minnesota, Minneapolis, 1969.

Miller, David Harry, and William W. Savage, Jr., eds. *The Character and Influence of the Indian Trade in Wisconsin.* Norman: University of Oklahoma Press, 1977.

Nesbit, Robert C. *Wisconsin, A History.* Madison: University of Wisconsin Press, 1973.

Nute, Grace L. *The Voyageur.* St. Paul: Minnesota Historical Society, 1955.

Peake, Ora B. *History of the U.S. Indian Factory System, 1795–1822.* Denver: Sage Books, 1954.

Petersen, William J. "Steamboating in the Upper Mississippi Fur Trade." *Minnesota History*, vol. 13, no. 3 (1932), pp. 221–243.

Peterson, Dale A. "Lumbering on the Chippewa: The Eau Claire Area. 1845–1885." Ph.D. thesis, University of Minnesota, Minneapolis, 1970.

Phillips, Paul C. *The Fur Trade.* 2 vols. Norman: University of Oklahoma Press, 1961.

Phillips, William C. "The American Fur Company, 1817–1827." Master's thesis, University of Wisconsin–Madison, 1931.

Portier, Louis B. "Capture of Mackinsaw, 1763." *Wisconsin Historical Collections*, vol. 8 (1879), pp. 227–231.

Quimby, George I. *Indian Life in the Upper Great Lakes: 11,000 B.C. to 1800 A.D.* Chicago: University of Chicago Press, 1960.

Raney, William Francis. *Wisconsin—A Story of Progress*. New York: Prentice-Hall, 1940.

Ray, Arthur J. *Indians in the Fur Trade*. Toronto: University of Toronto Press, 1974.

Ross, Frank E. "The Fur Trade of the Western Great Lakes Region." *Minnesota History*, vol. 19, pp. 271–307.

Sale, Randall D., and Edwin D. Karn. *American Expansion*. Homewood, Ill.: Dorsey Press, 1962.

Schafer, Joseph. *The Winnebago-Horicon Basin*. Madison: Wisconsin Institute of Sociology, 1937.

_____. *Four Wisconsin Counties*. Madison: State Historical Society of Wisconsin, 1927.

_____. *A History of Agriculture in Wisconsin*. Madison: State Historical Society of Wisconsin, 1922.

Smith, Guy-Harold. "Notes on the Distribution of the German-Born in Wisconsin in 1905." *Wisconsin Magazine of History*, vol. 13 (1929–1930), pp. 107–120.

Soltow, Lee. *Patterns of Wealthholding in Wisconsin Since 1850*. Madison: University of Wisconsin Press, 1971.

Stark, William F. *Ghost Towns of Wisconsin*.

Sheboygan: Zimmermann Press, 1977.

Trewartha, G. T. "The Prairie du Chien Terrace: Geography of Confluence Site." *Annals of the Association of American Geographers*, vol. 22 (1932), pp. 119–158.

Trowbridge, F. N. "Confirming Land Titles in Early Wisconsin." *Wisconsin Magazine of History*, vol. 26 (1943), pp. 314–322.

Turner, Frederick J. *The Character and Influence of the Indian Trade in Wisconsin*. Norman: University of Oklahoma Press, 1977.

Vogel, Virgil J. "Wisconsin's Name: A Linguistic Puzzle." *Wisconsin Magazine of History*, vol. 48, no. 3 (1965), pp. 181–186.

Walsch, Margaret. *The Manufacturing Frontier Pioneer Industry in Antebellum Wisconsin, 1830–1860*. Madison: State Historical Society of Wisconsin, 1972.

Wisconsin's Historic Sites. Madison: The Committee on Wisconsin Women, 1948.

Wright, G. A. "Some Aspects of Early and Mid-Seventeenth Century Exchange Networks in the Western Great Lakes." *Michigan Archaeologist*, vol. 13 (1967), pp. 181–197.

Wyman, Roger E. "Wisconsin Ethnic Groups and the Election of 1890." *Wisconsin Magazine of History*, vol. 51, no. 4 (1968), pp. 269–293.

Zeitlin, Richard H. *Germans in Wisconsin*. Madison: State Historical Society of Wisconsin, 1977.

CHAPTER 4

THE NORTHWOODS REGION

Physical features and human uses of land vary. The combination of environmental and sociopolitical conditions gives rise to special cultural landscapes or regions. Wisconsin has five regions based on predominant county land uses (Figure 4.1).

The northern third of the state is essentially a *forested region* with occasional pockets of agriculture and a few small towns. Logging was and remains important; but recreation and tourism is by far the most widespread and economically important land use. An outlier of the northern forest region is in central Wisconsin, in the Central Sand Plain. Although forests also predominate here and little of the total land area is used for farming, canning crops (vegetables for processing) are a distinctive agricultural activity in this area.

In the southeastern third of the state, the *agricultural region* is characterized by farms that use over half of the land. The highest value of farmland and buildings and value of crop production are found here, in what has always been the agricultural heartland of Wisconsin. A three-county outlier of this agricultural region is found in western Wisconsin along Interstate 94.

Milwaukee County is the only urban county. Other urban places occupy small portions of their counties. However, each city is an *urban region* by itself and is also similar to and related to other cities in the state. Extending to the west of Milwaukee is the *suburban region* of Waukesha County, and extending eastward from Minneapolis–St. Paul is the suburban landscape of St. Croix County. Suburban counties have experienced sharp declines in harvested acreage since the 1930s, yet they have a high concentration of amenity agriculture: sod farms, flowers for florists, greenhouses, nurseries, and horse stables and riding academies. On the edge of these suburban counties and in the immediately adjacent agricultural counties, urban and agricultural land uses are intermingled: truck dealers, manufacturing plants, supper clubs, residential subdivisions, dairy farms, pick-your-own apple orchards, and vegetable stands.

The *mixed farm and forest region* is wedged between the northern forest and southeastern agricultural regions. In this transition region, one-quarter to one-third of the total area is harvested cropland. The region excels in dairy farms and is the major part of the Wisconsin cheese belt.

The next four chapters deal with the state's major regions. "The Southern Agricultural Region," Chapter 5, discusses the agricultural counties of southeastern Wisconsin and the mixed farm and forest counties in the western and central parts of the state. Cities outside metropolitan Milwau-

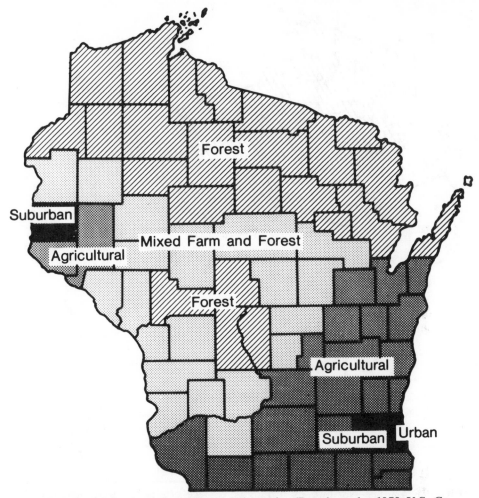

FIGURE 4.1 Major land-use types in Wisconsin. (Based on the *1978 U.S. Census of Agriculture* [Washington, D.C.: U.S. Government Printing Office, 1979])

kee are examined in Chapter 6, "The Urban Regions." Chapter 7, "The Milwaukee Metropolitan Region," deals with urban and suburban Milwaukee. The present chapter outlines the historical evolution of the northern forested region, known as the Northwoods.

Driving northward in Wisconsin, one has the feeling of entering a different region. The Northwoods has a distinctive look, smell, sound, and feel. The notion of a region exists because places possess physical and cultural attributes that set them apart in our minds from other places. If the distinctions are strong enough, both resi-

dents and outsiders perceive the place as different and unique. Sometimes the distinctiveness of a region is strong enough to be captured with a single word or phrase. The term "northwoods" invokes such a vivid image. We think of vast and dark evergreen forests, clear lakes, and rushing streams. In thinking about the region over time, images of Indians, fur traders, lumberjacks, miners, stump farmers, and Chicago tourists come to mind.

Geographers use the concept of a *vernacular region* to delimit distinctive places defined by ordinary people. A vernacular region is denoted by the common name or

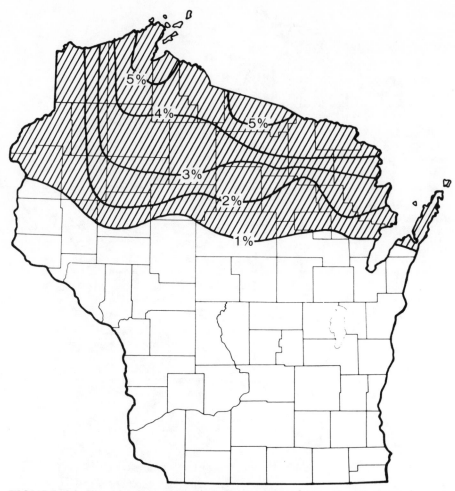

FIGURE 4.2 The Northwoods region. Percentage of "northern" terms in commercial telephone listings. (Ingolf Vogeler, J. Brady Foust, and Anthony R. de Souza, "The Northwoods Region: A Distinctive Area for Human Settlement," *Wisconsin Dialogue*, no. 3 [Spring 1983], p. 101. Reprinted by permission of the University of Wisconsin–Eau Claire.)

phrase that people who live in the area use and that is identified with the region by both residents and outsiders. "Northwoods" and its variations are such regional terms. The relative frequency of business names containing "northwoods," "northern," "north-bound," "northstar," and similar words was tabulated by Ingolf Vogeler, Brady Foust, and Anthony de Souza from the white pages of telephone books throughout Wisconsin. In Figure 4.2, which shows the results of this tabulation, the Northwoods region stands out clearly. South of

Highway 29, "northern" terms were few and far between, but they increased rapidly to the north—representing over 5 percent of all commercial listings in Bayfield and Vilas counties.

Much of the regional character of the Northwoods results from its resource base (described in Chapter 2), which is quite different from that of the rest of the state. This natural environment has been used in different ways by different groups of people, each successive group having had to earn a living from the land in the most productive way possible, given existing technology, the goals and needs of the inhabitants, and the local and national economy at the time. A study of the *sequent occupancy* of the Northwoods shows that each period of human settlement has played a role in producing the uniqueness of the region as we see it today.

The Indians, who now live mainly on reservations and in major urban centers, were the first inhabitants of the Northwoods. The next major resource users were logging and mining companies. With the depletion of white pine and other valuable timber and with the need for food in the northern mining towns, immigrant agriculturalists were attracted to the region. The limits of climate, soils, and distance from markets restricted farming, so that after the Great Depression, the Northwoods was largely abandoned by farmers. But with the post–World War II recreational boom, the region became Wisconsin's major recreational area.

INDIAN RESERVATIONS

Native Americans have occupied the northern section of the state for over 20,000 years. In the first part of the sixteenth century, they began trading furs for European products, first with the French, later with the British, and finally with U.S. traders.

After about 1820, when the number of fur-bearing animals was declining and the fur trade moving north into Canada, Wisconsin Indians had no useful role to play for the Europeans. Indeed, for white settlers they represented obstacles to lumbering and later to agricultural expansion. Consequently, the Indian nations of the Northwoods were forced to cede their lands, mostly from 1836 to 1842, and they were resettled by the U.S. government on reservations, which were generally the least-accessible and least-productive agricultural, lumbering, and mining lands in the state.

The Bureau of Indian Affairs (BIA), which is in charge of the U.S. reservation system,

was established within the U.S. War Department in 1824 and transferred to the U.S. Department of the Interior in 1849. Indian groups were initially treated as nations, which signed treaties with the U.S. government; in diplomacy and war they were treated as sovereign but dependent nations by the federal government. In 1871, the U.S. government abandoned the pretext of Indian sovereignty and reclassified Indians as "wards" of the state. Thereafter, the BIA attempted to "civilize" the Indians by assimilating them into the white society that had overrun them.

A fundamental change occurred in 1887 with the passage of the Dawes Allotment Act. Commissioner of Indian Affairs Thomas Jefferson Morgan outlined the new policy in 1889.

(1) The Reservation systems belong to the past, (2) Indians must be absorbed into our national life, not as Indians, but as American citizens, (3) the Indian must be "individualized" and treated as an individual by the government, (4) the Indian must "conform to the White man's ways, peaceably if they will, forceably if they must," (5) the Indian must be prepared for the new order through a system of compulsory education and (6) the traditional society of Indian groups must be broken up. (U.S., Department of Interior, *United States Indian Service,* 1962, p. 58)

Forced assimilation included allotting individuals tribal lands, selling "surplus" lands, sending children to compulsory boarding schools, and forbidding adults certain cultural practices, including religious ones. In Wisconsin, as elsewhere in the United States, the Dawes Act justified the presence of white institutions, such as government and religious day and boarding schools, on the reservations (Figure 4.3). Yet even in 1902 many people, including Wisconsin's conservative senator, John Spooner, known as a benevolent paternalist, realized that the Indians lived "in 'concentration camps' called reservations."

The failure of forced assimilation was

FIGURE 4.3 Indian reservation institutions, 1928. Mission, day, and boarding schools were also found on reservations in other states. (Based on information in Edward A. Fitzpatrick, *Wisconsin* [Milwaukee: Bruce Publishing Co., 1931])

recognized by the U.S. government in the 1930s. President Franklin D. Roosevelt gave Native Americans a New Deal with the Indian Reorganization Act of 1934, which supported strong cultural, political, and economic tribal groups on their reservations. A revolving federal loan fund aided the development of tribal natural resources. Day schools became focal points for community services and developments. These policies represented the first and only attempt by the federal government to rebuild tribal economies that had been distorted by territorial confinement and cultural genocide. Subsequent BIA commissioners

pursued policies that attempted to terminate all special government services to Native Americans. Yet, Native Americans and reservations persist.

The earliest reservations in Wisconsin were established in 1854, and all the large ones—Red Cliff, Bad River, Lac du Flambeau, Lac Court Oreilles, and Menominee (a county also)—are found in the Northwoods region. Of the 10 reservations, 3 have over 40,000 acres (16,188 ha) and 2 have 11,000–15,000 acres (4,451–6,070 ha). The largest, Menominee County and reservation, has 225,734 acres (91,354 ha) (Table 4.1). The total reservation land of

TABLE 4.1
Indian Reservations in Wisconsin, 1980

Reservations	Total Pop.	Employed, Earning Over $7,000 (Percent)	Unemployed (Percent)	Land (Acres)			
				Original Reservation	1980 Reservation	Tribal	Individual Allotments
Bad River	1,316	27	46	124,530	56,013	22,956	33,057
Lac Courte Oreilles	1,811	19	61	69,136	43,346	17,255	26,091
Lac Du Flambeau	1,485	33	42	71,030	44,649	30,149	14,500
Menominee	3,384	41	24	233,900	225,734	225,734	--
Mole Lake	280	14	64	--	1,694	1,694	--
Oneida	3,384	42	15	65,450	2,216	2,216	--
Potawatomi	390	11	65	--	11,666	11,266	400
Red Cliff	1,349	25	57	14,612	7,357	5,246	2,111
St. Croix	1,041	26	63	--	1,770	1,770	--
Stockbridge-Munsee	948	30	50	15,327	2,254	2,250	4
Winnebago	1,718	25	63	--	4,279	607	3,672
Total	17,106	Average 27	Average 50	593,985	400,978	318,893	79,835

Source: U.S., Department of the Interior, Bureau of Indian Affairs, Great Lakes Agency, Ashland, Wisconsin.

414,135 acres (167,600 ha) is misleading because not all land on the reservations belongs to Native Americans, individually or collectively. When Indians acquired individual allotments through the Dawes Act, they often found temporary relief from their poverty by selling their land to whites.

The Native American population of Wisconsin is the third largest east of the Mississippi River—after North Carolina and New York. Only four western states have a greater diversity of Indian cultures than Wisconsin with its three major linguistic stocks. Although their population grew from 11,200 in 1930 to 29,497 in 1980 (with a 56 percent increase between 1970 and 1980), Native Americans in Wisconsin have largely remained concentrated in areas with current or former reservations (Figure 4.4).

About 30 percent of the Native American population is urban: Twenty percent live in Milwaukee and 5 percent in Green Bay alone. About 25 percent of rural Indians are concentrated in five counties; Menominee County by itself accounts for 10 percent. Wisconsin is the only state east of the Mississippi to have a large number of reservations, yet the small number of Native Americans has left little lasting impact on the cultural landscape. On the Great Plains and in the Southwest, reservation landscapes are quite distinctive by comparison. Nevertheless, Wisconsin's reservations do share some features with the Great Plains and Southwest reservations, and their presence adds a distinctive character to the Northwoods. Having passed through a period of drastic cultural change, Native Americans have developed on the reservations their own characteristics of place based on their aboriginal cultures, persistent rural poverty, the religious and educational influences of Christian churches, and the ever-changing policies of the U.S. government as expressed by the BIA, Public Health Service, and other federal agencies.

The reservations of Wisconsin are mostly administered by the BIA at the Hayward agency, but some functions are performed by the Minneapolis area office. Each of four large northern reservations has at least one principal village, in which BIA and tribal social services are provided. These towns also provide the same commercial goods and services found in nearby white towns. The residential sections consist of two types of dwellings: BIA-sponsored houses and houses that were independently built. The uniformity of the public housing projects is in sharp contrast to the eclectic designs of the remaining Native American houses.

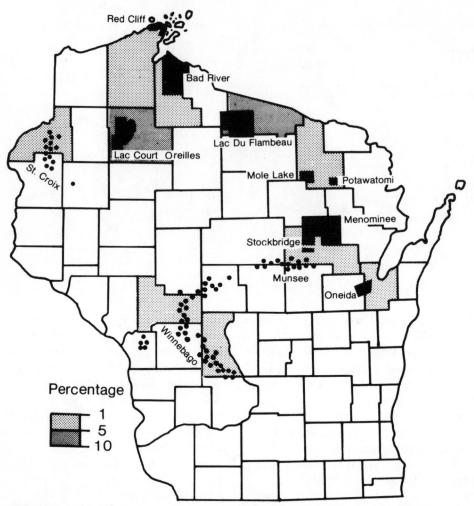

FIGURE 4.4 Indian reservations and settlements, 1980. (Black areas show reservations; black dots represent scattered tribal lands. The map also shows the distribution of Native Americans as a percentage of the total county population. (Data from the *1980 U.S. Census of Population and Housing* [Washington, D.C.: U.S. Government Printing Office, 1981])

At one time, every reservation had a mission school operated by the Roman Catholic church, such as St. Francis Indian Mission at Reserve (Figure 4.5). In the past, they were frequently boarding schools. Native American children were taken away from their parents and prohibited from speaking their own languages at these schools. Education was, and frequently still is, used to teach white cultural values and behaviors and to destroy, by neglect or by design, Native American cultures. Christian religions, particularly Roman Cathol-

icism, changed the burial practices of Indians, introducing individual burial, fenced off areas, and tombstones. As a result, Indian graveyards are the most diagnostic feature of the reservation landscape (Figure 4.6). The whitewashed wooden crosses reflect not only white religious institutions, but also the material impoverishment of contemporary Native Americans at the hands of whites (Figure 4.7).

With a revival of Native American political consciousness in the 1960s and 1970s, schools on the reservations are reflecting

FIGURE 4.5 Lac Court Oreilles Reservation. (left) North of Reserve is St. Francis Solanus Mission, with its largely nun-run school and Roman Catholic church. (Reserve, 1:24,000) (right) The wooden crosses in the cemetery indicate Indian graves. (Ingolf Vogeler)

FIGURE 4.6 (left) Indian cemetery on the Red Cliff Reservation. French names among Indians indicates blood ties with French fur traders. (Ingolf Vogeler) FIGURE 4.7 (above) Indian poverty and white wealth. Abandoned Native American cemetery and wealthy yacht club on Madeline Island. Summer commuter aircraft link Madeline Island with Minneapolis–St. Paul. Indian "houses" over the graves reflect the Europeanization of nineteenth-century Indian culture. (Ingolf Vogeler)

more of what these people want their children to learn. Churches on the reservation, likewise, are responding to a renewed awareness among Native Americans of their own cultural values and practices.

Largely concentrated in only a few areas of northern Wisconsin, Native Americans remain almost invisible. Ironically, contacts between whites and Native Americans are intensifying over natural resource use. Several reservations have attempted to require whites to purchase licenses for hunting and fishing on reservation lands. White anglers and hunters, who do not object to fishing licenses issued by the Wisconsin Department of Natural Resources, are fiercely opposed to Indians charging them to fish and hunt. Historically, Indian fishing and hunting rights, although guaranteed by treaties, were taken and/or limited by federal and state laws. Recent court rulings have upheld the Native Americans' treaty rights to hunt and fish on off-reservation lands in northern Wisconsin.

LOGGING AND LUMBERING, 1840s–1910s

In southern Wisconsin white settlers wanted Indian lands for farming, but in the Northwoods they wanted the timber resources. The lumber industry in Wisconsin was an extension of the eastern lumbering frontier. From Maine, New York, and Pennsylvania, speculators came to buy Wisconsin timberland, loggers and woodsmen to get out the logs, and sawyers to operate the mills (Figure 4.8).

Growth of the Lumber Industry

Early lumber mill towns were built on Lake Michigan or on the Mississippi River, but later lumbering spread up the Wisconsin, Black, Chippewa, St. Croix, Wolf, and Red Cedar rivers. Loggers cut timber closest to the rivers, regardless of land ownership; unauthorized timber cutting on the public domain in northern Wisconsin was similar to illegal lead mines in southeastern Wisconsin on Indian lands. The register of the Green Bay land office reported in 1849 that upwards of 15 million ft (4.5 million m) of pine lumber were being manufactured annually on the Green Bay watershed, "every foot of which is plundered off the public lands." Despite the appointment of special federal timber agents to enforce the law against timber stealing from the public lands, illegal logging continued in all major pineries, including along the Chippewa River, where one-third to one-half of the best pine had been cut by trespassers.

FIGURE 4.8 Logging camp. (Courtesy of the Chippewa Valley Museum, Eau Claire)

Focus: Lumberjack Lingo

A lumberjack in a hospital, when asked by the nurse how he got hurt, replied, "The ground loader threw the beads around a pine log. He claimed he had called for a Saint Croix but he gave a Saginaw; she gunned, broke three of my slats and one of my stilts and also a very fine skid." The nurse said, "I don't understand." His reply was, "I don't either. He must have been yaps."

Glossary

beads: chains used in loading logs.
ground loader: a member of the crew who attaches the tongs or loading hooks to the logs or guides the logs up the skids; same as bottom loader, hooker, hooker on, sender.
Saginaw: to retard the larger or butt end of a log in loading it up on a car; opposite of Saint Croix.
skid: (1) to drag logs from the place they are cut to the skidway, landing, or mill; same as drag in, dray in, snake, twitch; (2) a log or pole, commonly used in pairs, upon which logs were handled or piled; (3) the log or pole laid in a skid road to reinforce it; (4) a piece of hardwood about six feet long with studs on one side and two hooks on one end. It was placed on edge of dray to roll logs onto dray with a cant hook. The studs kept the log from slipping back.
slats: a person's ribs.
yaps: crazy, out of his mind.

Source: From L. C. Sorden, *Lumberjack Lingo* (Sauk City: Stanton & Lee, 1969).

Edward Paine was an example of the many lumber barons who gained control of the timber resources of the Northwoods. In the 1850s, Paine acquired timberlands north of Oshkosh, where he had established a mill. In violation of the Homestead Act, which required that buyers of land live on and work the land, Paine bribed the land office to acquire large tracts of prime timber stands—52,000 acres (21,044 ha) in Langlade County alone. Other lumber barons acquired land in similar fashion. In *Empire in Pine*, Robert Fries recounts in detail this epidemic land rush. The National Conservation Commission in 1909 found that "solid townships in northern Wisconsin had been acquired under the homestead law . . . the timber cut off . . . and not a single voter or inhabitant could be found in the township" (1951, p. 52). Such illegal land claims allowed Oshkosh in 1866 to have 50 mills that produced 85 million bd ft (2.5 million cu m), 8 million shingles, 14 million laths, and half of all U.S.-made sashes and doors.

The enormous forested area stretching from Maine to Minnesota supplied a vital raw material for the economic growth of the United States. Wood provided fuel and materials for barns, fences, houses, and public buildings, as well as for roads, railways, mines, and bridges. By the 1840s the forests of northern Wisconsin began to supply the American Manufacturing Belt, the treeless prairies of the Midwest, and the Great Plains with an abundance of lumber. Wisconsin lumber also found markets in Europe, South America, and the West Indies.

By 1860 Sheboygan, Manitowoc, and Kewaunee counties had 40 sawmills, cutting pine for the Milwaukee and Chicago markets. The whole region from Ozaukee to Door County was cut over by 1875. In 1841 every available mill site in the 48 mi (77 km) from Wisconsin Rapids to Wausau—the southernmost extent of pine—had passed into private hands. In 1848 the region had 24 mills operating and 45 saws; in 1857, 107 mills and 3,000 men were turning out more than 1 billion bd ft (29.4 million cu m) a year. By the late 1850s Green Bay was *the* shingle producer in the United States, but by the late 1860s La Crosse was the primary shingle producer.

In Wisconsin, the forest proper lay north of a line from Manitowoc to Portage and west to the St. Croix. The southern edge, about 30 to 50 mi (48–80 km) wide, was a hardwood tract, and to the north of it

FIGURE 4.9 (top) Log hauling. This load of logs represents 24,310 bd ft (641,784 cu m) of lumber. These men worked for the J. S. Owen Company in the Chippewa River Valley ca. 1910. (Courtesy of the Chippewa Valley Museum, Eau Claire) FIGURE 4.10 (bottom) Driving logs on the Chippewa River in 1906. (Courtesy of the Chippewa Valley Museum, Eau Claire)

lay a belt of mixed hardwoods and conifers. Most of the stands of conifers were concentrated along the headwaters of the Wolf, Menominee, Wisconsin, Chippewa, Black, and St. Croix rivers. The basis of Wisconsin's logging industry was the white pine and, to a much lesser extent, red pine and hemlock (Figure 4.9). Although pine rarely accounted for more than 60 percent of all trees, it was the only economically important species, hence the Northwoods region was called the *pinery*. White pine had special characteristics: It floated, was of great length and diameter, was lightweight yet strong, and was easy to use in carpentry work.

Successful early exploration of Wisconsin's forest resource depended on overcoming the low market value and high costs of production. An efficient water transportation system, vast forest stands, and a national and a regional market were the coincident factors responsible for the rise of Wisconsin's logging districts. Apart from the white pine itself, lakes and rivers played a major role in the growth of the early lumber industry. Lakes, such as the bow-shaped Half Moon Lake in Eau Claire, provided excellent facilities for holding and sorting logs. Before railroads penetrated the pineries of the region after the Civil War, the lumber industry depended on rivers for transportation (Figure 4.10). In the spring, reinforced by snowmelt and rains, the rivers provided transport energy. They also supplied waterpower sites for sawmills. In addition, they flowed toward the Great Lakes and the Mississippi River, which connected the lumber districts with the markets of the East and West. Lumber production in Wisconsin boomed after 1840. Less than 200 million bd ft (5.9 million cu m) of pine lumber was cut in 1853; that figure increased to over 3 billion bd ft (882 million cu m) in the peak year of 1892. Both softwood and hardwood timber production peaked in 1899 (Figure 4.11).

The logging camps had few amenities. An old timer recalled:

You worked all day in the rain, you came in at night and hung your old soggy clothes up around the one stove in the center of the room. They hung there and steamed all night. You slept there in that steam. That's the only bath you got. There was no other facilities; you got your steam bath there every night. There was no place to wash your clothes. If you wanted to wash up, the only thing you could do was to go out and hunt up an old oil can on Sundays, and boil up your clothes like a hobo down in the jungle. You move from one camp to another. You had to go with your roll of blankets on your back. You looked like a bunch of snails going down the highway. (*People, Pride and Politics: Building the North Star Country,* 1982)

As the lumbering industry grew, small communities evolved to supply the lumber camps with goods and services. Where abundant waterpower was available and where log sorting and storage facilities could be constructed, sawmill towns developed in proximity to the pineries. The larger

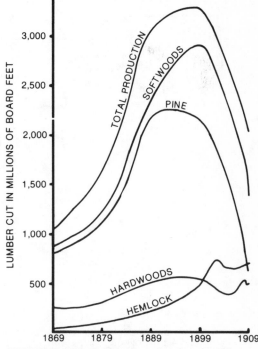

FIGURE 4.11 Lumber production in Wisconsin, 1869–1909.

logging towns included St. Croix Falls, Rice Lake, Chippewa Falls, Eau Claire, Wausau, Stevens Point, Rhinelander, and Marinette (Figure 4.12). Such towns were highly segregated socially and spatially; they were characterized by some low-density housing (a sprinkling of substantial homes of lumber barons, bankers, doctors, and merchants); a few high-density areas (rooming houses for workers); and a section for saloons and stores.

Labor Disputes and the Oshkosh Woodworkers' Strike

In 1889 lumbering and woodworking industries employed over 25 percent of all industrial workers in the state, and these industries dominated the state economy until 1900. With the industrialization of the logging mills, labor disputes intensified and strikes became common. Vernon Jenson (1945) wrote in his book *Lumber and*

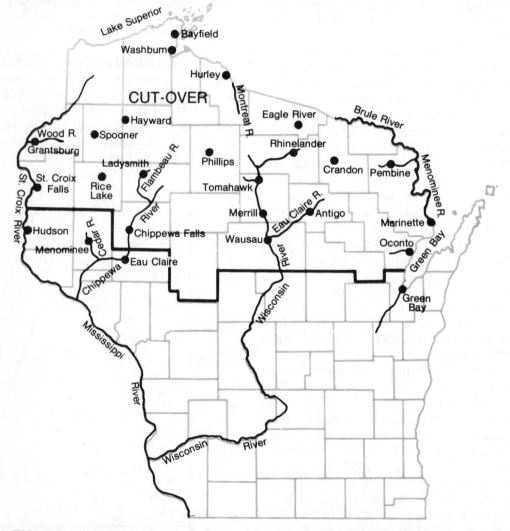

FIGURE 4.12 Logging towns and the Cutover region, 1850. (Based on information from Charles G. Mahaffey, "Changing Images of the Cutover: A Historical Geography of Resource Utilization in the Lake Superior Region, 1840–1930" [Ph.D. dissertation, University of Wisconsin–Madison, 1978])

Labor that "the heroic struggle of man to rise to higher planes of living is revealed in the attempts to form unions and improve conditions." The earliest organization of state woodworkers was the Chippewa Workingmen's Association, established in 1879. In 1881, in Eau Claire, this group organized one of Wisconsin's earliest and most well known strikes, aimed at the Weyerhauser Company for its long hours and payment of wages in company scrip rather than in cash. Many other strikes followed, including the famous Oshkosh strike of 1898.

In an 1894 survey of woodworkers in 45 U.S. cities, Oshkosh workers had the lowest wages. Machinists in the wood industry were making $1 for a 10-hour day; general factory workers earned 80 cents a day and sometimes as little as 40 cents a day. Children worked in factories and stores. Yet Oshkosh boasted that it was the second wealthiest city, proportional to its population, in the United States. Dr. Hixson, the author of this survey, which was published in the *Labor Advocate*, maintained that machinists in other cities earned two and three times the wages of Oshkosh machinists.

Low wages and high unemployment (1,500 workers unemployed in 1894) in Oshkosh led workers to make four requests of the Paine Lumber Company: (1) stop replacing men (at 96 cents a day) with women and children (at 66 to 56 cents a day) to save wages; (2) pay the workers once a week as the law required, rather than holding wages a full month; (3) increase wages; and (4) recognize the union. George Paine, owner of the factory, rejected the workers' requests and instead got the Oshkosh Manufacturers' Association to band together against the workers' demands. On May 16, 1898, the woodworkers went on strike. Although the union claimed only 1,600 members, most of the 2,800 woodworkers stayed out of the six mills. The national union promised workers weekly strike benefits of $3 or half their full average pay. In discussions with the factory owners, workers were told that the

mills had made no money in five years, yet George Paine's salary had increased from $40,000 to $60,000 annually in those five years. Workers in Oshkosh averaged 96 cents a day, whereas in the rest of the country woodworkers' wages ranged from $1.50 to $4 a day, depending on skill.

The strike became increasingly violent, and a striker was killed. As the strike continued, merchants claimed that for all practical purposes the city was in the hands of strikers. The merchants prevailed on the governor to send in the Wisconsin National Guard; 402 soldiers protected the city's bridges and the homes of scabs and guarded the sawmills. Women played an important role in the strike from its beginning. They often appeared at meetings and on picket lines in numbers equal to or greater than those of the men. But ethnic divisions remained: The old Oshkosh families of English background on the north side supported Paine; the German and Slavic (Polish) workers on the south side supported the strike.

The Oshkosh woodworkers' strike ended on August 20, 1898. Millowners agreed to several worker demands: (1) union membership would not be held against returning workers; (2) there would be no winter layoffs; and (3) pay would be increased in several weeks. But women and children working in the mills were not mentioned, and the union was given no recognition.

NORTHERN MINING, 1880s–1960s

In the late nineteenth century, mining in Wisconsin was concentrated in the Northwoods. For 80 years the Gogebic Range was the major mining area of northern Wisconsin (Figure 4.13). As one of six iron-ore-producing ranges in the Lake Superior region (plus Michigan's Copper Country), the Gogebic Range produced iron ore for the steel mills of Pittsburgh, Pennsylvania, Youngstown, Ohio, and Gary, Indiana, from 1885 to 1965. Mining involved much more than the exploitation of a mineral; the communities and people of the

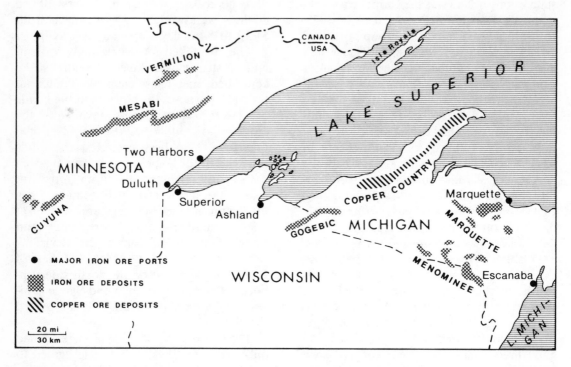

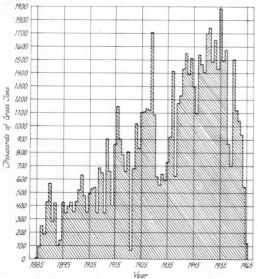

FIGURE 4.13 (top) The Gogebic Iron Range. Spanning the Wisconsin-Michigan border, it served as one of the seven iron- and copper-ore-producing areas of the Lake Superior region. FIGURE 4.14 (left) Annual iron-ore production from the Wisconsin section of the Gogebic Range, 1885–1965. (Based on data from *Lake Superior Iron Ores* [Cleveland: Lake Superior Iron Ore Association, 1952] and unpublished data from the Wisconsin Geological and Natural History Survey)

Gogebic Iron Range, situated in Iron County, added their own distinctiveness to northern Wisconsin.

The Product: Iron Ore

The Gogebic Range is a narrow, linear belt spanning the Wisconsin-Michigan border. The productive portion of this ore body was some 28 mi (50 km) in length, with approximately one-half in each state. Lower-grade ore deposits expanded the actual Gogebic Range both eastward into Michigan and westward into Wisconsin, but these reserves have not yet proven commercially viable. In Wisconsin, this rather lengthy extension of the Gogebic into Ashland County is referred to as the Penokee Range.

The first ore was shipped by rail from the Gogebic Range in 1884, when the Colby Mine near Bessemer, Michigan, began to produce; one year later the Germania Mine near Hurley, Wisconsin, shipped its first carload of ore to the new dock at Ashland. During the following eight decades Ashland, Wisconsin, on Lake Superior, served as the primary shipping port for ore from the entire Gogebic Range, although the Lake Michigan port of Escanaba, Michigan, was also used.

From 1884 to 1965, the Michigan side of the Gogebic Range exceeded Wisconsin's production by a ratio of about four to one. Some 318 million tn (288 million mt) of iron ore were shipped from the entire Gogebic during its productive life; just over 68 million tn (62 million mt) came from Wisconsin. During the 1930s and after, Wisconsin's relative share of overall production increased. Between 1885 and 1929, the mines of Wisconsin were responsible for providing only 15 percent of all iron ore produced on the Gogebic Range, but from 1930 to 1950 the figure rose to 26 percent and increased to 37 percent from 1951–1965.

On a year-to-year basis, the output of Wisconsin's mines fluctuated rather sharply (Figure 4.14). Smaller changes in production figures generally were tied to the annual iron and steel requirements of U.S. indus-

try, but larger transitions reflected major events in the nation and the world. Especially noticeable declines in shipments occurred during severe economic depressions, such as those experienced in 1893 and in the 1930s; in 1921 a drastic recession in the iron and steel industry contributed to a great drop in ore production. Iron-ore shipments, on the other hand, were highest during the periods of national prosperity that occurred throughout much of the 1920s, the late 1940s, and the early 1960s. The demand, especially for armaments and military equipment, that occurred during prolonged periods of international conflict resulted in high production in some years: Significant increases in shipments took place throughout World War I (1914–1918), World War II (1939–1945), and the Korean War (early 1950s).

Most of the Wisconsin mines were small operations that existed for short periods of time (Figure 4.15). The Montreal and Cary mines, situated just west of Hurley, were the major producers and the last two mines to close in Wisconsin. Together, the Montreal and Cary produced about 94 percent of all the iron ore from Wisconsin's Gogebic Range. Unlike Minnesota's massive Mesabi Range, where mining activities involved open-pit operations, the Gogebic consisted almost entirely of underground mines. Though all of the ore had not yet been exhausted by the time the mines closed, reduced deposits and progressively deeper shafts eventually made extraction more difficult and too expensive for mines to remain profitable. When the Montreal Mine shut down in 1962, it extended about 4,335 ft (1,321 m) underground, reportedly the deepest iron-ore mine in the world.

Mining Settlements

Mining towns are ephemeral settlements. Because the existence of mining communities is derived from the exploitation of finite resources, the depletion of resources means that unless other economic activities replace the towns' original function, the

100

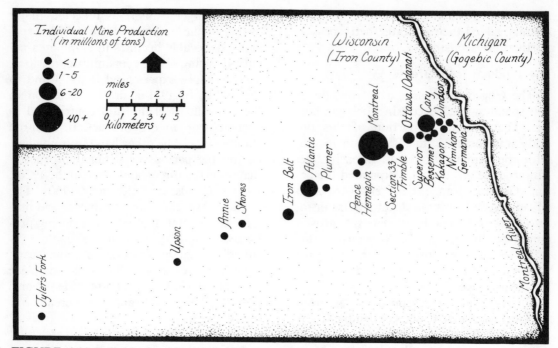

FIGURE 4.15 Individual mine production on the Gogebic Range. Many small mines produced iron ore for short periods of time on Wisconsin's Gogebic Range, but the Montreal and Cary mines provided the majority of the output. (Based on data from *Lake Superior Iron Ores* [Cleveland: Lake Superior Iron Ore Association, 1952] and unpublished data from the Wisconsin Geological and Natural History Survey)

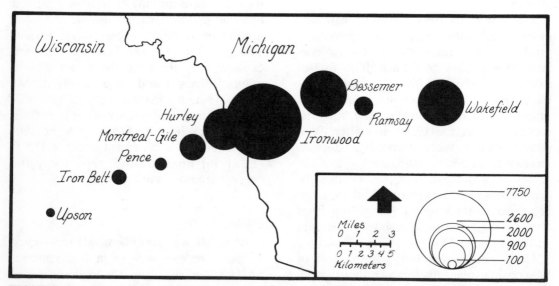

FIGURE 4.16 Population of the Gogebic Range communities, 1980. As in the past, the major settlements of the Gogebic Range are concentrated in Michigan. (*1980 U.S. Census of Population and Housing* [Washington, D.C.: U.S. Government Printing Office, 1981])

enclaves will cease to exist as viable settlements. This process is certainly evident on the Gogebic Range. Communities such as Hurley, Montreal, Pence, and Iron Belt still exist in Iron County, but they are no longer tied to the mining industry. These settlements are now oriented to tourism; or they act as service centers for small-scale agricultural and logging operations in the area; or they cater to the requirements of senior citizens and younger "new homesteaders," who have opted for a Northwoods life-style; or they function as bedroom satellites for commuters who work at the copper mine and mill located 45 mi (72 km) from the Wisconsin border in White Pine, Michigan. Hurley, the county seat, also houses many of the governmental services that are especially important to people who reside in economically depressed areas.

The 1980 population map for the region still reflects the dominant role that Michigan played in the historical evolution of the Gogebic Range (Figure 4.16). Because iron-ore deposits were greater on the east side of the Montreal River than they were on the west side, Michigan's mines, labor force, and communities have always exceeded Wisconsin's in size and importance. The three largest communities on the Gogebic Range have been and continue to be Wakefield, Bessemer, and Ironwood, Michigan. Hurley, with 2,000 residents, is the fourth largest Gogebic Range settlement and the dominant central place on the Wisconsin side. All communities on the Gogebic have declined in size since the zenith in mining activities, and several offer little more than faint visual evidence in the landscape of their once-booming existence. Others—such as Pratt, Benjamin, and Finney, Wisconsin—exist only as historic place names and so graphically portray the boom-and-bust syndrome often associated with mining towns.

Two basic community types provided the framework for settlement formation throughout the Gogebic Range and most of the Lake Superior mining region: townsites and "locations." Townsites such as Hurley, Iron Belt, and Upson were platted and developed primarily for speculative reasons. Though these settlements were oriented almost entirely to mining activities, and the companies often owned land and buildings within the communities, some independent political, social, and economic expression occurred. Commercial and public services were provided by individuals not employed by the mining industry, and individuals owned land and houses in townsites; hence, these places resembled typical U.S. towns and villages. The "locations," however, were quite different in organization and orientation. The term itself was derived from the surveying profession and referred to the residential enclaves that the mining corporations established on company-owned land. The locations, in certain respects, were small-scale versions of company towns found elsewhere in the United States, although company stores were seldom found on the Gogebic Range.

The locations were developed by companies to attract and maintain a stable and contented labor force. By providing low-cost housing for miners and their families, employers hoped that employees would not search for jobs elsewhere and that they would be less likely to question corporate management practices and regulations. To maintain a system of control, land and property in the locations were owned and managed by the companies, and housing generally was leased or rented to the worker residents. With home and work so closely linked, the companies were able to exert rather substantial influence over the lives, behavior, and deportment of their employees. A school, church, or community building might have been found in some locations, but opportunities were not available to develop consumers' cooperatives, labor groups, or socialist organizations, functions that did, however, develop in some of the townsites. Few activities in the locations were regulated more closely by the companies than those associated with vice. Saloons and taverns were outlawed entirely, which meant that they were

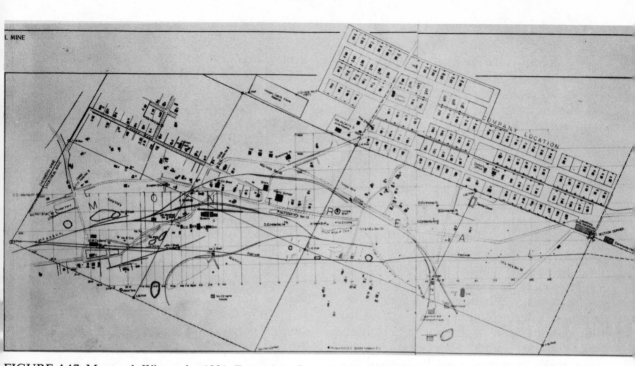

FIGURE 4.17 Montreal, Wisconsin, 1921. Examples of an unplatted "Old Location" and a rigidly laid-out "Company Location." (From A. O. Taylor's map in his manuscript improvement report on file in the Iron County Historica Society, Hurley)

simply relegated to the townsites, most notably Hurley.

At one time there were locations at the Atlantic, Cary, Ottawa, Germania, and other mine sites, but the premier example was and is found at Montreal, Wisconsin. Not only does Montreal still represent one of the largest, extant locations in the entire Lake Superior region, but the settlement also illustrates the progressive upgrading of facilities and amenities that the companies pursued as they sought to meet the changing aspirations of residents. The initial nucleus for Montreal—now termed the "Old Location"—was established in the late nineteenth century, when miners employed by the Oglebay-Norton Company of Cleveland, Ohio, settled along a few meandering streets adjacent to the mine site (Figure 4.17). In 1907, a rectilinear area was platted nearby and several houses were constructed; about 10 years later 50 pre-cut bungalows were added to the platted "Company Location." By the late 1970s, 46 percent of the 132 houses in the Company Location were owned by nonresidents from various

towns and cities in Wisconsin and the Midwest. The sounds and rather relaxed activities of skiers, tourists, young couples, and retired citizens have now replaced the regulated time schedules, whistles, rumbles, shouts, and other varied noises of miners and mining.

Hurley deserves special mention as a townsite because of its unique role as a "sin center" for the entire Gogebic Range. Taverns, prostitution, and gambling proliferated to such an extent that Hurley's Silver Street became famous throughout the Lake Superior region and the upper Midwest. Why Hurley supported so many vice-oriented functions is difficult to pinpoint exactly, but legal and governmental restrictions generally were not as strict in Wisconsin as they were in Michigan. Also, because most of the local headquarters of the mining companies were situated in Michigan, corporation executives might have sought to direct these activities into one concentrated area that was outside their community and state of residence. Every ore-producing range of the Lake Superior region had at least one town that served as a major watering hole for thirsty and thrill-seeking miners, but none achieved the notoriety and reputation of Hurley.

The People of the Gogebic Range

The people of the Gogebic Range established and developed the mining industry. Most written accounts tend to stress the U.S.-born residents or the officials and entrepreneurs who supervised the mines and established local businesses, but ultimately the thousands of anonymous residents—many of them immigrants from Europe—provided their backs and occasionally their lives to extract the red ore of the Gogebic.

During the initial years of development, the majority of the people on the Gogebic Range had been born in Europe. By 1900, just under 50 percent of the population had been born in Europe or Canada, but the figure undoubtedly increased to 65 or 75 percent of the total if the children of these immigrants were included. The U.S. Immigration Commission in 1911 noted that most of the early inhabitants who arrived on the Gogebic Range came from England, Ireland, and Sweden (Canada should also have been added to the list). The English immigrants came primarily from the mining region of Cornwall and were already familiar with underground mining operations. These "Cousin Jacks," as they were called, began to serve as mining captains and skilled workers in Michigan's Copper Country as early as the 1840s and assumed similar roles in the subsequent development of the six iron-ore ranges of the Lake Superior region. The Irish and Swedes first engaged in activities that required less previous experience, such as mine timbering, tramming, and common labor, and the Canadians were involved in a full array of occupations.

As eastern and southern Europeans began to emigrate in large numbers to the United States during the 1890s and early 1900s, some found their way to the Gogebic Range. These recent arrivals now took the unskilled jobs that were becoming more available in the mines. Finnish immigrants constituted the largest foreign-born group on the Gogebic, and indeed, the entire Lake Superior area. The first Finns came to the region during the late Civil War (1864-1865), when they accompanied Norwegians and Swedes recruited to replace northern Michigan copper miners who were fighting in the Union Army. At first the Finnish population grew slowly, but virtually all of their emigration was directed to the upper Midwest. By the 1890s, when vastly larger numbers of people began to depart Finland, a sizeable proportion of these emigrants headed for the same region where their compatriots had settled previously.

In 1900, the major foreign-born population on the entire Gogebic Range consisted of émigrés from (in order of numbers) Finland, Sweden, England, Italy, Canada, Germany, Austria, Russia, Norway, and Poland. When considered by itself, however, the Wisconsin side of the Gogebic displayed a somewhat different composition of foreign-born groups. The Finns still retained their number-one position, but they were followed by émigrés from Italy, Canada, Sweden, Germany, Austria, Norway, England, Russia, and Ireland (Figure 4.18).

CUTOVER AGRICULTURE, 1910s–1950s

Faced with a boom-and-bust mining economy and a declining logging industry at the turn of the century, workers looked for alternative employment. The migration of the lumber industry to the evergreen forests of the Pacific Northwest and to hardwood and yellow-pine regions of the South left behind a major economic problem for the Northwoods region. What was to become of the people and towns of the vast stump-studded Cutover? Agricultural settlement thus began in earnest.

Until late in the nineteenth century, the westward movement of agricultural settlement had bypassed the densely timbered region of northern Wisconsin. But as the lumber era faded, sawmill towns became

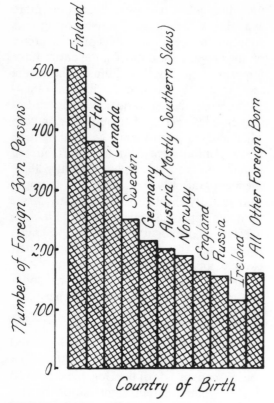

FIGURE 4.18 Foreign-born persons on the Wisconsin portion of the Gogebic Range, 1900. (Original manuscript schedules from the 1900 Federal Census, available at the State Historical Society of Wisconsin, Madison)

service centers for agricultural communities, and railroads opened new territory across northern Wisconsin, creating markets for agricultural production. Speculators began to redeem cutover land forfeited for taxes by logging companies or to purchase cutover land from lumber barons directly. Towns such as Ashland, Superior, Hayward, Rhinelander, Antigo, and Marshfield were the centers of a new land boom—this time for agricultural settlement, not for logging.

In an attempt to promote northern settlement and to provide settlers with information, the 1895 Wisconsin legislature established a state Board of Immigration to advertise northern Wisconsin land abroad. It also passed an act that authorized

the dean of the College of Agriculture at the University of Wisconsin in Madison to prepare a handbook describing the agricultural resource potentials for settlement in northern Wisconsin, which was defined as north of a line from Green Bay to Hudson. This illustrated volume told settlers of soil types, climate, the location and prices of land, appropriate crops, and prospects for dairying on the 8.5 million acres (3.4 million ha) of potential farmland in the 10-million-acre (4.1-million-ha) Cutover region. In the words of William Henry, the author of *Northern Wisconsin: A Handbook for the Homeseeker* (1895), the purpose of the handbook was to dispel "the great ignorance and even prejudice" that existed in the southern part of the state and elsewhere concerning the agricultural possibilities of northern Wisconsin (Figure 4.19). The various county immigrant bureaus were to acquaint settlers with the special advantages of each county in the New North (Figure 4.20). Although initially distributed free, by 1900 the handbook was selling for one dollar; over 50,000 copies were sold. In addition, 60,000 immigrant pamphlets were printed in English, German, and Norwegian that used illustrations from the handbook. Although Henry clearly promoted land sales, he warned prospective settlers of the arduous work ahead. The land would provide shelter, subsistence crops, and work in the forests, but prosperity would come only with long hours of clearing stumps from the fields (Figure 4.21).

Settlement on the stump-dotted land of northern Wisconsin was promoted by railroad and lumber companies, speculators, voluntary colonization societies, state boards of immigration, and the University of Wisconsin College of Agriculture. The Wisconsin Central Railroad, one of several railroads promoting agricultural settlement in northern Wisconsin after the forests had been removed for lumber, had agents in western Europe, the eastern United States, and in the Cutover itself. Railroad lands

FIGURE 4.19 Bountiful harvest in the Cutover. Settlers on the Menominee River Boom Company land in 1865. (W. A. Henry, *Northern Wisconsin: A Handbook for the Homeseeker* [Madison: Democrat Printing Co., 1895])

were praised throughout German-speaking countries in the 1880s. Settlers were offered land at $5 per acre ($12 per ha) with $50 down and the remainder in three yearly payments at 7 percent interest; agents received 10 percent commissions. Railroads were eager not only to sell their own land but also to promote the settlement of other northern lands to assure customers for their freight trains. By 1890 the Wisconsin Central had sold 250,000 acres (101,175 ha) of its 838,628-acre (339,392-ha) grant.

Lumber companies were sometimes in conflict with agricultural settlements in the Cutover. On the one hand, lumber barons, faced with diminishing forest resources in the 1880s and 1890s, wanted to sell their land to settlers. On the other hand, as the number of farm families increased, settlers wanted schools, roads, and other improvements for which the lumber companies would have to pay higher property taxes. Farming and lumbering, however, were

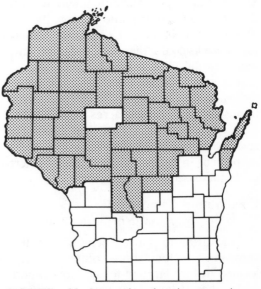

FIGURE 4.20 County immigration committees in Wisconsin.

FIGURE 4.21 Stump clearing, Medford, Taylor County, 1895. Stump lands were usually seeded in grass and used for pasture for several years, before stumps were removed by stump machines and horses. (W. A. Henry, *Northern Wisconsin: A Handbook for the Homeseeker* [Madison: Democrat Printing Co., 1895])

compatible in some areas. After the white pine had been cut, the nonfloating hardwoods required new techniques of logging and milling. Small sawmill towns utilized the hardwood forests and seasonally employed local laborers. Colonizing farmer-lumberjacks could, therefore, combine summer farming with winter logging.

The appeal of land was strong. Despite difficult conditions, about 20,000 new farms, representing 1 million acres (404,700 ha), were cleared between 1880 and 1900. The southern fringe of the Cutover gained about 20 percent in cultivated land; the northern parts increased by 10 percent.

Colonization Companies: Marketing Marginal Northern Land

In addition to state agencies and lumber companies, colonization companies were formed to lure farmers to the Northwoods with "cheap" land ($70 per acre, or $173 per ha), "free" stump-pulling services, and "at cost" agricultural supplies. Over 185

land colonization companies had home offices in Wisconsin after the turn of the century. Most of these companies were content merely to buy land on time and unload it as quickly as possible without considering the specific needs of settlers. However, a few firms did consider the real needs of stumpland farmers.

Benjamin F. Faast was one such entrepreneur. Richard Pifer, a Wisconsin historian, provided a detailed example of how Faast tried to get the Cutover settled. Faast was one land dealer who seemed to understand the difficulties of farming in the Cutover region, and he organized several companies to provide unusual services to help assure successful settlement. As early as 1908, the Faast Land Company sold "ready-made" farms to settlers in Rusk County. Buyers could expect to find at least 5 acres (2 ha) cleared of stumps and several buildings erected by the company. In addition, the company provided assistance to farmers through road construction and

TABLE 4.2
Colonization Companies in the Chippewa Valley, 1910–1920

Colonization Company	Company Land			Census Farm Familes 1910–1920	Company Farmers Percentage of All Farmers
	Land in Original Tract	Acres Unsold 1921	Farm Families Settled		
Chippewa Valley Colonization Company (Chippewa County)	26,000	4,000	225	650	35
Faast Land Company (Rusk County)	25,000	1,000	250	877	46
Rusk Farm Company (Rusk County)	15,000	2,000	150		
Wisconsin Colonization Company (Sawyer County)	50,000	20,000	350	435	69

Source: B. F. Faast, Auto Trip Through Wisconsin's Colonization Projects, June 28–29, 1921, available in the Area Research Center, University of Wisconsin-Eau Claire.

through its seed company and its experimental dairy farm.

Faast organized and was on the boards of directors of various colonization companies. In the Chippewa Valley, the single most important area for colonization efforts, he organized four such companies during the 1910s and 1920s (Table 4.2). Usually a handful of stockholders held a controlling interest in these companies, and the total number of stockholders only ranged from 30 to 100. Together, these companies, however, held 116,000 acres (46,945 ha), of which 89,000 (36,018 ha) were sold by 1921.

Faast's settlement philosophy is best illustrated by the methods of the Wisconsin Colonization Company. He had a dream that northern Wisconsin could become a land of prosperous yeoman farmers, but first it needed settlers and the settlers needed help to achieve this dream. The Wisconsin Colonization Company attracted settlers through advertising that gave graphic representation to Faast's dream of a northern dairyland, a land that would blossom with hard work and with the help of the company. After all, Sawyer County lay at the same latitude as the productive wheat lands of South Dakota; in addition, Wisconsin produced more corn, wheat, oats, potatoes,

clover seed, and hay per acre than Indiana, Illinois, and Iowa; and land prices were considerably lower in northern Wisconsin than in the older settled areas of the Midwest.

The company's advertising used popular images of U.S. life—home, family, and children. The promotional brochures portrayed a vision of the American dream and were designed to appeal to urban workers, recent immigrants, and renting farmers. Faast depicted farming in the Cutover region as a route to economic security and happiness. Railroads linked Sawyer County to large northern urban and mining centers and to the southern cities of Milwaukee and Chicago (Figure 4.22). The promotional literature proclaimed that Sawyer County's location assured "the highest price for what it has to sell and the lowest cost for what it buys."

To make his dairyland dream a reality, Faast believed that land dealers had to provide much more than the land itself. As a consequence, he emphasized the need for a small down payment and liberal terms. The company offered five made-to-order farm plans, complete with a choice of housing floor plans and outbuildings (Figure 4.23). For example in Plan No. 1, settlers

FIGURE 4.22 Sawyer County lies at the center of urban markets. This is an example of promotional material distributed by the Wisconsin Colonization Company. (University of Wisconsin–Eau Claire Area Research Center)

could secure 40 acres (16 ha), a 16 by 20 ft (5 by 6 m) one-room house, a small barn, land-clearing tools, and seeds with a $300 cash down payment on a final purchase price of approximately $1,500. Depending on the circumstances, the company either cleared some of the land or delayed the initial mortgage payment for 3 years and gave settlers 30 years to pay the balance. In the long run, Faast believed that liberal credit terms would benefit the company and the region. He expected farm-

ers to invest their early profits in farm stock, new buildings, and land clearing.

The concept of community-based agriculture was central to Faast's dream of a thriving northland. Successful farmers were not, in his view, individualists striving alone in the wilderness, but were members of a larger community where people worked together to build their future. The rural village provided a place to market farm crops and wood products, to buy supplies at reasonable prices, and to meet with

House No. 1

House No. 2

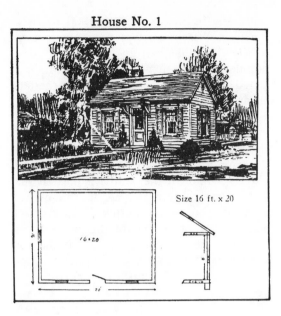

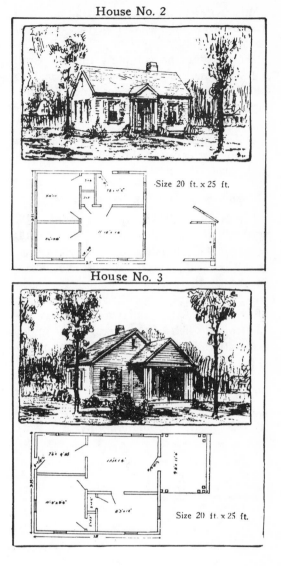

Size 16 ft. x 20

FIGURE 4.23 Wisconsin Colonization Company house plans. (University of Wisconsin–Eau Claire Area Research Center)

neighbors. Faast declared, in the company's promotional literature, that "the American small town should serve as the front yard or gateway to the country." The town of Ojibwa was built to fulfill this ideal. Situated next to the Chippewa River and the Omaha rail line, the townsite provided both scenic pleasures and easy access to national markets. The style of the store, restaurant, railway station, and other buildings was reminiscent of colonial architecture. For Faast, this was the only truly American

architectural form, and he wanted these buildings to set the tone for his model community. A Minneapolis town planning firm designed Ojibwa, which reflected the most current features of urban planning at the time: harmonious architecture, well-engineered traffic patterns, tree-lined curving streets, and centrally located public buildings and parks. Faast wanted to create an asthetically pleasing town that would serve all the needs of farmers for markets, consumer purchases, recreation, and social life in a 100-sq-mi (161-sq-km) area. On a smaller scale, Meadowbrook was designed in a similar way.

For a time the company thrived, land sales boomed, and the dream seemed to be coming to life. Between June 1917 and January 1920, 160 farmers occupied 8,339 acres (3,374 ha) of land purchased from the Wisconsin Colonization Company. In addition the company built 173 houses and 133 barns (Table 4.3).

Difficulties in Farming the Cutover

Throughout the Northwoods, about 8,000 settlers had inquired about land, and 90,000 acres (36,423 ha) had actually been cleared by 1920. The greatest progress was made in the southern row of counties—Clark, Marathon, and Chippewa. Here more than 60 percent of the land was in farms, although only half of the acreage was under cultivation. In the rest of the Cutover barely 7 percent was improved or in crops.

Colonization efforts paid off for speculators. In 30 years the New North had gained 341,000 people, for a total of 703,000 in 1920. Rural population increases were

especially impressive: From 1900 to 1920 northern Wisconsin was the only section of the state that had an increase in rural population. Foreign-born immigrants selected this region because other (better) lands farther south had already been settled. The heaviest influx of farm people occurred in the decade prior to World War I. By 1920, Norwegians, Swedes, and Finns predominated, followed by Germanic and Slavic people. In the southern part of the state, German settlers were the majority.

But despite the claims of land speculators and state agencies and the dreams of farm families, the Cutover was unsuitable for widespread agricultural development. After three and a half years of work only 15 percent of the land sold by the Wisconsin Colonization Company was under cultivation, and only 4 percent had been cleared of stumps. Company farmers had made little progress in changing the Cutover to productive farmland. After 1916 the Agricultural College of the University of Wisconsin operated land-clearing demonstration trains, on which the use of dynamite for stump removal was illustrated. In 1920 alone, 3.5 million lb (1.6 million kg) of dynamite were used to clear 75,000 acres (30,352 ha) in the Cutover (Figure 4.24). The "intrinsic wealth" of these improvements were estimated by promoters at $5 million.

As the years progressed, however, the prospects for success became increasingly bleak. The company's earlier growth had coincided with World War I, and the market for agricultural products had seemed insatiable. But when the war ended, "overproduction" brought on a national agricultural depression. And so the prosperity of company farmers located on the lands surrounding Ojibwa and Meadowbrook declined between 1920 and 1940.

Most did not prosper because the physical geography of the Northwoods severely restricted agricultural production. The soils of the Cutover are of lower quality for agriculture than are soils in the rest of the state. Soil types range from heavy red clay

TABLE 4.3
The Wisconsin Colonization Company
Improvements in Southern Sawyer
County, 1917-1920

Improvements		Total
Company Built		
Houses	173	
Barns	133	
Roads		
Brushed and Logged	46	miles
Made Passable	11	miles
Graded	2	miles
Telephone Lines	15	miles
Lumber Cut	1.4	million feet
Company Farmers	160	
Cleared Land Cultivated	324	acres
Stumpland Cultivated	1,117	acres
Meadows	58	acres
Land Occupied	8,339	acres
Due on Land	$247,098	
Value of All Assets	$538,218	
Cows	244	
Pigs	131	

Source: Manuscript data in the Area Research
Center, University of Wisconsin-Eau Claire.

FIGURE 4.24 Clearing the land with explosives. (Department of Agricultural Journalism, University of Wisconsin–Madison)

to light sand and are low in humus—organic matter necessary for high-yielding crops without the use of chemical fertilizers (which at that time had not yet been developed). These unproductive soils are also littered with boulders and stones dropped by glaciers 10,000 years ago. Late springs delay plowing, and early killing frosts threaten harvests. Although rainfall is about the same across the state, the lighter soils of the Cutover experience a greater frequency of drought when rainfall is less than normal. All these physical features limited the amount of land farmed, which in 1927 ranged from 1 to 10 percent in the far north to 10 to 30 percent in the southern portions; by contrast, 53 percent of the land in the rest of the state was farmed. After 10 years of settlement, less than 30 percent of northern farmers were still on the land; by 1940 the number had dropped to less than 16 percent.

To be sure, some farmers survived and even expanded their holdings. The Guy Squires family, for example, purchased 80 acres (32 ha) near Ojibwa around 1920. By

1931, the first year for which statistics are available, they had 1 acre (.4 ha) in potatoes, 7 acres (2.8 ha) in oats, and 7 acres (2.8 ha) in clover. By 1940 they had expanded their holdings by 50 percent, though they had added only 3 acres (1.2 ha) to cultivation. The Joe Teneta family was more typical of farmers who stayed on the land. Their holdings never increased beyond the original 80 acres (32 ha) purchased from the Wisconsin Colonization Company, although they were able to increase their cultivation from 4 acres (1.6 ha) in 1931 to 10 acres (4 ha) in 1940.

Families like the Squires and Tenetas were exceptional. For the most part, the land reverted to the control of Faast and his associates, who seldom were able to pay the property taxes. Although the College of Agriculture had promoted northern settlement in the late nineteenth century, by the 1940s the Agricultural Experiment Station at the University of Wisconsin was critical of settlement in the Cutover region. A 1941 Experiment Station research bulletin rated the quality of the land and the growing season very low compared with other areas of the state. These factors, when combined with the agricultural depression, the difficulties of clearing cutover land, and the long distances to markets, meant hard times for most farmers who tried to live out Ben Faast's dream.

Northern Agriculture from the Great Depression to the 1950s

Farming in northern Wisconsin was already difficult in the late nineteenth century; but by the 1920s, a sharp decline in agricultural prices resulted in farm abandonment, and land clearing essentially ceased. Colonization companies went bankrupt; tax delinquency became extensive, and local governments, which relied on property taxes, were nearing bankruptcy as well.

The collapse of farming in northern Wisconsin during the 1920s, climaxed by the stock market crash of 1929, was reflected in an increase in tax-delinquent land. Of the 11 million acres (4.4 million ha) in the 17 northern counties, 1 million acres (404,700 ha) were for sale as tax-delinquent in 1921; by 1927 land for sale had reached 2.5 million acres (1 million ha) or nearly 25 percent of all land in the north. More land was becoming tax-delinquent, but less was being bought. In 1921, 40 percent of all tax-delinquent land remained unsold; but in 1927, the unsold land had increased to 80 percent.

Furthermore, agricultural settlement had never really succeeded in the Cutover. After 40 years during which northern farming had been promoted by real estate speculators, railroad companies, county and state agencies, and colonialization companies, only 6 percent, or 660,000 acres (267,102 ha), had been cultivated. At this rate of forest-to-farm conversion, the northern Cutover areas would have been completely turned into farmland in 400 years! Until the early 1950s, the Cutover, which earlier referred simply to the lands from which pine had been cut, continued to be synonymous with a depressed area. Various

governmental responses, in the form of relief and work programs, attempted to alleviate social and environmental problems. Planning through county zoning ordinances was first practiced on a large scale in the Northwoods. Through land-use management, human settlement was more rationally adjusted to the particular physical conditions of local areas.

Three kinds of settlers lived in the Cutover during the Depression. First, there were experienced farmers, who by the 1940s represented the first generation of usually successful farmers. Second were settlers working in logging and mining. Third were urbanites, who were encouraged by state and federal agencies to seek a new, secure future in the "empty" and resource-rich Cutover region.

Although individual family and county variations in living conditions were considerable, the region remained depressed compared to the rest of the state. The 1950 living index—arrived at by combining the average dollar value of farm buildings with the percentage of farms having telephones, automobiles, electric lights, running water, and radios and calculated by county—ranged from 80 to 128, with a regional average of 97. In the remainder of the state, the range was 111 to 269, with an average index of 165. Social and areal differentiation was even more severe when considering the proportion of the population receiving public assistance. In June 1935, 25 percent of the Cutover inhabitants received some sort of public help; in the rest of the state, only 10 percent did. Strong dependence on public relief continued into 1939, when the percentages were 28 and 11, respectively.

Settlers were consequently unable to pay their property taxes. In 1956, the highest rates (56 percent and over) of tax delinquency were in the northernmost townships of the Northwoods (Figure 4.25). From the 1930s to the 1950s, the Cutover region continued to lose population. It had been the last region in Wisconsin to be settled by agriculturalists and the first to be abandoned. The outmigration was greatest among

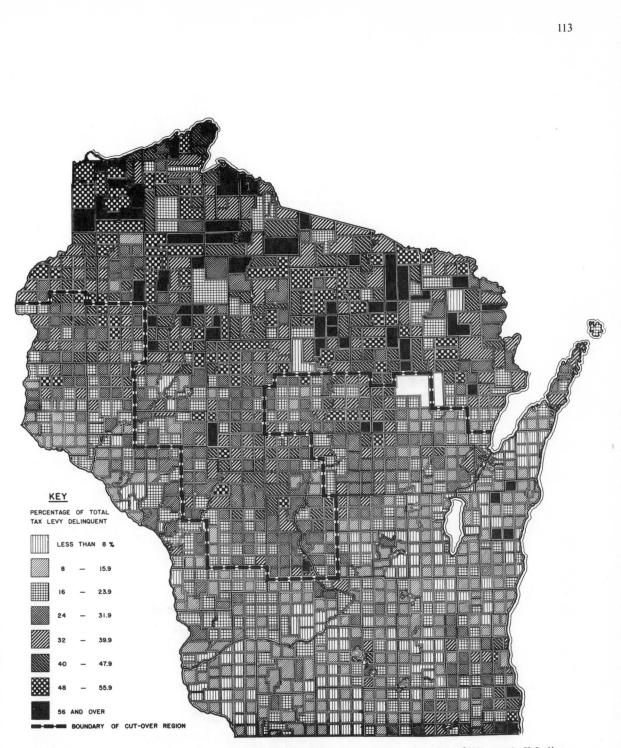

KEY

PERCENTAGE OF TOTAL
TAX LEVY DELINQUENT

LESS THAN 8 %

8 — 15.9

16 — 23.9

24 — 31.9

32 — 39.9

40 — 47.9

48 — 55.9

56 AND OVER

BOUNDARY OF CUT-OVER REGION

FIGURE 4.25 Tax-delinquency rates by township, 1936. (*The Cutover Region of Wisconsin* [Madison: Wisconsin State Planning Board, Bulletin no. 7, 1939])

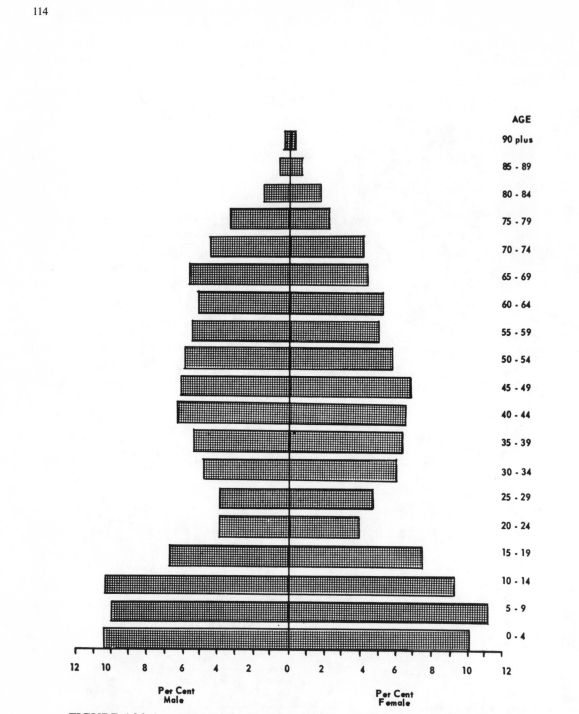

FIGURE 4.26 Age-sex pyramid for Price County, 1958. (Jon A. Doerflinger and D. G. Marshall, *The Story of Price County, Wisconsin: Population Research in a Rural Development County* [Madison: University of Wisconsin, Research Bulletin 220, 1960])

young adults. The 1958 age-sex distribution for Price County, which is representative of northern Wisconsin, shows the small number of young people remaining (Figure 4.26).

The collapse of the farming frontier in northern Wisconsin formed the basis for the state and county forest systems. Already in 1903 a Forestry Commission was established to acquire land in the Cutover for a state forest system. Many northern settlers and county governments objected to land being placed in state forests; they wanted the land sold to settlers, "who will make homes and farms for themselves" (Carstensen, 1958, p. 18). During the 1910s fierce legislative and legal battles raged between the conservationists and the agriculturalists. The massive tax-delinquent lands of the 1920s and 1930s, however, resulted in local units of government establishing township and county forests and parks. Today, Wisconsinites and out-of-staters enjoy the natural resources of the Northwoods without having to encounter the physical hardships and financial losses that had been the experience of settlers since the 1920s.

NORTHERN RECREATION AFTER THE 1950s

The Northwoods has long been a playground of the urban rich. In the first half of the nineteenth century, the area was dotted with vast hunting preserves and expensive private lodges owned by wealthy families from Milwaukee and Chicago. Numerous exclusive resort hotels provided a cool haven for the rich during the summer months (Figure 4.27). By 1897 hunters and anglers were spending 20,000 dollars an-

THE CHEQUAMEGON, ASHLAND, WIS.

FIGURE 4.27 The Chequamegon Resort Hotel, Ashland, 1882. The Chequamegon was typical of nineteenth-century resort hotels in size and offerings. It was one of many frequented by the rich, who swam, fished, and boated, doing ordinary things in exclusion from "ordinary" people. (James Baker, *Summer on the Shores of Lake Superior* [Milwaukee: Cramer, Aikens and Cramer, 1882])

nually enjoying northern forests and lakes.

Private recreational facilities resembling modern lakeshore leisure homes in form and function first appeared in northern Wisconsin in the late nineteenth century. These facilities were more recreational complexes than camps or cottages. They consisted of several buildings and were equipped, supplied, and staffed to be self-sufficient for summer and fall. Most of these complexes were constructed on lakes in remote areas that could be reached only by "packing in" or "buckboarding in" several miles after leaving the railroad. Very few existed, for they could be maintained only by exceptionally wealthy individuals—corporation heads, timber barons, railroad magnates, and other members of the elite. Many of these people were from Chicago or other large cities in northern Illinois or southeastern Wisconsin; some had acquired their fortunes in the region and were intimately familiar with its amenities.

With the introduction of the automobile in the 1910s and a subsequent expanding network of improved roads, private recreational lakeshore development in northern Wisconsin expanded. Many more lakes could be reached by far more people in considerably less time. Lakeshore cottages became economically feasible for the Chicago, Milwaukee, and Twin Cities upper middle class. By 1918 weekend summer homes in northwestern Wisconsin were appearing on most large and medium-sized lakes within a three-hour drive of the Twin Cities, including the larger lakes near Duluth-Superior and Eau Claire–Chippewa Falls.

During the Great Depression of the 1930s, several government programs were directly or indirectly related to recreation and the surface water resource of northern Wisconsin. The Civilian Conservation Corps (CCC) constructed parks, picnic areas, campgrounds, and public accesses along a number of the region's lakes and took the first truly comprehensive inventory of surface waters in northwestern Wisconsin. Other government agencies improved major

state highways. Most far-reaching in effect, however, was the massive social legislation relating generally to wages and working conditions that was enacted during the 1930s and during the first few years following World War II. Personal incomes and automobile ownership rates rose dramatically, summer vacations became a middle-class "necessity," and cars made it possible for urban families to "escape to Wisconsin" in increasing numbers.

The growth of post–World War II recreational development, whether private cottages or resorts, reinforced the perception by state agencies, local governments, and chambers of commerce that tourism was the best and perhaps only possible use of the natural environment of the Northwoods region. The best timber had been cut during the lumber era, and agriculture had proved unprofitable. What remained was a physical environment containing the woods and water that Americans expect to find when they seek outdoor recreation. Most of the area is covered by second- and third-generation timber, and many counties have abundant lakes and rivers. The progressive political leadership of Governor Gaylord Nelson and the state legislature established Wisconsin as a leader in preserving the natural environment. For example, the Outdoor Recreation Act of 1961 supported environmental planning, land acquisition for recreation, and the purchase of scenic easements.

After the 1950s and 1960s, shoreline development in northern Wisconsin reached explosive levels. Advertising by the recreation industry, now a giant in the region, made it seem illogical, even unacceptable, not to take one's family out to the water. Countless innovations in recreational technology made surface-water recreation easier, simpler, and safer: lightweight, leakproof aluminum boats and canoes; colorful and sturdy fiberglass launches; light boat trailers and reliable car-top carriers; powerful outboard motors to make water skiing a middle-class sport; foolproof spinning tackle; family-size pontoon boats; camping

FIGURE 4.28 Seasonal homes as a percent of total housing units. (Ingolf Vogeler, J. Brady Foust, and Anthony R. de Souza, "The Northwoods Region: A Distinctive Area for Human Settlement," *Wisconsin Dialogue,* no. 3 [Spring 1983], p. 112. Reprinted by permission of the University of Wisconsin–Eau Claire.)

trailers and camper vehicles of all forms, sizes, and prices; and prefab leisure homes that could be delivered to a lakeshore lot, assembled, and occupied in a matter of hours. All these devices stimulated the already intense interest in surface-water recreation and increased the already sizeable demand for private ownership of dwellings on or near water. By the 1970s, Wisconsin had over 120,000 vacation homes, mostly in the Northwoods.

Summer homes and cottages are clustered around lakes throughout the Northwoods region. In much of Vilas County over half of the residences are seasonal (Figure 4.28). In a study of lakeshore leisure homes in northwestern Wisconsin, Roland Nichols, a recreational geographer, found that they were owned by residents of Minnesota (40 percent), Wisconsin (35 percent), and Illinois (17 percent). Duluth–Superior, Twin Cities, and Chicago recreational owners were concentrated in their own particular part of the region. In Figure 4.29, the 30-percent-ownership isoline identifies sev-

eral cottage regions. Lakeshore cottage development varied with the size and accessibility of lakes. Small, remote lakes commonly had dispersed cottages, scattered along the shoreline out of sight from each other. On larger, more accessible lakes, and usually at a later stage of summer-home development, a linear settlement pattern emerged. Cottages were tightly packed with almost no vacant lots around most or all of the shoreline.

Wisconsin's reputation for fishing is reflected by the reasons resort vacationers give for coming to the state. Fifty-two percent of vacationers cite fishing, which is most important in the central and southeastern sections of the state. Water-related activities, second in popularity for visitors, are most important in the western and northern counties. Water-related recreation includes activities on Wisconsin's wild and scenic–designated rivers—among them the St. Croix, Bois Brule, Flambeau, Wolf, Pike, Pine, and Popple rivers, which are protected from commercial and residential uses—as

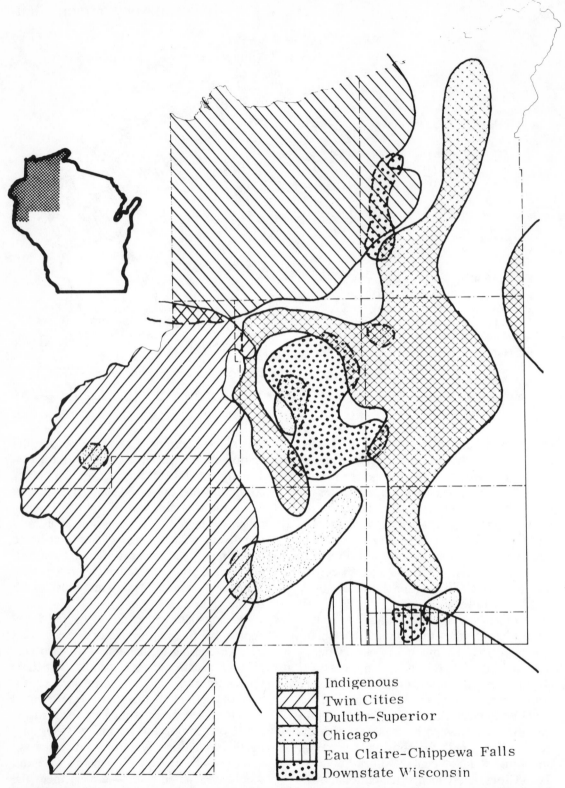

FIGURE 4.29 Cottage ownership regions in northwestern Wisconsin. Cottage owners are largely concentrated according to where they originate. (Roland Nichols, "Lakeshore Leisure Homes in Northwestern Wisconsin" [Ph.D. dissertation, University of Minnesota, Minneapolis, 1968])

well as on some truly commercialized recreational rivers. The Apple River, near Somerset, is the best-known example of a commercialized river; thousands of tourists, principally from Minneapolis–St. Paul, float down the river for about two and a half hours in inner tubes. So many people are attracted to this river that in 1977 the cost for picking up cans and litter was $15,000.

Many northern areas of the state, unsuitable for agriculture, have been returned to forest, and millions of these acres have been set aside for public use in federal, state, and county forests and parks. Over the Northwoods region, more than 150,000 acres (60,705 ha) per county are in recreational use (Figure 4.30). These lands are

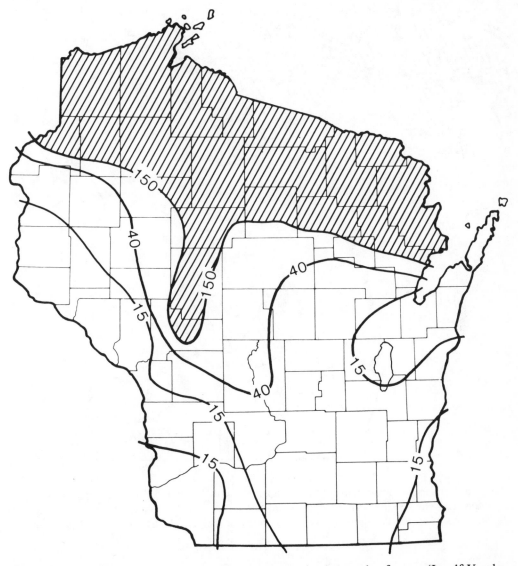

FIGURE 4.30 Recreational land per county. Data are in thousands of acres. (Ingolf Vogeler, J. Brady Foust, and Anthony R. de Souza, "The Northwoods Region: A Distinctive Area for Human Settlement," *Wisconsin Dialogue,* no. 3 [Spring 1983], p. 110. Reprinted by permission of the University of Wisconsin–Eau Claire.)

120

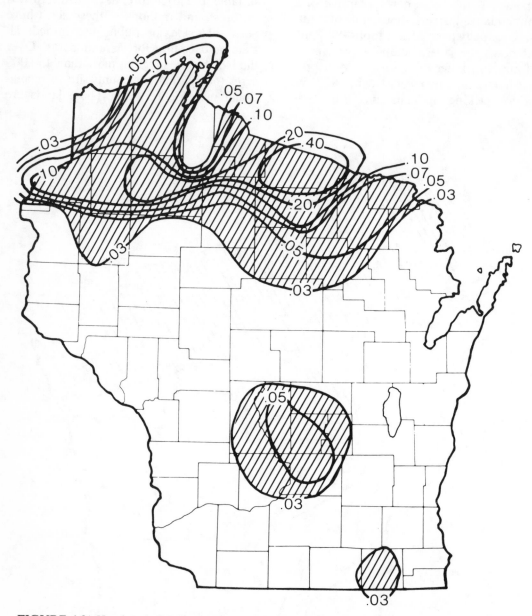

FIGURE 4.31 Hotel and motel rooms per capita. (Ingolf Vogeler, J. Brady Foust, and Anthony R. de Souza, "The Northwoods Region: A Distinctive Area for Human Settlement," *Wisconsin Dialogue,* no. 3 [Spring 1983], p. 111. Reprinted by permission of the University of Wisconsin–Eau Claire.)

visited by thousands of people during the summer, particularly July and August, and use is increasing during the winter for cross-country skiing and snowmobiling. The region is also dotted with thousands of private campgrounds, resorts, and other recreational facilities. Hotel and motel rooms on a per capita basis are heavily concentrated across the Northwoods (Figure 4.31).

*   *   *

In summary, the Northwoods is indeed a distinctive region. Locals and outsiders—whether Indians and fur traders, lumberjacks and lumber barons, dirt farmers and land speculators, or resort owners and big-city vacationers—have always perceived and recognized the special qualities of northern Wisconsin. The current diversity of Northwoods inhabitants reflects the major stages of human occupancy in this region. Understanding the historical geography of the Northwoods allows us to enjoy this region all the more today.

SELECTED REFERENCES

Alanen, A. R. "The Planning of Company Communities on the Lake Superior Mining Region." *Journal of the American Planning Association*, vol. 45 (July 1979), pp. 256–278.

Aldrich, H. R. *The Geology of the Gogebic Iron Range of Wisconsin*. Madison: Wisconsin Geological and Natural History Survey, Bulletin 71, 1929.

Barker, James. *Summer on the Shores of Lake Superior*. Milwaukee: Cramer, Aikens & Cramer, 1882.

Becker, Jeremy. *Strike!* Boston: South End Press, 1972.

Carstensen, Vernon. *Farms or Forests? Evolution of a State Policy for Northern Wisconsin, 1850–1932*. Madison: College of Agriculture, University of Wisconsin, 1958.

Clark, James I. *Cutover Problems: Colonization, Depression, Reforestation*. Madison: State Historical Society of Wisconsin, 1956.

———. *Farming the Cutover: The Settlement of Northern Wisconsin*. Madison: State Historical Society of Wisconsin, 1956.

———. *The Wisconsin Pineries*. Madison: State Historical Society of Wisconsin, 1956.

The Cutover Region of Wisconsin. Madison: Wisconsin State Planning Board, Bulletin No. 7, 1939.

Doerflinger, Jon A., and D. G. Marshall. *The Story of Price County, Wisconsin: Population Research in a Rural Development County*. Madison: University of Wisconsin, Research Bulletin 220, 1960.

Dorner, Peter, and Kenneth Hock. *Adjustments on the Farm and Transition out of Farming in Two Wisconsin Dairy Areas. 1950–1960*. Madison: University of Wisconsin, Research Bulletin 264, 1965.

Durand, Loyal, Jr. "The West Shawano Upland of Wisconsin: A Study of Regional Development Basic to the Problem of a Part of the Great Lakes Cut-Over Region." *Annals of the Association of American Geographers*, vol. 34, no. 3 (September 1944), pp. 135–163.

Dyck, Diedrich; J. R. Schmidt; and S. D. Staniforth. *Enterprise Changes on Part-Time Farms in Northern Wisconsin*. Madison: University of Wisconsin, Research Bulletin 231, 1962.

Faast, B. F. "Practical Policies of Land Colonization." *Journal of Land and Public Utility Economics*, vol. 1, no. 3 (July 1925), pp. 300–304.

Fapso, Richard J. *Norwegians in Wisconsin*. Madison: State Historical Society of Wisconsin, 1977.

Foust, J. B. "A Model of Recreational Travel into Wisconsin." Paper, Department of Geography, University of Wisconsin–Eau Claire, 1979.

Fries, Robert F. *Empire in Pine: The Story of Lumbering in Wisconsin 1830–1900*. Madison: State Historical Society of Wisconsin, 1951.

Gara, Larry. *A Short History of Wisconsin*. Madison: Kingsport Press for the State Historical Society of Wisconsin, 1962.

Gates, Paul W. *The Pine Lands of Cornell University: A Study in Land Policy and Absentee Ownership*. New York: Cornell University Press, 1943.

"The Great Oshkosh Woodworker Strike." *Green Mountain Quarterly*, no. 3 (May 1976), pp. 16–34.

Helgeson, Arlan. "Nineteenth Century Land Colonization in Northern Wisconsin." *Wisconsin Magazine of History*, vol. 36, no. 2 (Winter 1952–1953), pp. 115–121.

Henry, W. A. *Northern Wisconsin: A Handbook for the Homeseeker.* Madison: Democrat Printing Co., 1895.

Herzberg, Stephen J. "The Menominee Indians: From Treaty to Termination." *Wisconsin Magazine of History*, vol. 60, no. 4 (Summer 1977), pp. 267–329.

Hibbard, Benjamin H., and John Swenehart. *Tax Delinquency in Northern Wisconsin.* Madison: University of Wisconsin, Agricultural Experiment Station, Bulletin 399, 1928.

Hill, George W., and Roland A. Smith. *Man in the "Cut-Over," A Study of Family-Farm Resources in Northern Wisconsin.* Washington, D.C.: Rural Surveys Section, Works Projects Administration, and Madison: Agricultural Experiment Station, Research Bulletin 139, 1941.

Hole, Francis D. *Geography of Wisconsin.* Madison: Department of Geography, University of Wisconsin, 1980.

Hotchkiss, George. *History of the Lumber and Forest Industry of the Northwest.* Chicago: University of Chicago Press, 1898.

Jenson, Vernon. *Lumber and Labor.* New York: Farrar and Rinehart, 1945.

Kay, Jeanne. "Wisconsin Indian Hunting Patterns, 1634–1836." *Annals of the Association of American Geographers*, vol. 69, no. 3 (September 1979), pp. 402–418.

Kleven, Berhardt J. "Wisconsin Lumber Industry." Ph.D. dissertation, University of Minnesota, Minneapolis, 1941.

Knipping, Mark. *Finns in Wisconsin.* Madison: State Historical Society of Wisconsin, 1977.

Lake Superior Iron Ores. Cleveland: Lake Superior Iron Ore Association, 1952.

Loomer, C. W. *Land Tenure Problems in the Bad River Indian Reservation of Wisconsin.* Madison: University of Wisconsin, Research Bulletin 188, 1955.

Lurie, Nancy Oestreich. "Wisconsin: A Natural Laboratory for North American Indian Studies." *Wisconsin Magazine of History,* vol. 53, no. 1 (Autumn 1969), pp. 3–20.

Maladjustments in Land Use in the United States, Part VI. Washington, D.C.: U.S. Superintendent of Documents, 1935.

Maybee, Rolland H. *Michigan's White Pine Era: 1840–1900.* East Lansing: Michigan State University Press, 1964.

Nichols, Roland. "Lakeshore Leisure Homes in Northwestern Wisconsin." Ph.D. dissertation, University of Minnesota, Minneapolis, 1968.

People, Pride and Politics: Building the North Star Country, Labor Tape 3. St. Paul: Pandora Productions, 1982.

Pifer, Richard. *To Sell a Dream.* Eau Claire: University of Wisconsin Area Research Center, 1982.

Rosholt, Malcolm. *The Wisconsin Logging Book, 1839–1939.* Rosholt: Rosholt House, 1980.

Roth, Filbert. *On the Forestry Conditions of Northern Wisconsin.* Madison: Wisconsin Geological and Natural History Survey, Bulletin No. 1, Economic Series No. 1, 1898.

Sandfort, Ronald. "The Entrepreneurial Activities of Ben Faast: A Visionary Banker, Colonizer and County Developer of Northern Wisconsin." Master's thesis, University of Wisconsin–Eau Claire, 1974.

Schafer, Joseph. *A History of Agriculture in Wisconsin.* Madison: State Historical Society of Wisconsin, 1922.

Smith, James B. "Lumber Towns in the Cutover: A Comparative Study of the Stage Hypothesis of Urban Growth." Ph.D. dissertation, University of Wisconsin–Madison, 1973.

Twining, Charles E. *Downriver: Orrin H. Ingram and the Empire Lumber Company.* Madison: State Historical Society of Wisconsin, 1975.

U.S., Department of the Interior, Bureau of Indian Affairs. *United States Indian Service.* Washington, D.C.: U.S. Government Printing Office, 1962.

U.S., Immigration Commission. *Reports of the Immigration Commission: Immigrants in Industry, Part 18: Iron Ore Mining.* 61st Cong., 2d sess., Senate Document no. 633, serial 5677. Washington, D.C.: U.S. Government Printing Office, 1911.

Vogeler, Ingolf; J. Brady Foust; and Anthony de Souza. "The Northwoods Region: A Distinctive Area for Human Settlement." *Wisconsin Dialogue,* no. 3 (Spring 1983), pp. 100–115.

"The Wisconsin Loggers." *Harper's Weekly*, vol. 24 (1885), pp. 196, 203.

Wisconsin Woodland Indian Project, Rhinelander School District. Contact Robert Hanson, district administrator of Rhinelander School District, Acacia Land, Rhinelander, Wisconsin, 54501.

Zeitlin, Richard H. *Germans in Wisconsin.* Madison: State Historical Society of Wisconsin, 1977.

Zelinsky, Wilbur. "North America's Vernacular Regions." *Annals of the Association of American Geographers*, vol. 70, no. 1 (March 1980), pp. 1–16.

CHAPTER 5

THE SOUTHERN AGRICULTURAL REGION

The southern part of Wisconsin has always been the heart of the state's agricultural lands. Human factors, such as proximity to mining and Great Lakes port towns, and physical factors, such as fertile soils and a longer growing season, produced the most developed agricultural landscapes in the state. Although Wisconsin's agriculture is today best known for dairying, other types of farming were important in the past.

WISCONSIN'S AGRICULTURAL HISTORY

The evolution of Wisconsin's agriculture reflects national, indeed, international, market conditions. The earliest settlers grew food and kept livestock largely for their own use; subsistence agriculture lasted into the 1840s in the southeastern part of the state and until the 1860s in the north. The first widespread cash crop was wheat, and it played a distinctive role in the state's agricultural history. With the collapse of the wheat boom, commercial diversified farming emerged. But very quickly, specialized dairy farming appeared, and by the 1910s Wisconsin had taken the lead in the national dairy industry. This supremacy has been maintained for over 70 years (Table 5.1).

Wheat Farming

From the 1840s to the 1880s wheat was the most important cash crop grown in Wisconsin, which was unique among U.S. states in the rapid rise and decline of wheat farming (Figure 5.1). Wheat was first planted on the Rock County prairie in 1844. Wisconsin was settled at precisely the time that new inventions in grain-harvesting machinery were being manufactured, so that by 1850 McCormick reapers, made in Chicago, and locally manufactured reapers, such as Esterly and Beloit, were used in the prairie fields of the state. The shortage of working people because of the Civil War encouraged the mechanization of wheat harvesting, particularly the use of threshing machines.

Reapers were common even on the smaller farms and bonanza wheat farms

TABLE 5.1
Evolution of Wisconsin
Agriculture by Region

| Farming Type | Important Decades by Region | |
	Southeast	North
Subsistence	1830s	1860s
Wheat	1840s–1870s	1860s–1880s
Diversified	1850s–1880s	1890s–1910s
Dairy	1890s–1980s	1910s–1980s

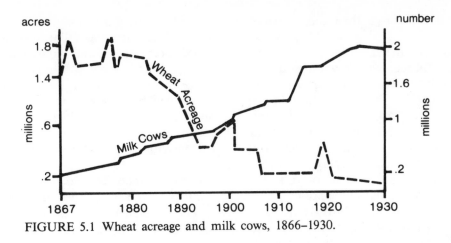

FIGURE 5.1 Wheat acreage and milk cows, 1866–1930.

predated those in the Red River Valley of Minnesota by 20 to 30 years. In Dane County, for example, the DeForest farm consisted of 2,200 acres (890 ha), 1,000 acres (404 ha) of which was in grain. The 800 acres (324 ha) of wheat were harvested by eight reaping machines and 60 men. The first major wheat production year was 1849, representing twice the highest production for any previous year. By 1855, the wheat harvest had been doubled again, and it reached 14 million bu (.5 billion lt) in 1857. In the "golden year," 1860, Wisconsin ranked third in U.S. wheat production and produced 17 percent of all U.S. wheat. Wisconsin was known as America's bread basket.

Wheat specialization spread across the state, as it had across the United States. Rock County was first in wheat production in 1849, but by 1859 Green Lake, one of the newer counties bordering the Fox River, had taken over first place, and then in 1869 Green Lake was surpassed by St. Croix, in north-central Wisconsin. By the 1850s, however, with the depletion of soil fertility, wheat yields were already declining. Rock County slipped to fifth place in 1859 and thirty-first in 1869. But new land was cleared and wheat continued to be planted because the Civil War assured high wheat prices. The abundance of Wisconsin wheat on the world market drove western European wheat prices down and farmers there to bank-

ruptcy. Ironically, many of these same farmers emigrated to the New World, often to the same state that had caused their distress—the region that had been the source of their problem became the region from which they sought a solution.

In southeastern Wisconsin wheat growing had ceased by 1879; in the newer settlements of the southwest, wheat continued to be grown on the ridges of the Driftless Area, although the alluvial valley lands were no longer used for the crop. In the densely forested northern areas of the state wheat was never a major crop. Land there could not be cleared rapidly, and what was cleared was best planted in several crops for diversification than in one highly speculative crop, such as wheat.

Diversified Farming

Although wheat production increased by almost 6 times between 1849 and 1879, corn and oats increased by 12; hay production increased by almost 7 times. During this period the state's agriculture was becoming diversified; the one-crop wheat system was being replaced by crop and livestock farming. By 1850 the state's agricultural counties were divided into two distinctive regions. Feed crops—corn, oats, and hay—predominated in the southern two-tier counties including Sauk, Richland, and Crawford. To the north of these counties, cereals—wheat, rye, and barley—

covered more acreage than did livestock feed crops.

Several specialized crops also became important. Tobacco was grown in southern and western Wisconsin and potatoes in central Wisconsin. Tobacco continues to be grown as a cash crop on many dairy farms, but potatoes, once a cash crop on dairy farms as well, are now largely grown on specialized farms in large acreages. Tobacco sheds characterize the tobacco-producing areas of the state, but the once-common potato cellars, partially aboveground and partially dug into the side of hills, remain only as historic relics of a distinctive but outmoded agricultural system. Early potato cellars may still be found in Waushara, Waupaca, and Portage counties.

The Development of Dairy Farming

By 1860, commercial dairying was already a regular business for some farmers. These early dairy farmers were widely scattered in southeastern and southern counties. Kenosha, Racine, Milwaukee, Walworth, and Green counties were the largest per capita producers of butter (25 lb, or 11 kg, or more), but most farmers only kept several cows for their own use.

Intensive dairying developed rapidly from the 1860s to the 1890s. Three major circumstances account for the widespread growth of dairy farming in Wisconsin. First, New Yorkers who came to Wisconsin in large numbers from the 1830s to the 1850s brought with them the knowledge and skill of scientific and commercial dairying. Prior to Wisconsin's prominence in dairying, New York was exemplary for good breeding practices and well-run dairy operations. New Yorkers frequently headed local movements to build cheese factories and to organize breeder associations and other kinds of dairy improvement societies in Wisconsin. They demonstrated that the practice of breeding "dual-purpose" cows, for both beef and milk, should be replaced by breeding for milk only.

A second influence was the research and extension work of the College of Agriculture at the University of Wisconsin in Madison. The college encouraged dairying and provided short courses and winter classes (the first in 1887) to dairy farmers. Research at the college resulted in the Babcock milk tester (which measures the amount of butterfat in milk), bacteriological tests for detecting diseases, and practical methods of pasteurizing milk. The college also held farmers' institutes throughout the state, the earliest in 1886, at which scientists and farmers shared experience and knowledge.

The third factor was the willingness of foreign-born immigrants to make practical use of dairy knowledge. Eager for easy profit in the new wheat areas of the Dakotas during the 1870s and 1880s, many of Wisconsin's U.S.-born settlers sold their Wisconsin farms to the newly arriving Germans, Scandinavians, and Bohemians, who had no choice but to work "hard and persistently, the long year through" to make a living. To these immigrants, milking cows twice a day, feeding and tending cows, delivering milk to the factory, and working in the fields was all in a day's work.

During the 1870s, several developments helped strengthen the cheese industry in Wisconsin. In 1871 refrigerated railroad cars became available to deliver cheese shipments to East Coast markets. At the 1876 Centennial Exposition in Philadelphia, Wisconsin cheese and butter rated second after New York's.

The development of Wisconsin's dairy farming had four distinctive stages:

1. During the pioneer phase, 1830s–1840s, dairying was for home use only.
2. From 1840 to 1870 fluid-milk production became important around major cities, competing with wheat, the then dominant cash crop.
3. Dairy specialization on farms occurred from 1870 to 1890. Improved dairy breeds, improved feeds, fast refrigerator rail service, a system of cheese factories, promotion by the Wisconsin Dairyman's Association (founded in 1872), and emphasis on dairy science and education

by the University of Wisconsin in Madison—all these developments made Wisconsin cheese and butter competitive with East Coast dairy products. During these 20 years, Wisconsin went from ninth to fourth place nationally in the number of milk cows.

4. By 1910, milk sales accounted for one-third of all cash farm income in Wisconsin. Wisconsin achieved national leadership in 1920, ranking first among the states in milk and dairy products.

Although the number of dairy farms in Wisconsin increased during the twentieth century, the Great Depression was a major setback to dairy farmers. Wisconsin milk production levels remained the same, but gross farm income of leading agricultural products declined by 41 percent between 1929 and 1931. This represented the sharpest decline in agricultural prices and farm incomes ever recorded for the state. In fact, farm incomes in 1932 were below farm incomes in 1910, despite increases in production of 28 percent. In reaction to declining farm prices during the 1920s and 1930s, Wisconsin's farmers conducted livestock and milk strikes, particularly during 1933. In that year, the Farm Holiday Association called a meat animal strike throughout the Midwest, and Wisconsin farmers joined in this protest to get higher prices for their products.

DAIRYING IN WISCONSIN TODAY

To him who loveth the cow, to him shall all other things be added—feed, ensilage, butter, more grasses, more prosperity, happier homes, and greater wealth.
—William D. Hoard, a leading
Wisconsin proponent
of modern dairying

Wisconsin is "America's Dairyland," as the state's license plates proclaim. A total of 1.8 million dairy cows produced 22.7 billion lb (10.3 billion kg) of milk, which represented 17 percent of the U.S. total in 1981. Milk accounted for $3 billion in cash receipts or 57 percent of all cash receipts from farm commodities in the state. Wisconsin ranks much higher than its nearest rivals—California, New York, and Minnesota—in total milk production and in the number of milk cows. The relative importance of Wisconsin dairy farms in the United States is best illustrated by a *cartogram*: Figure 5.2 depicts the size of each state by the number of its dairy farms. By using relative space, rather than the accustomed absolute space, the cartogram demonstrates the national importance of Wisconsin dairying.

The U.S. dairy region extends from New England to the Great Plains. The Northern Forest and Cutover lies to the north; the Corn-Soybean Belt, to the south; and the Spring Wheat Belt, to the west. The geography of the Dairy Belt is well suited to this form of agriculture. Only 10,000 years ago, mile-high glaciers covered this part of the continent, leaving the topography undulating or rolling with morainal deposits. The poorly drained, often stony soils can best be used for hay and pastures—necessary ingredients for dairy farming (Figure 5.3).

The New England–New York section of the Dairy Belt is primarily a fluid-milk market area, whereas in the western part, including Wisconsin, much of the milk is used for processed dairy products. Almost 80 percent of Wisconsin's milk production is manufactured into butter, cheese, and other products. As the nation's leading cheese-producing state, Wisconsin produced 1.6 billion lb (.7 billion kg) in 1981,

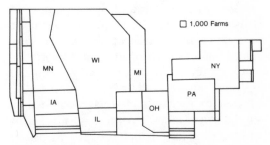

FIGURE 5.2 Cartogram of U.S. dairy farms.

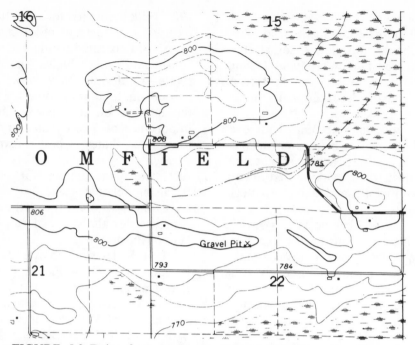

FIGURE 5.3 Dairy farm landscape. The topographic map shows the rolling topography with its poorly drained areas and gravel pit. The solid black squares represent houses, and the open rectangles stand for the large dairy barns. (Pop Sippi, 1 : 24,000)

37 percent of the U.S. total. Wisconsin is also the leader in butter production—295 million lb (134 million kg) in 1981, or 24 percent of the U.S. total—as well as the number one producer of sweetened and unsweetened condensed milk, buttermilk, whey, and whey products.

Half of Wisconsin's dairy farms are classified as Grade B milk producers, whose milk is manufactured into dairy products. Two-thirds of all Grade B milk produced in the United States is marketed by Wisconsin, Minnesota, and Iowa. Grade A milk, produced for fluid milk, is also turned into dairy products because more is produced than is consumed in fluid form.

Only about 20 percent of Wisconsin's milk is consumed directly; in contrast, 92 percent of Florida's milk is consumed in fluid form. Under federal law, marketing orders, established in the 1930s to assure an adequate supply of milk in all parts of the country at stable prices, divide the United States into 46 federal milk markets.

Wisconsin is divided into two milk market order districts: Minneapolis–St. Paul and Chicago-Milwaukee. Each federal milk marketing order defines a marketing area. This is not necessarily the area in which milk is produced, but is the area in which milk is sold to consumers. Only Grade A milk dealers are regulated. The distribution of Grade A milk as a percentage of all milk production by county shows the shape of the Chicago-Milwaukee and Minneapolis–St. Paul milksheds (Figure 5.4). Because almost all of the few farms in Iron and Vilas counties produce fluid milk, this northern concentration is less significant than Figure 5.4 indicates.

In Wisconsin, milk cows are concentrated in the southern two-thirds of the state, with the largest cow densities found from Green Bay to Watertown. The two

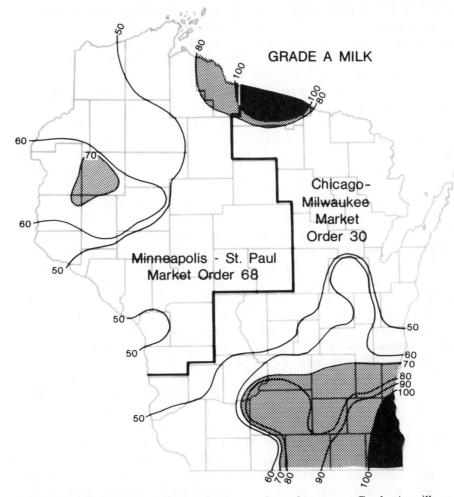

FIGURE 5.4 Grade A milk production and market areas. Grade A milk as a percentage of total milk production by county. (Based on data from *Wisconsin Dairy Facts* [Madison: Wisconsin Agriculture Reporting Service, 1982])

"holes" in this distribution are the urban counties of Milwaukee, Racine, Kenosha, Janesville, and Beloit and the recreational townships of Walworth County in the southeast; and the counties of the Central Sand Plain.

Wisconsin farmers are typically members of marketing, farm supply, and service cooperatives. Only Minnesota has more co-ops than Wisconsin. Other states have greater values of business or have more co-op members than does Wisconsin, but cooperatives are very much a part of life in rural Wisconsin, where dairy farmers have organized themselves into coopera-

tives to have greater control over the prices they receive for their work. In 1973 the 236 cooperatively owned dairy processing plants in Wisconsin purchased 51 percent of the milk produced in the state.

The Seasonal Cycle of Dairying

With a restrictive physical environment and a short growing season, Wisconsin dairy farmers grow crops primarily as feed rather than as cash crops. During one year a milk cow eats about 50 percent of its intake of roughage from pastures; the other 50 percent of its feed must come from harvested crops. This includes 2.8 tn (.12

mt) of hay, 5.5 tn (.24 mt) of silage, and for five winter months, 2.1 tn (.09 mt) of grain. Wisconsin ranks number one in the nation for "all hay" and "corn for silage," fourth for oats, and sixth for "corn for grain" (Wisconsin Department of Agriculture terms). The primary sources of feed are corn (57 percent) and oats (22 percent).

Corn is easily Wisconsin's most important crop, accounting for over 9 percent of the state's cash receipts in 1980. In contrast to Corn Belt states such as Illinois and Iowa, Wisconsin has historically grown corn largely for dairy-cattle feed. But new species of corn that mature in a shorter growing season have allowed farmers to grow more corn for cash and to grow it farther north. As corn production has gradually spread northward, corn has become an important cash crop. In 1960, only 18 percent of the state's corn production was sold; the rest was used on farms as feed. By 1981, 50 percent of the corn crop was sold. Wisconsin may be rapidly becoming a Corn Belt state.

Wisconsin has slightly fewer cattle than people. Of the 4.5 million cattle and calves in 1982, almost 58 percent were kept for milk. The number of milk cows in 1982 was about 100,000 less than in 1930, yet milk production has more than doubled. The average milk production per Wisconsin cow increased from 5,680 lb (2,576 kg) in 1930 to 12,441 lb (5,643 kg) in 1981, higher than milk production per cow in every country in the world, though lower than milk production in 10 other U.S. states. The quality of Wisconsin's dairy cattle and its high production of calves allows it to sell its animals to other states and to foreign countries. Almost 158,000 dairy cattle and calves were shipped from Wisconsin in 1981. About 60 percent were sold to adjacent Midwest states, although Texas and Florida bought 5,198 and 2,069, respectively.

The black-and-white Holstein-Friesian dairy breed is the biggest milk producer and the most numerous in the state and the nation, comprising 79 percent of the state dairy herd and 85 percent of the national dairy herd. Guernsey, Brown Swiss, and Jersey breeds produce less milk but more butterfat per cow. Jersey cows account for 13 percent and Guernseys for another 5 percent of the state's herd. Wisconsin's dairy stock originated from the world's oldest specialized dairy region, the Friesian areas along the North Sea in Europe. In the last 100 years, however, U.S. breeders have made substantial improvements on the European originals.

Dairy cows must be bred to produce milk. Outside Madison, the American Breeders Association produces renowned cattle semen. It is only one of several such exclusive companies in the nation. In air-conditioned barns, pedigreed bulls have a very active sex life. They are expected to perform three times a day on an average of two days a week. Every time these studs are "worked," they produce enough semen to fill 350 to 450 small glass ampules—each capable of fertilizing a cow. Through artificial insemination, a popular sire will produce 50,000 offspring a year and as many as a million of them in a career. Frozen ampules are delivered directly to farms, where the lowliest dams can be bred to the greatest bulls for $2.50 to $25. Only about 1,000 bulls are needed to keep the country's 11 million cows with calf.

Farmers arrange breeding and freshening periods (it takes nine months after breeding for a cow to give milk, or freshen) to milk about the same number of cows each month. In the past, milk production was much higher during the summer months and relatively low in the winter months. During the 1930s, freshening cows during the fall became common and thus, winter milk production increased. However, state milk production per cow still varies substantially between summer and winter seasons (Figure 5.5). During the fall and winter, when cattle depend on silage, cows produce less milk. In March, cows are calving and milk production jumps, peaking in May when summer pastures are available.

Fieldwork on dairy farms is also adjusted

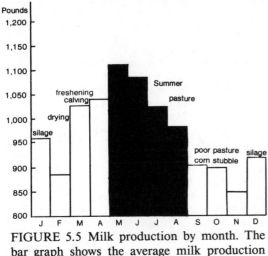

FIGURE 5.5 Milk production by month. The bar graph shows the average milk production per cow, which is greatest during the summer months.

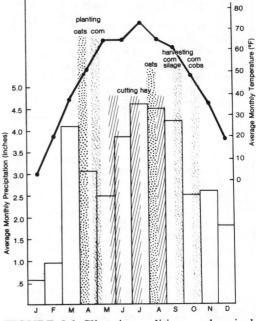

FIGURE 5.6 Climatic conditions and agricultural work.

to the seasons and daily weather conditions (Figure 5.6). As temperature and rainfall increase, corn and oats are planted in April and May. Two or even three cuttings of hay provide the bulk of winter feed. Harvesting of row crops starts with corn for silage in September and corn for grain in October or later. The cycles of weather, fieldwork, and milk production are interrelated to create the special character of Wisconsin's dairyland, in which dairy farming has its own particular way of life. Almost all dairy farms are family operated: Family members, usually a husband, wife, and children, do the work. Dairying is labor-intensive: Cows must be milked and fed twice—on some farms three times—a day, seven days a week; crops must be planted and harvested; hay must be baled and machinery repaired and maintained. The hours worked each month are essentially the same, although they do peak during the summer.

By California and Florida standards, Wisconsin's dairy farms are small. In 1981 about one-third of Wisconsin's dairy cows were in herd sizes of 30 to 49 and another third in herd sizes of 50 to 99; only 10 percent of the state's dairy cows were found in herds over 100; the average herd size

was 41 cows. In California, the average dairy herd size doubled during the 1970s to more than 300 cows, or seven times the size of the average Wisconsin dairy herd. The average Grade A herd in central Arizona's milk market is above 400 cows; in southeastern Florida, it is above 800 cows. And in New Mexico's rapidly growing dairy industry, new herds range from 700 to 2,000 cows. Such large commercial type dairy farms are destroying family farms in the traditional northern Dairy Belt and shifting milk production to the South. In a few decades, Wisconsin's dairy industry could well be overshadowed by that of California or Florida. Perhaps Florida's license plates will one day read "America's Dairyland."

The Dairyland Cultural Landscape

Dairying in Wisconsin has produced its own cultural landscape. Dairy farmsteads have a distinctive regional character, which has been studied by many prominent geographers, among them Glenn T. Trewartha, Clyde F. Kohn, and Loyal Durand, Jr. Dairying requires greater investments

---

Focus: Dairy Farming: A Hard Row to Hoe

What is it like to be a dairy farmer in Wisconsin? In 1982 the Farmers Union Milk Marketing Cooperative studied the Smith family, who operate a dairy farm—typical of the 48,500 dairy farms in the state—in Marathon County. The Smiths milk 34 cows, a popular-sized herd in Wisconsin.

John and Betty Smith get up at 5:30 A.M. and, together, begin to milk the herd at 6 A.M., finishing at 8 A.M. They take an hour for breakfast and household duties. Then John leaves for the field to plow or for town to pick up feed, while Betty launches into the household chores. The work cycle pauses at the noon lunch hour, then runs again from 1 to 5 P.M. After another hour break, the evening milking begins at 6 P.M. and continues until 8 P.M. Again, husband and wife work as a team.

On the average workday John works 11 to 12 hours, and Betty 4 to 5 hours in farm-related activities and again as many hours on housework. During the haying and seeding seasons John works an additional 4 hours daily and Betty an additional 5 to 6. The children also do chores, but most of their time is consumed by school, homework, and youth activities.

Sunday is not a day of rest on any dairy farm. It still means several hours of work for the family. Day in day out, year in year out, the cows must be milked and fed and milking equipment cleaned. Chores never stop. If farmers like the Smiths hope to take any days off during the year, they must arrange to have their cows milked by relatives, friends, or by their children staying home.

The Smiths live with uncertainty. They cannot precisely control the production of their cows; they cannot throw a switch and turn them off like machines when the market becomes glutted and prices drop; they cannot predict or control the effects of weather. In the autumn of 1974, for example, an early killing frost hit the prime agriculture areas of central Wisconsin, cutting corn production by 20 percent. Excessive moisture in the spring of 1975 hampered planting and destroyed crops. The worst ice storm in the state's history struck in March 1976.

According to the Farmers Union Milk Marketing Cooperative, the Smith family had a net gain of $7,794 from their dairy-farm operations in 1976. The capital investment of the farm in land, buildings, livestock, and equipment was approximately $185,000. On that basis, the Smiths either received 4.2 percent return on their investment and no wages, or they received no return on their investment and about $1.70 per hour for their over-100-hour workweek!

---

in buildings than does the cash grain farming found in southern Wisconsin counties. Large barns with attached milk houses for cooling and storing milk and tall silos are the salient features of this cultural landscape. Additional smaller buildings may include granaries, corncribs, machine sheds, and a relic chicken shed or pigpen (Figure 5.7).

Wisconsin has been a pioneer in the building of silos. Square and rectangular stone silos built inside barns were most common until the 1890s. In 1880, L. W. Weeks had the first aboveground silo built in Oconomowoc. In 1898, Arthur Mc-Grevch had the world's largest silo built at Lake Mills; it was 64 ft (19.5 m) in diameter and 60 ft (18 m) high and held as much as 200 acres (81 ha) of corn. By 1888, the United States had 91 silos; 60 of them were in the township of Lake Mills, Wisconsin. After the 1890s, round wooden silos attached to barns were popular. With

silage, farmers could keep larger herds of dairy cows during the winter, and the cost of keeping cows was lower than with dry feed. Many arguments, however, were used against silos and silage: Cows would lose their teeth, silage would burn out their stomachs, calving would be difficult, and silage would affect the quality of milk. Some even claimed silage made their cows drunk (the moist and chopped-up corn or hay usually used for silage ferments slightly and smells sweet, like beer). As late as 1908, a few creameries refused to accept milk from farmers who fed their cows silage. Today, every dairy farm has at least one silo, and many have three or four of different ages, heights, and building materials. The blue-and-white thermoslike Harvestores are the most recent innovation in storing silage.

Wisconsin is the home of Harvestores. A glass-coated steel beer vat was erected on Swiss Tom Farms, near Beloit, in 1945 to serve as a new kind of silo. The glass-coated surface prevented silage from freezing and rust from forming, and because the container was airtight, silage could not spoil. Because of the tremendous weight of the silage, coalmining equipment was used to bore it out at the bottom of the silo, and a large plastic bag at the top of the structure allowed changes in gas pressure to be equalized. The first 100 Harvestore silos were manufactured in 1949. In the 1980s these blue silos are found throughout the state, especially in the southern half and particularly in the southeastern portion, where the high cost of these silos can be more readily financed. Indeed, Harvestores are good indicators of high farm indebtedness because they cost about twice as much as similar-sized cement silos. The dairy farmsteads of southeastern Wisconsin are the biggest and most prosperous in appearance, frequently characterized by two or more Harvestores. In the northern part of the state, dairy farmsteads reflect the harder conditions of farming in general; hence, in the north, Harvestores are generally absent.

The size, quality, and design of dairy barns does not vary by ethnic group, as commonly held. Only the first generation of immigrants built ethnically distinctive buildings; subsequent generations built what worked best for agriculture in the region. The typical Wisconsin dairy barn is rectangular, has two stories, with a gable, gambrel, or gothic roof (Figure 5.8). The first story houses the livestock and gives access to the silage. A row of windows, often along the south wall, is a common trait of dairy barns. The second story is used for storing baled hay and sometimes grain. Most Wisconsin barns are banked: the north-facing first story is set into the ground, allowing wagons to be driven directly into the second story. (See also Chapter 1.)

The round barn is a distinctive Wisconsin contribution to U.S. rural architecture. In 1889, F. H. King at the University of Wisconsin–Madison designed a "distinctively practical barn"; it featured easier feeding (because of a central silo) and had a greater storage capacity using fewer building materials than rectangular barns. Innovative farmers adopted this new style of barn throughout the state. Today, round and octagonal barns are testimony to the

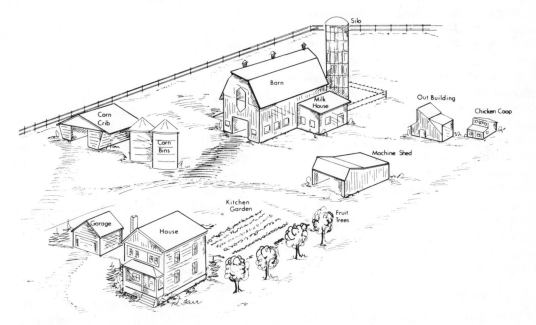

FIGURE 5.7 A dairy farmstead.

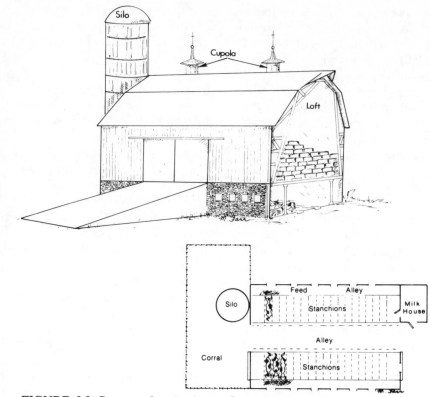

FIGURE 5.8 Cross-section (top) and floor plan (bottom) of a dairy barn.

innovative agricultural research done by the University of Wisconsin.

Midwest dairy farmers, in contrast to New England dairy farmers, grow almost all the feed for their cattle. This is achieved by using a corn-oats-hay rotation system. Corn is cut while still green as silage or allowed to mature and used as grain. Because genetic engineering has allowed the development of corn that matures in fewer and fewer days, Wisconsin dairy farmers can plant early-maturing varieties of corn for grain. In recent years, more corn has been grown for grain and less for silage. Instead, chopped green hay has been used for silage. Oats are grown mainly as a nursery crop for hay and used as supplemental feed for cows, especially during the winter months.

Cheese Regions

Wisconsin's milk production is largely processed. About 69 percent is converted into cheese, 5 percent into butter, 4 percent into condensed, evaporated, and other milk products. The consumption of dairy products in Wisconsin is so routine that bars *automatically* make milk-based cocktails, such as grasshoppers, with ice cream! Of total milk production, fluid milk only accounts for 20 percent, 7 percent of which is consumed within the state. Wisconsin produces 37 percent of all cheese made in the United States and through advertising has achieved a national reputation for its cheese. Indeed, rumor has it that Minnesota cheese is trucked into the state to enable companies to sell their product as Wisconsin cheese! Cheese is such an important tourist attraction that the Wisconsin Division of Tourism publishes a map of cheese factories that give tours.

Cheese production is highly concentrated in the Lakeshore, Southwestern, and Central cheese regions (Figure 5.9). Although cheese factories still dot the landscape, the small family-run cheese factories are dying out and being replaced by large-volume,

FIGURE 5.9 Cheese regions. (Based on Gordon R. Lewthwaite, "Wisconsin Cheese and Farm Type: A Locational Hypothesis," *Economic Geography,* vol. 40, no. 2 [April 1964], pp. 95–112)

large-scale processing plants. From 1870 to 1963 Wisconsin had about 1,000 cheese factories, but by the 1980s, less than 600 remained. Nevertheless, the location of the Cheese Belt has not changed since the turn of the century.

The comparative perishability of various dairy products and their differential abilities to bear freight rates are reflected in zonal patterns of milk utilization. On the one hand, fluid-milk production—the most perishable and bulky of milk products— is dominant in the urban milksheds of Milwaukee and Chicago. On the other hand, because cheese retains 10 percent of the bulk of milk, and butter uses only 5 percent,

cheese regions are appropriately wedged between the southeastern condensery belt and the great butter region, which extends across western Wisconsin. (Condenseries remove the water from milk, reducing its bulk and producing condensed milk and dried milk products.)

Gordon R. Lewthwaite argued that the location of cheese factories in Wisconsin may be explained by two factors: the absolute intensity of dairy farms (number of dairy farms per square mile) and the degree of dairy specialization (on each farm, percentage of income from milk production). The present pattern of cheese factories had its origin, for the most part, in the horse-

and-wagon era. In the period before the automobile, cheese factories were located in proximity to a large number of specialized dairy farms. Cheese factories, unlike creameries, paid higher prices for milk because they completely utilized the milk proteins and the butterfats. Higher milk prices from cheese factories allowed small-scale farmers to operate and encouraged them to specialize in milk production, to the exclusion of most other agricultural production.

The intensity of milk production resulted from more than the mere numbers of milk cows. Specialized dairy farmers, frequently holding small acreages, were likely to produce more milk per cow than less-specialized dairy farmers. This was particularly true on the smaller farms of the Southwestern Swiss-cheese and Lakeshore regions. But a large number of dairy farms in a given area was not adequate in and of itself for the location of cheese factories. These farms also had to be specialized in dairy production. In the warmer southeastern corner of the state, competing interests in hogs, beef cattle, and cash grains detracted from dairying. In cooler central and northern Wisconsin, intensive dairying failed to develop on the poorer Sand Plain and in the Cutover. Where dairying was *both* intensive and specialized, the cheese industry usually became predominant. Thus, the Cheese Belt is localized in a wedge-shaped zone of intensive and specialized dairying.

Wisconsin, in 1981, produced primarily American Cheddar (48 percent of all cheese produced). Brick cheese was still mainly produced in the county of its origin, Dodge. Swiss and Limburger production were concentrated in Green and adjacent counties. Italian cheese (14 percent) was the most important of the foreign cheeses, of which Wisconsin produced 80 to 90 percent of the U.S. total. Foreign-cheese production is extremely localized, and the importance of foreign cheeses, particularly Swiss, is related to the geography of ethnic groups. The Swiss settled in New Glarus in 1846 and spread over most of Green County,

the southwestern corner of Dane, and the eastern parts of Iowa and La Fayette counties. Although the Swiss settlers in Wisconsin were not expert cheese makers, they were acquainted with European Swiss-cheese-making practices. At first Swiss cheese was made at home for family consumption; but after 1870, when the first cheese factory was built in Green County, Swiss cheese was produced for commerce.

SPECIALTY CROPS

Although Wisconsin's agriculture is a livestock economy, several crops—canning crops, cranberries, and tobacco—are particularly important in a few areas and create distinctive farm landscapes. Intensive cash crops are principally concentrated in the midwestern Dairy Belt. The relatively low returns from dairying and the availability of family farm labor make auxiliary income sources especially attractive to dairy farmers. Although usually only about 5 to 10 percent of the crop acreage on dairy farms is planted in truck crops, collectively the concentration of vegetables, tobacco, and other specialty crops is impressive. Wisconsin is second to California in vegetable acreage.

Canning Crops

Wisconsin is a major producer of vegetables, especially processed vegetables (Figure 5.10). In 1981, according to U.S. census figures, the state ranked first in processed sweet corn, green peas, snap beans, beets, and cabbage as sauerkraut; third in lima beans; and fifth in cucumbers for pickles. Wisconsin had a less dominant position in fresh vegetables: third in the nation in carrots, fourth in cabbage, and seventh in potatoes. Although relatively few acres (about 305,000, or 123,433 ha) were planted in these crops, their value was extraordinarily high. For example, fresh cabbage brought $2,631.67 per acre ($6,579.18 per ha) and cabbage for kraut yielded $904 per acre ($2,260 per ha) (Table 5.2).

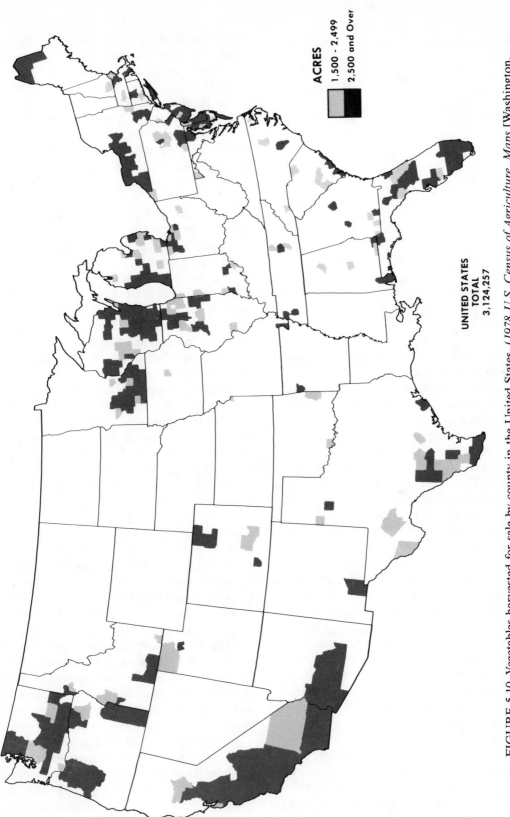

ACRES

1,500 - 2,499

2,500 and Over

UNITED STATES
TOTAL
3,124,257

FIGURE 5.10 Vegetables harvested for sale by county in the United States. (*1978 U.S. Census of Agriculture, Maps* [Washington, D.C.: U.S. Government Printing Office, 1979])

TABLE 5.2
Wisconsin's Vegetable Crops, 1981

Type	Acres Harvested		Value ($) Per Acre
Fresh Vegetables			
Cabbage	1,800		2,631.67
Carrots	4,500		1,710.00
Lettuce	950		2,021.05
Onions	1,400		2,782.14
Potatoes	53,500		1,496.00
Subtotal	62,150	Average	2,128.00
Processed Vegetables			
Sweet Corn	113,400		324.82
Sweet Peas	84,200		324.82
Cucumbers (pickling)	7,100		957.04
Snap Beans	70,200		445.30
Beets	4,500		554.44
Lima Beans	4,000		357.00
Cabbage (for kraut)	3,500		904.00
Subtotal	322,900	Average	552.00
Total	385,050		

Source: 1982 Wisconsin Agricultural Statistics (Madison: Wisconsin Agriculture Reporting Service, 1982, pp. 44-52).

Dairy farms contract with canning companies to grow canning crops. Farmers can diversify their income by growing a canning crop, and the contracts assure them at least a minimum source of income, but with the lower risks comes loss of independence. Under these contracts, canning companies decide when to plant, spray, and harvest the crop. They also often provide the agricultural supplies and specialized harvesting equipment. Farmers provide only the land and their labor; they functionally become employees of the canning companies, but without receiving the benefits of other employees, such as paid vacations and health coverage. Because canning contracts play only a minor role on any one farm, the negative aspects of contract farming are minimized in Wisconsin. In the southern United States, poultry farmers have no other income, and therefore contract farming has destroyed the independence of farmers and lowered their economic well-being.

Traditionally, canneries received crops from farmers adjacent to the canneries. The high concentration of canning plants from Madison to Fond du Lac reflects this early development. Many of these plants now have substantial quantities of crops trucked in from the Central Sand Plain. With cen-tral pivot irrigation, this formerly barren sandy area now specializes in vegetables and has become one of the most productive agricultural areas of the state. For example, potatoes and snap beans are localized in Portage County, in the "Golden Sands" (Central Sand Plain). But sweet peas and sweet corn are still concentrated in Fond du Lac, Dodge, and Columbia counties.

Wisconsin cannery towns, such as Waunakee in Dane County, Beaver Dam in Dodge County, and Clintonville in Waupaca County, are economically and visually dominated by the canning plant. During the packing season, from about mid-June to October, the work force often increases 100-fold. Plants are operated on two eight-hour shifts, six days a week, with trucks arriving continually. The canning companies depend on local seasonal workers—students and "homemakers"—and on Chicano migratory workers.

By 1900, Wisconsin farmers had already begun using migrant workers. Workers of European origin were recruited from low-income areas in cities, including Sheboygan, Milwaukee, Chicago, St. Louis, and Kansas City. This early use of migrants was tied to the expansion of sugar-beet and vegetable production. In the 1920s the use of Spanish-speaking migrants (U.S. citizens living in Texas, as well as Mexican nationals) became prevalent. During the 1930s about 3,000 Texas-based farm workers came to the state annually. Since the 1960s, over 90 percent of Wisconsin's migrant workers have been Spanish-speaking, primarily from the Rio Grande Valley in south Texas (Figure 5.11). During the 1940s Wisconsin imported male workers from Jamaica, the Bahamas, British Honduras, and Mexico, and from 1943 to 1946 German and Italian prisoners of war were also used to harvest Wisconsin crops.

Migrant workers peaked at about 15,000 in the 1950s. In 1956 Wisconsin ranked tenth in its number of migrant farm workers, outranked in the Midwest only by Michigan. But the mechanization of canning crops and orchards has reduced the number of migrant workers in Wisconsin

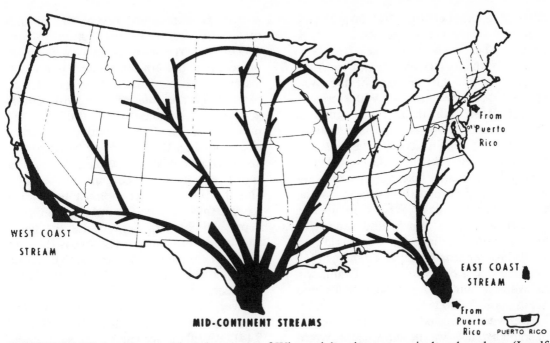

FIGURE 5.11 Source area and travel patterns of Wisconsin's migratory agricultural workers. (Ingolf Vogeler, *The Myth of the Family Farm: Agribusiness Dominance of U.S. Agriculture* [Boulder, Colo.: Westview Press, 1981], p. 230. Reprinted by permission.)

sharply. Mechanical harvesters were developed for sugar beets, potatoes, and snap beans in the early 1950s. The cherry industry, once the largest employer of migrant workers—having used 6,000 in 1949—is now mechanized (although few orchards remain in the state). In 1968, 40 percent of the cherry crop was harvested by machine; by 1978 almost the entire crop. Difficulties in mechanizing the cucumber harvest has meant that cucumber growers employed almost 27 percent of all migrant workers in the state in 1978; potato growers employed 6 percent, the second largest number.

The use of herbicides in vegetable production has also reduced the need for migrant workers. In the past, many migrants had been employed for weed control in intensively grown crops with a high value per acre, such as onions and mint. By 1968, more migrant workers were employed in food processing plants than in fieldwork. But despite the numbers and more noticeable ethnic background of agricultural migrants, local agricultural workers have ac-

tually always been employed in even larger numbers. For example, in 1968 local workers were 15,460 and migrant workers were 9,262 or a 1.66:1 ratio; by 1975 local workers represented 15,015 and migrants were 4,340 or a 3.46:1 ratio. Mechanization, use of herbicides, and passage of more stringent federal and state migrant labor laws have drastically reduced the number of migrant workers employed in Wisconsin since the 1970s.

Cranberries

Of the five U.S. states that grow cranberries, Wisconsin and Massachusetts produce 82 percent of the national total. Wisconsin accounts for half of that. The state has the highest yields per harvested acre, and in 1981, at $4,781.41, cranberries had the highest value per acre of all Wisconsin crops. Onions were the next highest with only half as much value per acre.

The first commercial production of cranberries started at Berlin, Wisconsin, in 1850 in the swamps of former Lake Oshkosh.

After 1870, cranberry production was concentrated in the bed of former Lake Wisconsin. These two large lakes had been created by meltwater as the two ice lobes (Chippewa and Green Bay) of the Wisconsin glaciation retreated. Water erosion in Lake Wisconsin finally wore a gorge at the Wisconsin Dells, and the lake drained into the Wisconsin River. The flat and poorly drained lake bed developed into swamps and smaller lakes. Over thousands of years, the decomposition of organic material in former Lake Wisconsin created large beds of peat, muck, and sand—the ideal growing medium for cranberries.

By 1900 approximately 1,200 acres (468 ha) were under cultivation near Cranmoor, in Wood County. During the 1970s and 1980s about 7,000 acres (2,833 ha) of cranberries were harvested. The northern region of cranberry bogs was developed after World War I and expanded after World War II. Wisconsin growers also migrated to the West Coast where they helped start the cranberry industries of Oregon and Washington.

Topographic maps reveal the unique quality of cranberry production (Figure 5.12). Cranberry plants are bog plants grown on acid peat beds in central and, to a much lesser degree, in northern Wisconsin. Cranberry bogs are intermingled with ponds and marshes that are the result of impeded natural drainage. Ponds existing at a higher elevation than the bogs must be dammed, and the dams must have water-control gates. Canals are dug from the dams to the bogs, and the bogs themselves must be leveled so that they may be flooded to a uniform depth. Ditches are dug around the fields and lateral ditches are dug across them at frequent intervals (Figure 5.13). These ditches bring water in and drain the fields as needed.

Every three years 1 in. (2.5 cm) of sand is spread on the ice in the winter (Figure 5.14). When the ice melts, the sand sinks down and covers the runners, allowing them to root, to produce more, and to be harvested more easily by machines. Sanding is also done before and after cranberries are planted. Sand provides aeration and

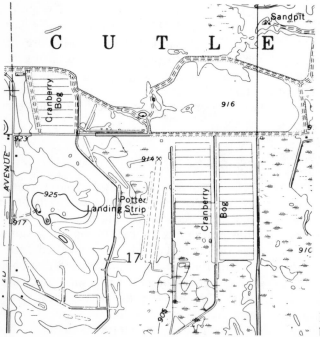

FIGURE 5.12 Topographic map of cranberry bogs. (Shennington, 1:24,000)

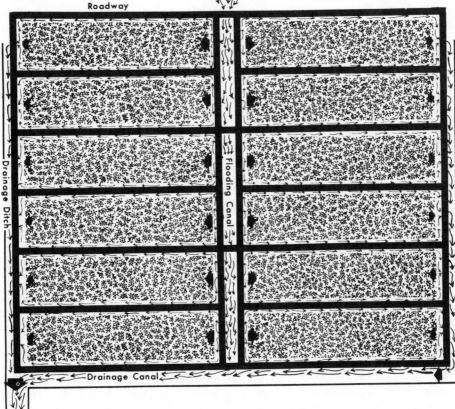

FIGURE 5.13 Drainage in a cranberry bog. (*Cranberry Growing in Wisconsin* [Madison: University of Wisconsin, College of Agriculture, Extension Service, Circular 654, July 1966], p. 11)

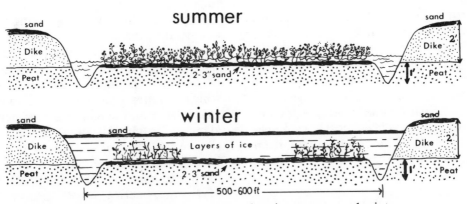

FIGURE 5.14 Cross-section of a cranberry bog in summer and winter.

lower humidity beneath the vines. Sandpits, which dot the landscape, provide the source for winter sanding (Figure 5.12).

To prevent frost damage, commercial cranberry fields are flooded with water, which insulates the plants, during the winter and during long cold spells in the spring and fall. During the harvest season, the crop is flooded up to 6 in. (15 cm) so the berries float for easy harvesting. Frost is such a critical weather factor in cranberry production that the Wisconsin Cranberry Frost Warning Service provides farmers with at least twice-daily weather and frost probability forecasts.

A few large-scale producers, many of them corporations, harvest the bulk of the cranberry crop. The farmsteads characteristic of Wisconsin's Dairy Belt are absent. On a cranberry farm, the large owner's or manager's house is usually surrounded by several smaller houses for the full-time work force. Machine sheds house the special cranberry-harvesting equipment and trucks, and the larger farms also have sorting sheds. The many dirt landing strips are used by dusting planes to spray the cranberry crop (Figure 5.12). Most of the Wisconsin crop goes to the Ocean Spray plant at Babcock for cleaning and grading and then to Kenosha, which has the world's biggest cranberry facilities, for processing and warehousing.

Cranberry farmers, like other specialty-crop farmers, must rely on seasonal agricultural workers to quickly harvest perishable crops. During the late nineteenth century, local farmers in central Wisconsin hired Polish farmers (too poor to make a living on their own land) and farm laborers, from up to 30 mi (48 km) away, for five to six weeks. The larger bog owners employed principally Indians. Although cranberry harvesting has been mechanized, seasonal agricultural labor—migrants from Texas and local workers—is still needed.

Tobacco

Although Wisconsin is not a major tobacco producer, its tobacco cultivation

creates one of the most interesting rural landscapes in the Midwest. In the early spring, white cheesecloth-covered seedling beds appear on tobacco farms. Tobacco seeds are started in these protected spaces; later, only the strong plants are transplanted into the adjacent fields. Distinctive tobacco barns, or sheds, as they are called in Wisconsin, are a persistent feature of this rural landscape (Figure 5.15).

A typical tobacco shed is about 28 ft (8.5 m) wide, 15 ft (4.6 m) to the eaves, and 25 ft (7.6 m) to the gable (Figure 5.16). The length of a shed reflects the amount of tobacco a farmer grows—each 12- to 16-ft (3.6–4.9-m) "bent," or sectional division, can hold the tobacco from about 0.5 acres (.2 ha). The capacity of a shed can be estimated by counting the number of roof ventilators: one ventilator for each bent. The sheds have a frame-and-board construction with large doors at both ends. On the sides of the sheds, vertical slats are opened during the autumn to cure the tobacco hanging inside on horizontal tiers of poles laid parallel about 4 ft (1.2 m) apart across the bents. The 4-ft-long (1.2-m) tobacco lath stick, bearing five or six tobacco stalks, is laid across the poles.

Tobacco is cured or dried in one of three ways: by smoke, smoke-free heated air, or fresh air. These three methods are referred to as fire, flue, and air cured (Figure 5.17). In western Kentucky and Tennessee, farmers make smoky fires in the bottoms of tobacco-hung barns. This oldest method of curing produces very strong tasting tobacco and is little used today. Throughout the Carolinas, Georgia, and Florida, flues conduct clean heated air into the barns. Overall, air curing is the most widespread method, which requires that barns have moveable side boards and sometimes roof vents, to allow air to circulate around the tobacco (Figure 5.16). Wisconsin tobacco is air cured, hence its barns share a great deal in common with tobacco barns in other regions of North America where tobacco is air cured.

Among cash crops, tobacco cultivation

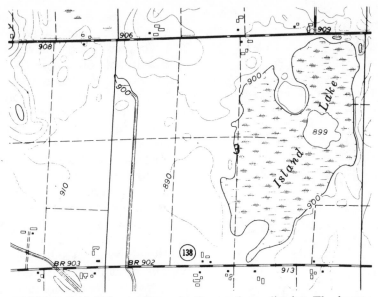

FIGURE 5.15 Tobacco farms in the southern district. The longer open rectangles are tobacco barns. (Rutland, 1:24,000)

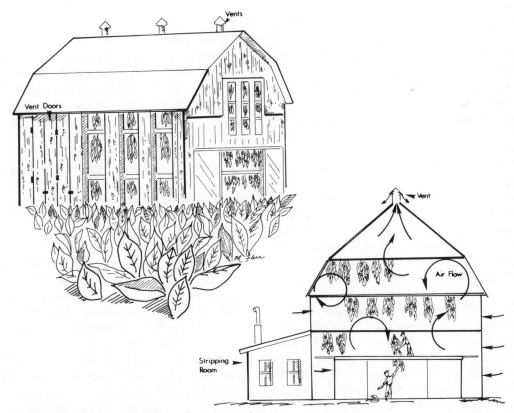

FIGURE 5.16 Cross-section of a tobacco barn.

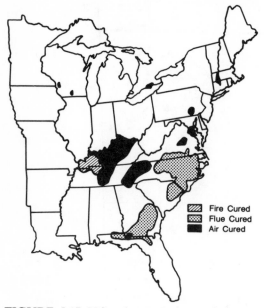

FIGURE 5.17 U.S. tobacco-curing regions.

requires the greatest amount of labor—in Wisconsin, about 189 hours of labor per acre (473 hr per ha) per year. One cow requires about 77 hours of labor annually. Because many tobacco farmers also have dairy herds, their work demands are considerable. For example, for a farm with 3 acres (1.2 ha) of tobacco (the average in western Wisconsin) and 41 milk cows (the state average herd size), the annual labor requirement would be 567 hours for tobacco and 3,157 hours for the cows, exclusive of all other farm chores. To meet these seasonal labor demands, tobacco farmers hire local workers and/or exchange labor with neighbors and relatives. Tobacco farming is family farming, and family incomes are improved by tobacco, which has one of the highest values per acre, over $2,000 in 1981.

Tobacco is produced in two small regions in Wisconsin. The southern tobacco district is centered in Stoughton and Edgerton; the western one, in Vernon and adjacent counties (Figure 5.18). Historically, both areas produced cigar binder tobacco, but today they produce chewing tobacco. Commercial tobacco production started in the state during the 1850s. With a peak production of 70 million lb (32 million kg) in 1903,

tobacco has declined to about 26 million lb (12 million kg) in 1981.

Tobacco is a highly regulated crop. The location of tobacco in Wisconsin and in the rest of the United States is determined by federal farm legislation. In the early 1930s, low tobacco prices caused by overproduction threatened the viability of many smaller farmers. In 1933, the U.S. Agricultural Adjustment Act encouraged farmers to reduce their tobacco acreage by 50 percent in order to increase prices. Those who did so received $33 to $35 per acre ($82.50 to $87.50 per ha) for taking tobacco land out of production. The tobacco allotment program substantially reduced the areal production of tobacco in the United States. In Wisconsin the acreage devoted to tobacco dropped from 28,000 (11,331 ha) in 1932 to 7,500 (3,035 ha) in 1934. The acreage allotment program was, and continues to be, restricted to particular states, counties, and individual farms that have a history of growing the crop.

Each farm is allocated an exact amount of land—to the nearest hundredth of an acre. Allotments are inspected by U.S. Department of Agriculture officials and penalties are imposed for exceeding the allotted acreage. Legally, allotments are attached to the land, and therefore cannot be transferred from one farm to another. The consolidation of tobacco production into the hands of a few large growers has consequently been prevented. Year after year, tobacco farmers vote for this program because it guarantees them a base price and a minimum income from their tobacco production. In 1981, tobacco continued to be harvested in Wisconsin on 13,400 acres (5,433 ha). The annual Northern Wisconsin Tobacco Exposition in Chippewa Falls attests to the fact that tobacco culture is very much alive. One notable event at the exposition is the tobacco-chewing contest. The 1979 champion, Charles Berge, stepped up to the mark, chewed, tensed, and reared back, letting fly a mighty expectoration of tobacco for a distance of 17 ft, 4 in. (5.28 m)!

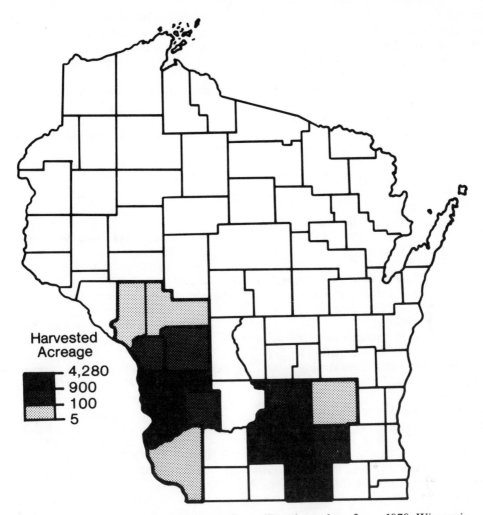

FIGURE 5.18 Wisconsin tobacco regions. (Based on data from *1979 Wisconsin Agricultural Statistics* [Madison: Wisconsin Agriculture Reporting Service, 1979])

What kinds of people grow tobacco and why are they so concentrated in particular areas? Rural geographers Karl Raitz and Cotton Mather found that the best explanation for the location and distribution of tobacco farms in Wisconsin was ethnicity. Based on ethnic maps, platbooks, and field surveys, they found that tobacco producers in western Wisconsin had predominantly (about 70 percent) Norwegian backgrounds and were Lutherans (over 96 percent). When members of other ethnic groups—Germans or Irish, for example—grew tobacco, they tended to have a Norwegian in the family.

Information on how to grow and harvest tobacco continues to be transmitted largely by this ethnic group in Wisconsin.

SELECTED REFERENCES

Bastian, Robert. "Southeastern Pennsylvania and Central Wisconsin Barns: Examples of Independent Parallel Development?" *The Professional Geographer*, vol. 27, no. 2 (May 1975), pp. 200–204.

Clark, James I. *Wisconsin Agriculture*. Madison: State Historical Society of Wisconsin, 1956.

Dairy Plant Directory. Madison: Wisconsin Department of Agriculture, Trade and Consumer Protection, 1978.

Durand, Loyal, Jr. "The Migration of Cheese Manufacture in the United States." *Annals of the Association of American Geographers*, vol. 42, no. 4 (December 1952), pp. 263–282.

――― . "The American Dairy Region." *Journal of Geography*, vol. 48 (1949), pp. 1–20.

――― . "Dairy Barns of Southeastern Wisconsin." *Economic Geography,* vol. 19 (January 1949), pp. 37–44.

Fish, N. S. "The History of the Silo in Wisconsin." *Wisconsin Magazine of History*, vol. 8 (Winter 1923), pp. 160–170.

Highbee, Edward. *American Agriculture.* Chapter 20, "The Economic Geography of Dairy Farming," pp. 257–284. New York: John Wiley & Sons, 1958.

Kohn, Clyde F. "The Use of Aerial Photographs in the Geographic Analysis of Rural Settlements." *Photogrammetric Engineering*, vol. 17 (1951), pp. 759–771.

Lewthwaite, Gordon R. "Wisconsin Cheese and Farm Type: A Locational Hypothesis." *Economic Geography*, vol. 40 (1964), pp. 95–112.

Logan, Ben T. *The Land Remembers.* New York: Viking Press, 1975.

Mather, Cotton; John Fraser Hart; and Hildegard Binder Johnson. *Upper Coulee Country.* Prescott, Wisc.: Trimbelle Press, 1975.

McNall, P. E.; H. O. Anderson; A. R. Albert; and R. W. Abbott. *Farming in the Central Sandy Area of Wisconsin.* Madison: University of Wisconsin, Agricultural Experiment Station, Bulletin 497, 1952.

O'Neil, Paul. "How Now World's Greatest Cow?" *The Atlantic Monthly*, September 1973, pp. 47–51.

Raitz, Karl, and Cotton Mather. "Norwegians and Tobacco in Western Wisconsin." *Annals of the Association of American Geographers*, vol. 61, no. 4 (December 1971), pp. 684–696.

Schafer, Joseph. *A History of Agriculture in Wisconsin.* Madison: State Historical Society of Wisconsin, 1922.

Trewartha, Glenn T. "Some Regional Characteristics of American Farmsteads." *Annals of the Association of American Geographers*, vol. 38, no. 3 (September 1948), pp. 169–225.

――― . "The Green County, Wisconsin, Foreign Cheese Industry." *Economic Geography*, vol. 2 (1926), pp. 292–308.

Vogeler, Ingolf; J. Brady Foust; and Anthony R. de Souza. "The Northwoods Region: A Distinctive Area for Human Settlement." *Wisconsin Dialogue,* no. 3 (Spring 1983), pp. 100–115.

Whitbeck, R. H. "Economic Aspects of the Glaciation of Wisconsin." *Annals of the Association of American Geographers*, vol. 3, no. 1 (1913), pp. 62–87.

Wisconsin Agricultural Statistics. Madison: Wisconsin Agricultural Reporting Service, 1983.

Wisconsin Dairy Facts. Madison: Wisconsin Agricultural Reporting Service, 1983.

CHAPTER 6

THE URBAN REGIONS

Geographers study urban places at two quite different scales. At one scale, they study the *internal* structure of individual cities by examining such things as land-use patterns, transport networks, ethnic and social distributions, and neighborhoods. Chapter 7 examines the internal structure of Milwaukee. At a much larger scale, geographers consider cities as part of an *urban system*. When Wisconsinites visualize the state's cities, they think of the familiar map of cities and transportation networks. Transportation networks link cities to other cities and to their surrounding trade areas. Collectively, cities, trade areas, and interaction among cities and trade areas make up an urban system. This chapter concentrates on the urban system of the state by focusing on three aspects: the historical evolution of Wisconsin's urban system, the spacing and size of cities in the system, and the role of manufacturing in the state's urban economy.

HISTORICAL EVOLUTION OF THE URBAN PATTERN

Urban systems are evolutionary in nature. At any given time, the pattern of cities reflects the current resource base and the skills available to exploit that resource base, the existing level of transportation technology, interconnections in the national and international economy, and many other factors. No pattern can be understood, however, without considering the past. In the United States, for example, as European settlement expanded, cities on the edge of the frontier during one time period became established centers catering to farmers in the settled agricultural countryside of the next time period. Given today's technology and settlement pattern, many cities would perhaps be much better off in another location. The investments of the past, the *locational inertia*, however, precludes the abandonment of a poor site and the rebuilding of a large settlement at a new one. We pay for past mistakes, and like all evolutionary systems, we find many wrong turns and dead ends. In this section, we will examine the pattern of settlement in Wisconsin as an evolutionary process, in which the pattern at any given time is the result of both present and past conditions.

Figure 6.1 shows the urban pattern in the state in 1850, which was the first year for which census data for urban places in the state were available. Only Milwaukee and Racine had more than 5,000 people; the rest of the settlements were considerably smaller. The settlement frontier generally followed the line from Green Bay to Prairie du Chien. Although the northwestern two-thirds of the state had been exploited by hunters, trappers, and French fur traders, permanent white settlements did not exist. Settlements that existed in the south reflected two factors: the transportation technology of the times and resource exploitation. Certainly all the cities along Lake Michigan took advantage of lake trans-

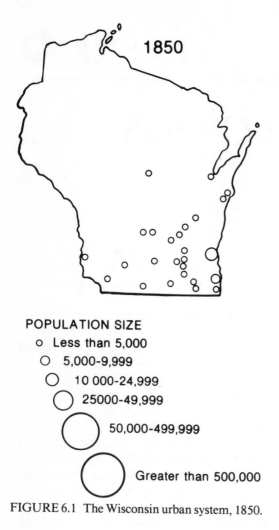

POPULATION SIZE

○ Less than 5,000

○ 5,000-9,999

○ 10 000-24,999

◯ 25000-49,999

◯ 50,000-499,999

◯ Greater than 500,000

FIGURE 6.1 The Wisconsin urban system, 1850.

portation, and Mississippi and Wisconsin river cities developed along river transportation routes. Some of the other smaller settlements in the south, such as Platteville, were based on lead and zinc mining; still other small settlements exploited timber resources.

Figures 6.2 through 6.4 show the development of the Wisconsin urban system between 1870 and 1980. Cities are shown by size category rather than actual population. The symbols on the maps show the changes in size levels from decade to decade. This is especially helpful in isolating the "growth centers" of a particular period. The Milwaukee metropolitan region—consisting of Milwaukee, Waukesha, Washing-

ton, and Ozaukee counties—is treated as a single entity on all the maps. There are so many smaller centers in this region that showing them would unnecessarily complicate the maps; growth in the area really reflected the fortunes of Milwaukee, and the Milwaukee urban region is essentially a single node in the state's urban system.

In 1870, the Civil War was over and the nation was entering a period of rapid growth and industrialization (Figure 6.2). Milwaukee had grown quickly during the preceding two decades to well over 25,000 people. The frontier had moved northward to an east-west line running roughly from Green Bay to the Twin Cities. Even in 1985 this line, which parallels Highway 29, generally separates the agricultural southern part of the state from the forested, recreational Northwoods. Between 1850 and 1870, several cities moved up two levels in the urban hierarchy, including Madison and Fond du Lac. Numerous other cities, founded during this period, were to become primary nodes of the Wisconsin urban system: La Crosse, Eau Claire, Wausau, Oshkosh, and Superior.

1880 marked the beginning of the golden age of the U.S. industrial revolution. Steamboat travel became prevalent on both rivers and lakes, and the rail net was expanded rapidly. In 1880, Milwaukee's population reached 100,000, but the populations of the rest of the state's cities remained under 25,000. La Crosse and Eau Claire had both jumped one level in the preceding decade. La Crosse's growth was the result of steamboat travel on the Mississippi. Eau Claire and Wausau, on the other hand, were at the edge of the great softwood forest, the pinery, that covered most of the northern part of the state, and the exploitation of this vast resource began to thrive in the 1880s. Eau Claire, Wausau, and Green Bay became the gateway cities to the Northwoods, and much of their economies for the next 30 years depended heavily on lumbering. The settlement pattern of smaller lumber towns also began to emerge at this time.

In the decade preceding 1890, the pop-

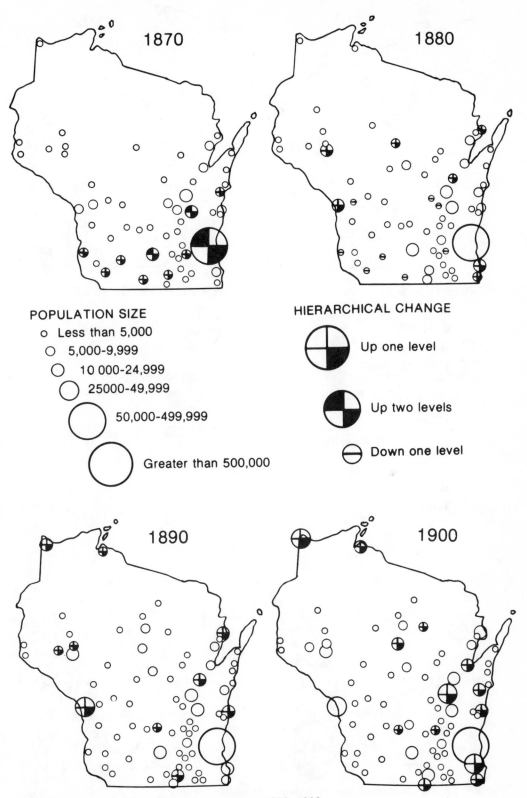

FIGURE 6.2 The Wisconsin urban system, 1870–1900.

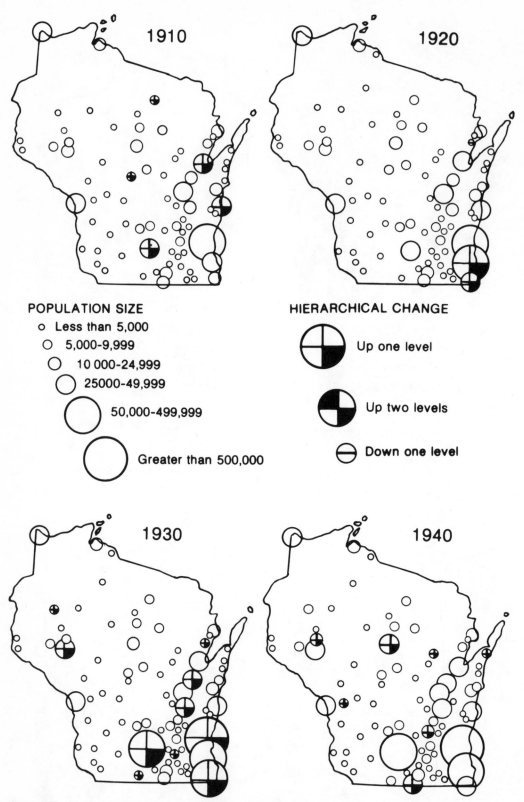

POPULATION SIZE
- ○ Less than 5,000
- ○ 5,000-9,999
- ○ 10 000-24,999
- ○ 25000-49,999
- ○ 50,000-499,999
- ○ Greater than 500,000

HIERARCHICAL CHANGE

Up one level

Up two levels

Down one level

FIGURE 6.3 The Wisconsin urban system, 1910–1940.

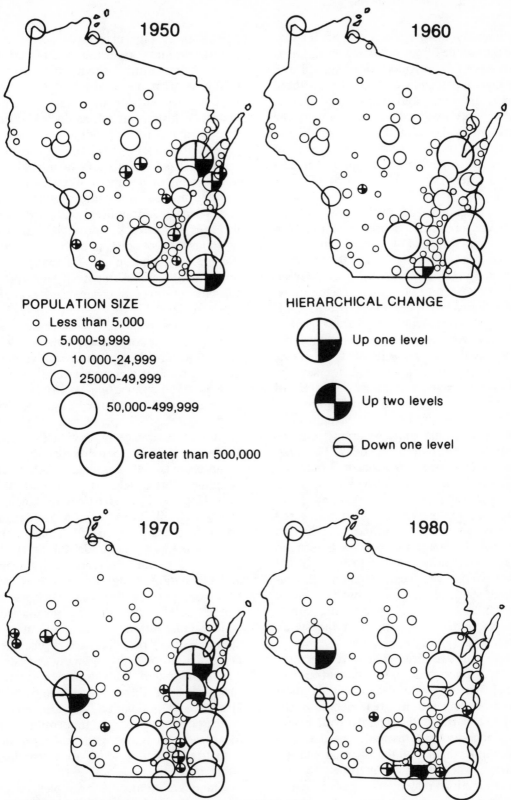

POPULATION SIZE

- Less than 5,000
- 5,000-9,999
- 10 000-24,999
- 25000-49,999
- 50,000-499,999
- Greater than 500,000

HIERARCHICAL CHANGE

Up one level

Up two levels

Down one level

FIGURE 6.4 The Wisconsin urban system, 1950–1980.

ulations of La Crosse, Superior, Sheboygan, and Janesville all grew by one level, based on river or lake transportation. Agricultural settlement gradually covered the southern part of the state, and many small market and "county seat" towns arose to serve the surrounding agricultural population. Figure 6.2 also shows the founding and growth of secondary lumber towns in the north. The period after 1890 through 1920 (Figures 6.2 and 6.3) was one of both massive industrialization and immigration in the more densely settled southern and eastern parts of the state. Differential growth occurred, but the populations of Beloit, Madison, Kenosha, Racine, Sheboygan, Green Bay, Oshkosh, and Manitowoc each jumped one or more levels during the period. Outside of the industrialized corridor, growth was slow and reflected the stabilizing pattern of agricultural settlement. By 1930, Milwaukee's population had topped the half-million mark, and the basic pattern of settlement in the state was set (Figure 6.3).

In other words, the *location* pattern of 1930 was not markedly different from the urban location pattern of today. The 1930 map shows the urbanized Madison–Milwaukee–Green Bay corridor, the manufacturing clusters of the Fox and Rock river valleys, the more widely dispersed service centers of the northern and western parts of the state, and the small isolated recreational and agricultural centers of the Northwoods. The location pattern has remained stable to the present, but differential growth has occurred, producing subtle changes in the size pattern of the state's settlements (Figure 6.4).

How can two cities that were the same size at a given time have different growth rates in the following decades? This question is considered in great detail in the next two parts of this chapter, but essentially one city captures functions that provide employment (and therefore population growth), whereas its competitors do not. These functions may be transportation and port facilities, as was the case for La Crosse, Superior, and all the cities along Lake

Michigan. A city may have access to a natural resource, as in the case of turn-of-the-century lumber towns such as Eau Claire, Wausau, and Green Bay. A city may have government functions such as a university or a state capital, as does Madison. The primary force in differential urban growth for most of Wisconsin's history, however, has been manufacturing. The establishment of a papermill at Green Bay or Fond du Lac, or an auto assembly plant at Kenosha or Janesville, or outboard-motor factories at Milwaukee provided hundreds or thousands of jobs, and therefore population expanded in the following years. Subsequent establishment of new plants elsewhere promoted urban growth at different nodes.

The cities most likely to attract new employment opportunities, however, were those that already had certain advantages and had reached a certain size. This principle is called a *deviation-amplifying effect* or *circular and cumulative causation*. Both of these terms simply mean that some locational advantage or growth (for whatever reason) leads to more locational advantages or growth. Geographer Alan Pred simplified this concept into diagrammatic form (Figure 6.5). Starting with a new or enlarged local industry, jobs are created not only in the plant itself but also in the service sectors (retail trade, public works, etc.). This in turn increases employment and population enough for the city to support some new enterprises, such as expanded retail establishments or an educational institution. Or the city may be able to expand port facilities or become a new node on the evolving highway system. This development leads to new or enlarged industries, and the process snowballs. Growth and population size also lead to increased invention and innovation. New ideas lead to new, enlarged, and "spin-off" industries, and new ideas are nurtured in larger cities.

There are numerous examples of this model in the evolution of Wisconsin's urban system. The first deep-water port facilities

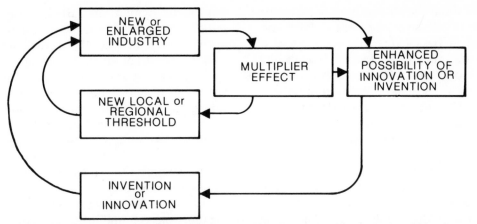

FIGURE 6.5 A model of urban growth. (Modified from Alan Pred, "Industrialization, Initial Advantage, and American Metropolitan Growth," *Geographical Review,* vol. 55 [1965], pp. 158–185)

on Lake Michigan in the state were built at Milwaukee. Once those facilities were in place, Milwaukee was able to attract the heavy industries that required a deep-water port. The heavy industrial infrastructure that developed, in turn, attracted more industrial investment. Milwaukee was also the logical place for the first airport able to handle the new jets of the 1950s. Once that airport was operating, other activities were attracted to the area and the process once again snowballed.

For another example, consider the development of the interstate highway system in the state. The Interstate 94 link was built primarily to connect Milwaukee and the Twin Cities, but Eau Claire, for example, was large enough and in the right location to be included as a secondary node on the network. Once that connection was made, however, the interstate highway gave the city an enormous advantage over rivals lacking such a transportation artery. By the same token, Eau Claire was the only city in the region of sufficient size to justify the building of an airport able to handle commercial jet traffic. These location features also gave the city an advantage over other centers in the region hoping to attract new employment sources.

Why do cities exist? Why do people live in urban clusters? Why are cities arranged

the way they are? Answers to these questions help us understand the pattern of settlements in Wisconsin. Worldwide, cities have been founded for cultural, social, political, military, and religious reasons, but they persist for *economic* reasons. Cities provide employment opportunities. People who left farms in the nineteenth and early twentieth centuries migrated to urban areas because jobs were to be found there and were lacking in rural areas. The presumed glamour of the "big city," compared to rural life, was a secondary reason. Although the big surge of rural-to-urban migration has ended, young people still leave small towns and rural areas in the state to find jobs in larger cities.

What kinds of employment do cities provide? An urban economy can be divided into two simple parts. Some income can be earned by providing goods and services for the residents of the city. This internal circulation of money is called *nonbasic* employment by urban economists and geographers. Cities are not self-sufficient, especially in terms of food and energy, so cities must export in order to pay for their imports. Export income constitutes the *basic* sector of the urban economy. Employees in the basic sector create wealth by exporting goods and services to areas outside their city. The economic life of a city then depends upon the basic sector, because the number of nonbasic jobs rises or falls with changes in basic employment. Suppose a new manufacturing plant moves into a small town and creates 100 new jobs. Further assume that its total output is sold outside the city. This is all basic employment. These workers in turn spend most of their wages locally, creating jobs for salesclerks, physicians, police, firefighters, and numerous other nonbasic workers.

Geographers use the concept of a basic to nonbasic ratio to measure the impact of changes in basic employment. The basic side of the ratio is always set to unity, or 1. Suppose that each job in the basic sector supports 0.5 jobs in the nonbasic sector, resulting in a basic-nonbasic ratio of 1:0.5. Any increase in basic employment leads to an increase in total employment equal to the number of basic jobs times the sum of the two numbers in the basic-nonbasic ratio. Thus, in our example (with 100 basic jobs and a 1:0.5 ratio) total employment would increase by 150 (100 x 1.5). The reverse is also true; a loss of jobs in the basic sector means a loss in nonbasic employment. The closing of a large manufacturing plant in a small town, for example, will have an effect on employment beyond the jobs lost directly in the plant itself. The nonbasic sector is also called *settlement-serving,* and the number of employees in this sector follows settlement size. Settlement size, however, follows changes in the basic sector. As cities grow, therefore, they must add people in both sectors, but size is ultimately determined solely by the size of the basic sector.

Basic employment can be divided into two parts. Urban places exist to provide goods and services to their surrounding market areas. Wausau, for example, sells goods and services to a large area surrounding the city, and these sales are basic in that they bring money into the city. A farm-equipment dealer in this town will certainly sell products to the surrounding farmers. This basic activity is termed *settlement-forming* trade. The second kind of

basic employment is called *settlement-building* trade and consists of all income derived from beyond the immediate surrounding market area. For example, all basic grocery sales will be made in the surrounding market area, but a manufacturing plant producing machine tools may sell its entire output to distant market areas. A university, military base, or other government institution brings money into the local economy, and most of the income comes from beyond the local trade area.

The same general set of settlement-serving functions is found in all places of similar size. The size of the market area limits the amount of settlement-forming income. The market area of a city cannot be expanded without encroaching on the territory of competing cities, so that basic income from settlement-forming trade is somewhat fixed and can only expand as population grows. New jobs can be created, however, with the addition of settlement-building activities, which allow centers to "transcend" the limits placed upon them by their market-area trade. Assume for example that the state is going to build a new campus of the University of Wisconsin system or a new prison. Several small towns are being considered as potential sites. Each town is pretty well dependent on trade with the surrounding market area, and the number of jobs is rather fixed. The one that gets the new facility will be able to add jobs above the limits imposed by the market area and will experience a growth spurt not shared by its rivals.

CENTRAL PLACES: THE SIZE AND SPACING OF CITIES

An urban system has two easily observed attributes: *size* and *spacing* of all urban places. The spacing of Wisconsin's urban places is not uniform (Figure 6.6). Urban places are rather concentrated in some areas and thinly scattered in others. Some cities play a larger economic, social, and cultural role and serve a much bigger market area than others. Economic, social, and cultural

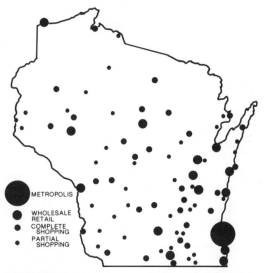

FIGURE 6.6 Spacing and size of Wisconsin urban centers.

power and market area size are almost exclusively a function of population size. The urban dominance of the southeastern and eastern part of the state is very apparent: Most of the state's population lives in an almost continuous string of cities called the Madison–Milwaukee–Green Bay urban triangle.

Geographers use *central place theory* to explain the size and spacing of urban places. Central place theory, however, deals only with settlement-serving trade. A few basic concepts of central place theory vastly improve our understanding of the urban system of Wisconsin. According to *central place theory*, settlements are arrayed in an interlocking hierarchy. Small settlements and their market areas nest within the market areas of larger settlements in an orderly fashion. Each economic activity has a specific *threshold*, which is the minimum amount of business or minimum number of people required to support a single firm of a particular business type. Thresholds for selected functions in Wisconsin are given in Table 6.1. Notice that the activities we generally think of as typical of small centers, such as taverns, filling stations, and grocery stores, have low thresholds, whereas functions that are typical only of larger

towns and cities, such as department stores or speciality shops, require much larger populations to support them.

A second important concept in central place theory is the *range* of a good. The range is the maximum distance consumers are likely to travel to purchase a given good at a given price. Goods with small thresholds and small ranges are called low-order goods. Small settlements, as a rule, can offer only low-order goods and can attract customers only over short distances. Larger settlements offer goods with higher thresholds and attract consumers over larger distances. The market areas of several low-order central places "nest" within the larger trade area of a higher-order central place. In Figure 6.7, the market area of the higher-order center includes the population of the lower-order areas. The higher-order center can therefore offer goods and services that the lower-level centers cannot.

If the basic economic life of every city depended exclusively on trade with the surrounding trade area (settlement-forming trade), all cities of a given level would be very similar in size. However, the situation is complicated by the presence of settlement-building activities and other factors. Chicago is the highest-order center in the Midwest. In the upper Midwest, Milwaukee and Minneapolis–St. Paul are second-order central places. Wisconsin cities such as Green Bay, Wausau, Eau Claire, and La Crosse are third-order central places and are fairly similar in size. Wisconsin, however, has many cities that do not fit neatly into this steplike hierarchy.

Madison is the prime example. Whereas other cities in the third level of the upper Midwest hierarchy have an average population of about 50,000, Madison has a population of 200,000. What accounts for this "excess" population of 150,000 people? Madison has settlement-building functions that other cities of the same level do not have. These include state government functions and the University of Wisconsin–Madison. The jobs created by these institutions bring in basic income but are

TABLE 6.1
Thresholds for Selected Functions
in Wisconsin

Function	Threshold (People)	Function	Threshold (People)
Taverns	77	Dentists	563
Food stores	92	Supermarkets	587
Fuel-oil dealers	164	Hotels	603
Filling stations	186	Appliance stores	607
Feed stores	247	Liquor stores	613
Beauticians	268	Electric repair shops	631
Insurance agencies	293	Barber shops	632
Farm implements	309	Furniture stores	637
Restaurants	316	Drugstores	638
Hardware stores	372	Auto-parts dealers	642
Auto repair shops	375	Banks	643
Lumberyards	380	Laundromats	649
Motels	384	Women's clothing stores	678
Shoe repair shops	387	Bakeries	687
Real estate agencies	418	Dry cleaners	692
Auto dealers	420	Shoe stores	712
Building materials	444	Movie theaters	716
Plumbers	468	Jewelry stores	722
Variety stores	475	Optometrists	726
Hospital and clinics	490	Florists	726
Physicians	493	Billiard halls	742
Veterinarians	494	Sheet-metal works	747
Lawyers	497	Men's clothing stores	752
Radio-TV sales	521	Public accountants	757
Freight lines and storage	535	Photographers	794
Drive-in eating places	537	Frozen-food lockers	1,000

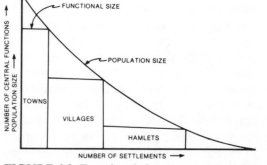

FIGURE 6.8 Functional size versus population size at the lower levels of the Wisconsin urban hierarchy.

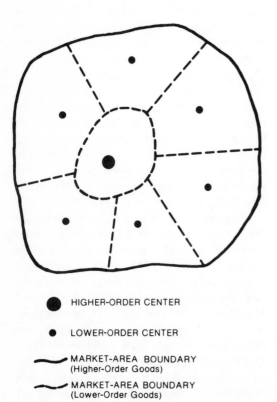

● HIGHER-ORDER CENTER

• LOWER-ORDER CENTER

〰 MARKET-AREA BOUNDARY
(Higher-Order Goods)

〰 MARKET-AREA BOUNDARY
(Lower-Order Goods)

FIGURE 6.7 Market-area "nesting."

not dependent upon trade with the immediate surrounding market area. Madison also has some large manufacturing companies (for example, Oscar Mayer), which are settlement-building. Collectively, these functions raise the population of Madison by the number of settlement-building jobs times the basic-nonbasic ratio.

Duluth-Superior is another example of an anomaly. Its port and manufacturing functions are settlement-building, which raise its population well above the expected third-order average. Obviously, not every city can be a port or a state capital or have a large university or a huge military base, but each city may have some settlement-building activities that support different numbers of people and contribute to the economic life of the city. If a manufacturing plant closes, settlement-building and associated settlement-serving jobs will be lost, but that part of the economy supported by trade with the market area (settlement-forming) should remain stable.

Two cities may belong to the same level of the urban hierarchy, therefore, but have different population sizes. This difference depends upon the mix of settlement-building functions and the basic employment supported by them. These differences are fairly clear at the upper end of the urban hierarchy, but do the same kinds of population variations exist at the lower end?

In a classic study of smaller central places in Wisconsin, geographer John Brush studied the three lowest levels of the urban hierarchy—hamlet, village, and town. These places are mostly dependent upon trade with the surrounding countryside. Brush found that on the basis of their *functional size*, which is measured by the number and kinds of business types in each center, these centers could be arranged in a clear, steplike hierarchy. But based on population, the centers formed a rather smooth curve from the largest town to the smallest hamlet— the larger hamlets were only slightly smaller than the smallest villages, and the largest villages only slightly smaller than the smallest towns. In Figure 6.8, the horizontal

lines show the functional sizes of each level, and the vertical lines show the population of each center.

Brush found four reasons for the size differences within levels. First, significant differences in average family size occurred among the centers. A hamlet with an average family size of six would have a larger population than one with an average family size of four, yet the number of families (wage-earners) would be the same. Second, some centers were close enough to higher-order central places for commuting to take place. People lived in the lower-order places, but commuted to La Crosse or Whitewater, for example, to work. Their basic income therefore did not depend upon trade with the surrounding area. Third, some centers had a fairly large number of retirees, whose income was derived from pensions, social security payments, and savings, but whose spending helped fuel the settlement-serving, nonbasic sector and therefore increased the population size. Finally, Brush found that some of these centers had settlement-building activities, such as small manufacturing plants, county courthouses, or educational institutions, which also increased their population.

John Borchert, urban geographer, also studied central places. He systematically divided the cities in the upper Midwest into a hierarchy of central places, shown with the representative functions for each urban level in Figure 6.9. Milwaukee is the only metropolitan wholesale-retail center in Wisconsin; much of the western part of the state is focused on the Minneapolis–St. Paul urban area. The general structure of the Wisconsin urban system is shown in Figure 6.10. Lower-order centers are connected to higher-order ones to show the patterns of the Wisconsin urban hierarchy.

The distribution of wholesale-retail centers across the state reflects the state pattern of population density. They are closer together in the Madison–Milwaukee–Green Bay triangle than they are in the more sparsely settled northern and western parts of the state. The string of cities following

158

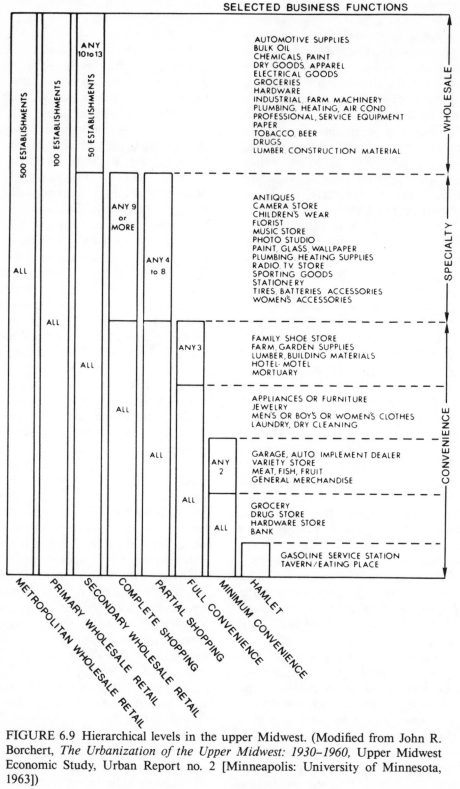

FIGURE 6.9 Hierarchical levels in the upper Midwest. (Modified from John R. Borchert, *The Urbanization of the Upper Midwest: 1930–1960,* Upper Midwest Economic Study, Urban Report no. 2 [Minneapolis: University of Minnesota, 1963])

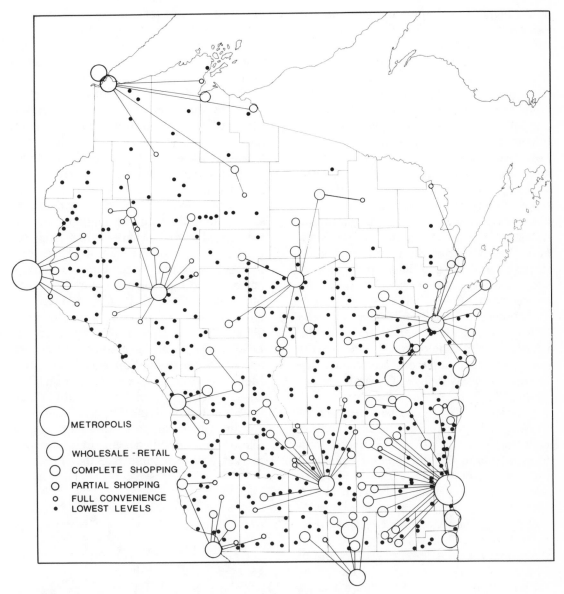

FIGURE 6.10 Hierarchical levels of Wisconsin's urban system.

Highway 29 across the state (Green Bay, Wausau, Eau Claire) shows a very regular spacing, and the hinterlands of each center appear to be roughly the same size. In the southeastern quarter of the state, however, the regular central place spacing is disrupted by the higher population densities and settlement-building functions found here. This section of the state is part of the massive industrial complex called the American Manufacturing Belt. The industrialized lakeshore that begins in Gary, Indiana, continues northward into Wisconsin through Kenosha, Racine, Milwaukee, Sheboygan, and Manitowoc to Green Bay. The Fox River Valley is part of this complex and includes the cities of Appleton, Oshkosh, and Fond du Lac. Madison, with its large assortment of settlement-building functions, forms the western margin of this industrial region in the state, and the Rock River Valley carries the theme southward through Janesville and Beloit in Wisconsin, where the industrial corridor continues on to Rockford, Illinois, and beyond.

The lines in Figure 6.10 give us some idea of the extent of market areas for the wholesale-retail centers in the state, but the sizes and shapes of these hinterlands can be more precisely defined. Geographers use *Reilly's Law* to measure the "pull" of a city, which is assumed to be a function of its size. The trade-area "breaking point" between two cities can be calculated by a formula stating that the breaking point in miles from city A = $D_{AB}/[1 + \sqrt{(P_B/P_A)}]$, where D_{AB} is the distance between city A and city B, P_A is the population of city A, and P_B is the population of city B (see Fig. 6.11). Figure 6.12 shows the trade areas of the primary wholesale-retail centers and of Milwaukee based on Reilly's Law. The breaking point between Eau Claire and La Crosse is almost midway between these cities, whereas the breaking point between Madison and Janesville occurs much closer to Janesville. In terms of square miles, Wausau has a very large trade area compared to Milwaukee. The area encompassed by Wausau's trade area, however, has a very

low population density compared to Milwaukee's population density, which is the heaviest in the state; Milwaukee's market area contains well over 1.5 million people, whereas Wausau's has only slightly over 300,000. Where population densities are low, centers must serve larger areas in order to meet the thresholds of the functions that they offer; higher population density means that the same population may be reached in a much smaller area.

None of the wholesale-retail centers in the state are supported exclusively by settlement-forming activities—by the sale of goods and services to the surrounding market areas shown in Figure 6.12. Each has some settlement-building activities that support a much larger population than would be possible if the place had to rely solely on trade with the market area. As mentioned before, Madison has large educational and governmental settlement-building functions, and Superior-Duluth has port and manufacturing functions. The other wholesale-retail centers in Wisconsin all have some manufacturing employment. Green Bay, La Crosse, and the cities on Lake Michigan all have some major port-transport functions. Superior, Eau Claire, Menomonie, La Crosse, Stevens Point, Oshkosh, Green Bay, Whitewater, and Parkside have campuses of the University of Wisconsin, which support considerable populations not directly dependent on the local market area. In Table 6.2, the important

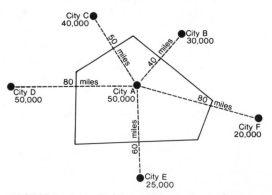

FIGURE 6.11 Reilly's Law: calculation example.

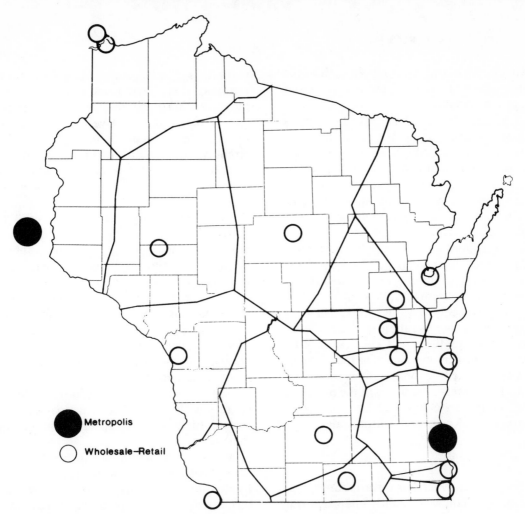

FIGURE 6.12 Primary wholesale-retail market areas in Wisconsin.

TABLE 6.2
Examples of Settlement-Building Functions for Selected Cities in Wisconsin

Function	City						
	Madison	Eau Claire	Wausau	Superior	Appleton	Oshkosh	La Crosse
Manufacturing	Oscar Mayer	Uniroyal	Wausau Paper Mills Co.	Fraser Ship-yards, Inc.	Zwicher Knitting Mills	Kimberly Clark Paper Co.	Trane Co.
Service Activity	University Hospital & Medical Ctr.	Middlefort Clinic	Mutual Emplyrs. Insurance Co.	Superior Memorial Hospital	Aid Assn. for Lutherans	Mercy Medical Ctr.	Anderson Clinic
Education	University of Wisconsin-Madison	University of Wisconsin-Eau Claire	UW-Center Marathon Co.	University of Wisconsin-Superior	Lawrence Univ.	University of Wisconsin-Oshkosh	University of Wisconsin-La Crosse
Government	State Capital	County Seat	County Seat	County Seat	County Seat	County Seat	County Seat
Transportation	Interstate Jet Airport	Interstate Jet Airport	Jet Airport	Port Facilities	Jet Airport	Jet Airport	Interstate Jet Airport

settlement-building functions of each of the wholesale-retail centers in the state are listed in greater detail.

The populations of lower-order centers are also augmented by settlement-building activities. These activities are often increasingly concentrated in a few (or single) activities in the lowest levels of the hierarchy. Some partial-shopping settlements are almost completely dependent upon a single manufacturing plant as the major settlement-building activity, for example. Other small centers depend upon the trade generated by traffic on the interstate highway system, tourism (e.g., Wisconsin Dells), a state university (e.g., River Falls), or a major health-care facility (e.g., Marshfield). Also, many of the small centers in Wisconsin depend upon tourism as the primary settlement-building force. This is especially true of the lower-level places in the northern third of the state, such as Spooner, Hayward, Eagle River, and Rhinelander.

MANUFACTURING

South from Madison toward Janesville, the cultural landscape subtly changes from one totally dominated by agriculture or woodland to one dominated by cities and industrial land uses. Although Wisconsin is generally perceived as an agricultural state, manufacturing is a very important sector of the state's economy. Manufacturing accounts for one-third of all the jobs in the state and about the same proportion of total earnings. Wisconsin's manufacturing exports were over $2.2 billion in 1976. It ranked twelfth nationally in manufactured exports and eleventh in value added both by manufacturing and manufacturing employment, even though the state ranked only sixteenth in population. In 1980, over a half-million people were employed in Wisconsin's factories.

Geographers are interested in *why* things are located *where* they are. If a map shows that a particular type of manufacturing is highly concentrated in one area and almost absent in another, geographers want to ex-

plain this spatial distribution. Why, for example, does Wisconsin have high employment in the manufacture of engines and turbines and relatively little employment in textile manufacturing? Also, different types of manufacturing are not evenly distributed over the state, but rather are concentrated in specific parts of Wisconsin. Why?

The concept of *orientation* is used to discuss location patterns of manufacturing and to develop a typology of manufacturing types. Some types of manufacturing are raw-material oriented and their spatial distribution reflects the distribution of key raw materials. For example, paper manufacturing reflects the present and past distribution of the forest and water resources required by this industry, whereas engines, construction machinery, and motor vehicles are oriented toward specialized labor sources. Other industries may be oriented toward energy sites or specific markets for their outputs.

Many types of manufacturing have location patterns that cannot be explained by the present-day distribution of raw materials, energy, labor, or markets. Past conditions must be considered to understand present patterns. Many manufacturing sites were chosen in the past to take advantage of raw materials, markets, or other factors that existed at that time and represented a considerable investment. Breweries, for example, were founded in Wisconsin in the nineteenth century because the state was being settled by an ethnic group (German) that provided both a market for beer and the expertise required to produce it and because raw materials (barley and hops) could be produced easily and cheaply locally. As the patterns of raw materials and markets change, traditional locations may not be as profitable as potential new ones, but the investment made in the past keeps the locational pattern stable over a fairly long time. This is called *industrial inertia* and has been a very important location factor in Wisconsin's manufacturing sector.

Which specific types of manufacturing

TABLE 6.3
Wisconsin Manufacturing Employment

Industry	Total Employment (Thousands)			
	1965	1971	1975	1980
Food and kindred products	58.3	57.2	61.5	54.3
Textile mill products	6.7	6.6	5.6	3.9
Apparel	8.1	6.5	6.5	6.0
Lumber and wood products	16.8	16.0	16.7	21.9
Furniture and fixtures	7.3	7.7	9.0	9.3
Paper and allied products	41.6	43.4	42.0	41.2
Printing and publishing	22.9	25.5	27.1	31.2
Chemicals and allied products	6.8	10.5	9.0	10.0
Rubber and rubber products	8.7	11.7	13.7	18.9
Leather and leather products	15.7	13.6	11.5	9.1
Stone, clay, and glass products	7.1	7.8	7.3	8.6
Primary metals	29.0	27.4	32.0	30.3
Fabricated metal products	38.7	42.4	44.4	59.2
Nonelectrical machinery	106.2	99.2	111.1	128.5
Electrical machinery	55.5	45.8	48.2	56.6
Transportation equipment	45.6	36.5	41.2	32.9
Instruments and related products	6.1	8.5	8.7	11.9
Total	491.9	479.6	507.3	571.4

Source: U.S., Bureau of the Census, Census of Manufacturers,
various years.

are absolutely and relatively important in Wisconsin? In terms of total employment, nonelectrical and electrical machinery, transportation equipment, food processing, and paper production have consistently been the most important types of manufacturing (Table 6.3). A large number of employees does not necessarily indicate that the state is a leading producer of that particular product, however, in terms of total national production.

One way to specify the relative importance of industries in the state is to use the *location quotient*, which measures the relative strength of an industry in terms of national employment. The quotient is calculated by dividing the percentage contribution of a given type of manufacturing to Wisconsin's total manufacturing employment by the industry's contribution to national manufacturing employment. A location quotient of 1, or unity, means that the importance of the industry to Wisconsin is exactly the same as its national importance. A quotient greater than 1 indicates that the type of manufacturing is more important in the state than it is nationally and represents an industrial concentration, whereas a quotient less than unity indicates the opposite. Location quotients for Wisconsin manufacturing are shown in Table 6.4.

Raw-Material-Based Industries

Food Processing. Wisconsin is a very important agricultural state, and outputs from its farms form the raw materials used by many types of manufacturing. Food processing was the second leading industry in the state in terms of employment until the mid-1970s (Table 6.3). By 1980, however, the industry dropped to fourth place as an employment source, but it still employed over 50,000 people and accounted for about 10 percent of total manufacturing employment. The specific types of food processing found in the state reflect its agricultural specializations—dairy products, vegetables, and meats. The first two industries have already been discussed in Chapter 5.

Wisconsin's position on the edge of the

TABLE 6.4
Location Quotients for
Wisconsin Industries

Industry	Location Quotient
Dairy products	3.69
Meat products	1.24
Preserved fruits and vegetables	13.60
Beverages	1.91
Wood containers	1.72
Wood buildings	1.20
Papermills	5.13
Commercial printing	1.18
Leather tanning	4.76
Iron and steel foundries	2.89
Cutlery, hand tools, hardware	1.43
Plumbing and heating fixtures	2.66
Engines and turbines	7.29
Farm and garden equipment	3.97
Construction machinery	1.98
Metalworking machinery	1.31
Refrigeration and service machinery	1.58
Electrical industrial apparatus	3.85
Motor vehicles and equipment	1.38

Corn Belt provides the raw materials for processed meats, and the state is a major exporter of processed meat products, mainly wieners and sausages. Meat processing is concentrated mostly in the eastern side of the state, where Milwaukee, Dane, and Brown counties all have important meat-processing facilities. The Oscar Mayer plant in Madison, with 4,000 employees, is probably the most well known example. German and Polish immigrants who settled eastern Wisconsin brought the skills and traditions of processing meats into sausages, and they founded most of these companies, although many are now owned by large food conglomerates.

Wood Products. The manufacture of wood products is another type of manufacturing strongly tied to the raw materials of the state. The white-pine and hardwood forests of the past were the basis of a forest-product industry. This industrial infrastructure remains even though today much wood is imported to Wisconsin from the Pacific Northwest to be manufactured into wood doors, windows, and similar products. The first phase of the wood-products industry begins with the production of timber. Al-

though not as important today as in the past, a large amount of raw-material wood is still produced in the state. The distribution of logging camps and contractors is highly concentrated across the forested northern tier of counties (Figure 6.13). Major wood-processing mills are found at Marshfield, Oshkosh, Merrill, and Ashland. The next stage in the process is sawing or planing. Then, "bolts" and other rough-sawn products of the sawmill or planing mill are used to produce more-finished wood products. Wisconsin is the leading producer of wood windows in the nation, second in wood doors and hardwood plywood, third in hardwood veneer, and a leading producer of millwork.

Wood is also the primary raw material in the making of paper. Almost 50,000 employees work in this industry, making Wisconsin a leading producer of a wide range of paper products (Figure 6.14). Paper manufacturing industries require lots of water, which accounts for the location of all mills on major streams, especially along the upper Wisconsin and lower Fox rivers (Figure 6.15).

The American Manufacturing Belt: Wisconsin's Contribution

A large proportion of the manufacturing in the United States takes place in the rectangle defined by Boston, Washington, D.C., St. Louis, and Chicago. This area is called the American Manufacturing Belt. Manufacturing plants and employment are slowly shifting to other parts of the United States, such as to the Sun Belt and to foreign countries, but the American Manufacturing Belt remains extremely important because of industrial inertia, an abundant and skilled labor supply, raw materials, and markets that exist within the region. This area grew into one of the world's primary industrial areas for several reasons. Settled early and densely, this part of the United States had abundant raw materials on its periphery, especially coal, iron ore, and petroleum, which were needed by heavy

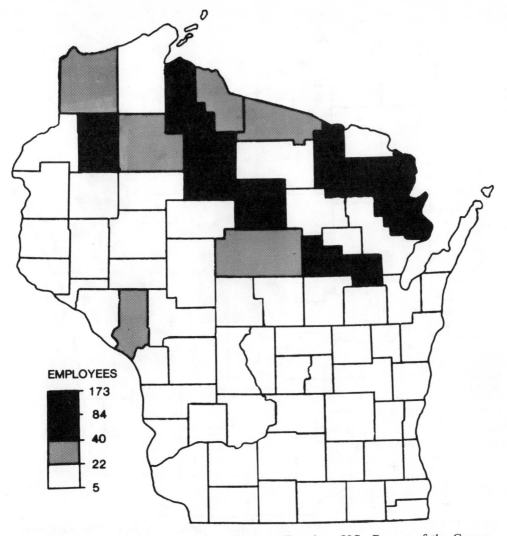

EMPLOYEES

173

84

40

22

5

FIGURE 6.13 Logging camps and contractors. (Based on U.S., Bureau of the Census, *1980 County Business Patterns, Wisconsin* [Washington, D.C.: U.S. Government Printing Office, 1980])

industry. The Great Lakes and the Mississippi and Ohio rivers were crucial transportation arteries. Industries producing iron and steel, transportation equipment, petrochemicals, and other kinds of heavy manufacturing were concentrated within this region. Wisconsin, because of its location on the periphery of the Manufacturing Belt, is a region with a long history of "industrial colonialization"; that is, larger corporations have established branch plants or acquired small companies in the state to supply them with inputs for their larger operations in the belt proper.

Most of southeastern Wisconsin is within this huge manufacturing complex. Cities like Milwaukee, Racine, and Janesville have an employment structure that is quite different from that of the cities that lie outside the Manufacturing Belt. They are much more dependent upon manufacturing employment, and their economies are tied to the economy of the rest of the Manufacturing Belt, rather than to the production of agricultural products or to the service or tourist trade so typical of the rest of

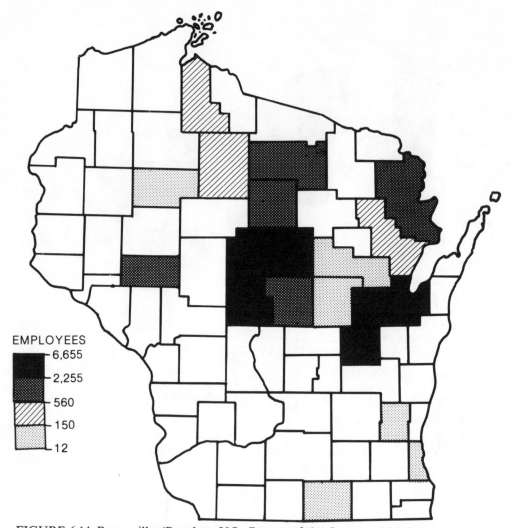

FIGURE 6.14 Papermills. (Based on U.S., Bureau of the Census, *1980 County Business Patterns, Wisconsin* [Washington, D.C.: U.S. Government Printing Office, 1980])

EMPLOYEES
- 6,655
- 2,255
- 560
- 150
- 12

FIGURE 6.15 Aerial view of the Pope and Talbot papermill in Eau Claire. (Courtesy of the Pope and Talbot Company)

the state. The urban system of the southeast contains the manual and technical skills needed for almost every type of manufacturing.

The Manufacturing Belt itself is a huge producer of raw materials for industry. Most of the raw materials entering a manufacturing plant have already undergone some processing so that they are in reality the finished products of yet another type of manufacturing. For example, most plants producing machine tools do not produce their own steel; foundries do not produce their own pig iron. Many of the small manufacturing plants in Milwaukee sell their entire output to other plants in the city or to plants in nearby cities in the Manufacturing Belt. Thus the industrial pattern of southeastern Wisconsin, and the manufacture of several industrial products in which the state specializes, can only be understood with reference to Wisconsin's location on the edge of the American Manufacturing Belt, where the raw materials are produced that form the inputs to Wisconsin's factories and where a major market utilizes Wisconsin outputs.

Primary Metal Industries. Primary metal production is important to Wisconsin's industrial structure. Over 30,000 people are employed in these industries, which experienced an increase of over 10,000 workers in the 1970s. The most important type of primary metal industry is the foundry. Many large foundries exist in larger manufacturing plants that are counted in the industrial statistics only by the end product they produce. For example, plants producing machinery may have large foundries as part of the manufacturing process, but they are classified as machinery plants. Many foundries do, of course, produce end products besides castings or other parts for larger companies. The raw materials for Wisconsin's primary metalworking operations come mostly from the Chicago-Gary steel region.

The Macwhyte Wire Rope Company in Kenosha is a large wire-drawing operation employing over 500 workers. More than 1,000 people work making carbon- and alloy-steel tubing at the Babcock and Wilcox Company plant in Milwaukee. Gray-iron foundries in the state employ almost 10,000 people; the largest are the Neenah Foundry (1,500 workers) in Winnebago County and the Brillion Iron Works (800 workers) in Calumet County. International Harvester Company has a malleable-iron foundry in Waukesha employing over 600 people. Nineteen steel foundries collectively employ over 4,000 people, and they are all concentrated in the Milwaukee-Manitowoc-Kenosha corridor.

In addition, a cluster of foundries for nonferrous metals is found in the southeast. Aluminum and aluminum-based alloy castings as well as brass, bronze, copper, and copper-based castings are important.

Fabricated Metal Products. A large variety of products are classified as fabricated metal products, including metal cans, cutlery, tools and hardware, and plumbing fixtures (Figure 6.16), and as fabricated structural steel, such as I-beams, wire, springs, and pipe. Employment in this sector grew by over 10,000 people in the 1970s. Wisconsin is the nation's leading producer of metal sanitary ware and of stamped and spun utensils (cooking and kitchenware made of aluminum) and is second in utensils other than those made from aluminum. The state is also an important producer of boilershop products (metal tanks), steel and aluminum cans, mechanics' hand tools, builders' hardware, gas cylinders, metal flooring and siding, and ferrous and nonferrous forgings. Again, the location of the fabricated metal products industry is largely concentrated in the Manufacturing Belt counties (Figure 6.17).

Nonelectrical Machinery. Much of the state's export income comes from the sale of heavy machinery such as engines, tractors, construction machinery, draglines, ore-crushing equipment, and cranes. Almost one-quarter of the factory jobs in Wisconsin

FIGURE 6.16 Vitreous china casting in a Kohler plumbing fixtures plant. Operations like this get most of their raw materials from the Manufacturing Belt. (Courtesy of Kohler Company)

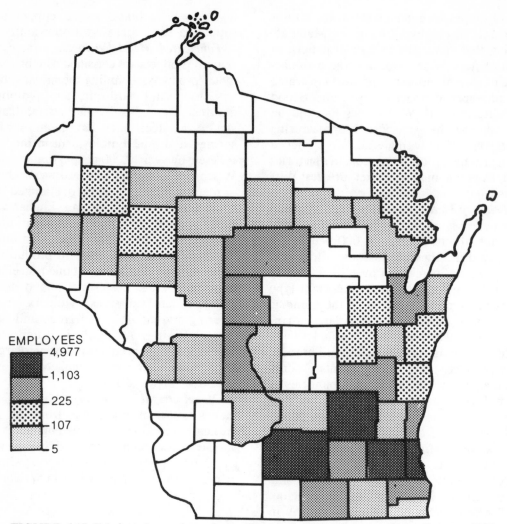

FIGURE 6.17 Fabricated metal products. (Based on U.S., Bureau of the Census, *1980 County Business Patterns, Wisconsin* [Washington, D.C.: U.S. Government Printing Office, 1980])

may be traced to this industry, which employs 110,000 people. The largest subcategories are engines and turbines (20,000 workers), construction/mining/material-handling machinery (20,000), general industrial equipment (17,000), and farm machinery (17,000). The location pattern for the heavy-machinery industry can be explained by its situation in the Manufacturing Belt, in proximity to the iron and steel industries, and by the early need for manufacturing in the state to serve agriculture and the forestry and mining industries.

Engine production is characterized by very large operations. Wisconsin is the world's leading center for the manufacture of internal combustion engines, excluding auto and aircraft engines. It produces both small air-cooled engines for a variety of applications, as well as large heavy-duty engines. Briggs and Stratton engines, perhaps the best known of Wisconsin's product line, are used on lawn mowers, snow blowers, and a variety of other machines. The company employs almost 10,000 people in several plants in Milwaukee. Other large producers include Mercury Marine, at Fond du Lac, Cedarburg, and Oshkosh, whose almost 4,000 employees make outboard and stern drive units; Evinrude, in Milwaukee, with almost 2,000 employees making outboard units; and Lawson Engine Division, which employs almost 1,800 people at New Holstein making Tecumseh small engines.

Wisconsin has a favorable location for the farm and garden machinery and equipment industry because of raw-material sources (metals and engines) and large markets. This industry's largest concentration is in Racine, where the J. I. Case Company employs over 5,000 people making farm machinery; Allis-Chalmers has over 3,000 employees in its tractor plant in Milwaukee. The state also has numerous producers of small garden-type tractors, including Simplicity at Port Washington, Jacobsen at Racine, and Ariens in Calumet County.

The production of construction, mining, and material-handling machinery and equipment is also concentrated in the southeast corner of the state and, like the production of engines, is dominated by large operations. Bucyrus-Erie in Milwaukee makes both mining and construction equipment (primarily cranes and draglines) and employs almost 3,000 people. At the Manitowoc Company in Manitowoc, 2,000 workers make mostly large cranes and excavators. Drott Manufacturing, a division of J. I. Case, is located in Wausau and has 1,000 workers. Rexnord in Milwaukee makes rock-crushing and mineral-processing machinery, and Allis-Chalmers has some mineral-processing-machinery operations there also. The Harnischfeger Corporation of Milwaukee employs almost 4,000 people making large industrial hoists.

Metalworking Machinery and Equipment. Almost 10,000 people are employed in this industry, but most work for rather small operations. There are some large plants—notably Kearney and Trecker Corporation, which employs about 1,700 Milwaukee workers to make mostly milling machines, and Giddings and Lewis, Inc., in Fond du Lac and Kaukauna, with 1,800 workers. But about 250 other companies employ approximately 4,000 tool and die makers, so that most of the plants are rather small. A. O. Smith of Milwaukee is the largest of these small companies, with about 500 employees making special tools and dies. Other companies make machine-tool accessories, such as drill bits, and some plants produce power-driven hand tools.

Motor Vehicles and Motor Vehicle Equipment. Wisconsin is among the top eight states in the production of motor vehicles and motor vehicle equipment. Almost 35,000 workers are employed in this industry in Wisconsin. The American Motors assembly plant at Kenosha employs more than 12,000 people at peak production, and the company's body plant has about 3,000 employees. General Motors has a car and truck assembly plant at Janesville with over 6,000 workers. Trucks and truck bodies are produced at Oshkosh, Clintonville, and Milwaukee. The manufacture of motor vehicle parts is also an extremely important Wisconsin industry. In Milwaukee, A. O. Smith produces vehicle frames and spark plugs (3,500 workers), and at the General Motors AC Spark Plug operation, 1,500 workers make catalytic convertors. Vehicle axles are produced at Oshkosh.

Industrial Inertia

In southeastern Wisconsin specialized labor skills developed and matured to provide generation after generation of tool and die makers, machinists, welders, and other skilled workers for the factories located in the polygon bounded by Madison, Manitowoc, Kenosha, and Beloit. Once this labor-input-market industrial infrastructure developed, industrial inertia kept the pattern relatively stable. The general pattern was established during the period of U.S. industrial expansion, which lasted from 1880 to 1920. By the end of the massive foreign immigration in 1920, which provided most of the labor for Wisconsin's industrial mills, the basic infrastructure in the industrial corridor of the state had been established. Most of Wisconsin's companies were founded and were operating prior to World War II, when the American Manufacturing Belt reached maturity.

In the late 1970s and early 1980s, however, the industrial infrastructure of the United States was undergoing rapid change. Many types of manufacturing were shifting operations to new facilities in the Sun Belt or overseas. Much of the industry of the Manufacturing Belt was perceived to be old, outdated, and expensive to operate. This was especially true of the primary metals and transportation-equipment industries, which were particularly hard hit by unemployment during the recessions of the early 1980s.

CONCLUSION

The economy of the United States has undergone great changes in this century, and many of the trends toward massive urbanization and large industrial infrastructures have been reversed in recent years. For example, throughout most of human history, the trend in transportation costs has been steadily downward, reflecting both new technologies and falling energy costs. Suddenly in the 1970s the costs of all kinds of transportation increased, because all were dependent on petroleum. Rising gasoline prices and lowered speed limits essentially increased the distance between urban places in the state. The total effects of rising energy costs on the urban system are hard to predict, but increases in the retailing sectors of smaller settlements may occur as people shop in closer towns rather than traveling 10 to 20 mi (16 to 32 km) to higher-order places.

Also, manufacturing is no longer the driving force underlying urban employment. The United States has shifted from a nation based on manufacturing to one based on the tertiary or service sector, which is much less tied to physical resources, freight transportation, and large-scale infrastructures. Today, the movement of people and information is important, and geographers are more concerned with the location of office space than with new factories. Manufacturing itself has shifted from heavy industry, such as steel, petro-

chemicals, and transport equipment, toward "light" and "high-tech" products. With these shifts in the economic structure of the United States, amenities, or quality-of-life factors, have become increasingly more important.

Throughout most of U.S. history, the pattern of migration was rural to urban. Metropolitan areas grew as the countryside was depopulated. Small towns that once existed to serve a higher-density rural population declined or died as farm populations fell. Even if central cities did not grow, as was the case throughout much of the 1950s and 1960s, their suburbs did. In the 1970s, a population turn-around began. Rural and nonmetropolitan areas experienced growth. Counties in northern Wisconsin, for example, which had lost population through out-migration almost every decade in this century, exhibited population growth. Generally, it was the "high-amenity" counties such as Vilas, with its water and forest recreational resources, that grew. In the upper Midwest, throughout most of the 1960s and 1970s, cities were the major growth poles; these will continue to grow in the rest of the century as the old, large industrial areas stagnate.

Geographers Brian Berry and Frank Horton have suggested that differential urban growth is the result of two effects. The first is an *industry-mix effect,* which means that cities that happen to have the growth industries of a particular period will grow more rapidly than their rivals. The growth industries of the 1980s and 1990s are high tech and information based, and those settlements that have or can attract these industries have the best chance of growth and prosperity. These industries, often described as "foot-loose," are attracted to research and development facilities, transportation facilities, and, most important, to physical and cultural amenities. This effect helps to explain the boom in the Sun Belt and the growth and prosperity of cities like Stevens Point (headquarters of Sentry Insurance, an information-based company), Chippewa Falls (with Cray Research, a producer of one of the largest mainframe computers in the world), and Marshfield (with very specialized medical facilities).

The second effect identified by Berry and Horton is a *competitive-shift effect,* which begins with the set of all centers that have benefited from a particular industry mix and explains the differential growth of those centers. The competitive-shift effect indicates that those centers with more of the resources and other needs of the growth industries of the period will experience the most rapid growth. Given the trends of recent years, these centers will be those with skilled labor forces, air-transport facilities, and educational institutions. Most important are quality-of-life factors, such as climate (Sun Belt), size (small towns), and recreational resources (Colorado). This would seem to indicate that the smaller cities in Wisconsin (those with 10,000 to 100,000 people) will grow at the expense of the older, industrial-corridor cities. Smaller urban places near these new growth centers will also benefit from the changing economic structure of the United States

SELECTED REFERENCES

Abler, R.; J. S. Adams; and P. Gould. *Spatial Organization: The Geographer's View of the World.* Englewood Cliffs, N.J.: Prentice-Hall, 1971.

Berry, Brian, and F. E. Horton. *Geographic Perspectives on Urban Systems.* Englewood Cliffs, N.J.: Prentice-Hall, 1970.

Borchert, J. R. "Instability in American Metropolitan Growth." *Geographical Review,* vol. 73 (1983), pp. 12–149.

———. "Major Control Points in American Economic Geography." *Annals of the Association of American Geographers,* vol. 68 (1978), pp. 214–232.

———. "American Metropolitan Evolution." *Geographical Review,* vol. 57 (1967), pp. 301–332.

———. *The Urbanization of the Upper Midwest: 1930–1960.* Upper Midwest Economic Study, Urban Report No. 2. Minneapolis: University of Minnesota, 1963.

Brush, J. E. "The Hierarchy of Central Places in Southwestern Wisconsin." *Geographical Review,* vol. 43 (1953), pp. 380–402.

Christaller, W. *The Central Places of Southern Germany.* Translated by C. W. Baskin. Englewood Cliffs, N.J.: Prentice-Hall, 1966.

Pred, A. *Major Job Providing Organizations and Systems of Cities.* Washington, D.C.: Association of American Geographers Commission on College Geography, Resource Paper No. 27, 1974.

Semple, R. K. "Recent Trends in the Spatial Concentrations of Corporate Headquarters." *Economic Geography,* vol. 49 (1973), pp. 309–318.

Smith, D. M. *Industrial Location: An Economic Geographic Analysis.* New York: John Wiley & Sons, 1971.

Stewart, C. T., Jr. "The Size and Spacing of Cities." *Geographical Review,* vol. 48 (1958), pp. 222–245.

CHAPTER 7

THE MILWAUKEE METROPOLITAN REGION

Metropolitan Milwaukee is the economic heart of Wisconsin. The four-county Milwaukee metropolitan area covers less than 3 percent of the state's area, but contains 30 percent of its population and about 38 percent of its workers (excluding government and railroad employees and self-employed persons). Workers in the four metropolitan counties receive over 40 percent of the state's wages and salaries. The influence of Milwaukee, as the primate city of Wisconsin, extends throughout the state and beyond, although for some functions the proximity of Chicago, which is only 85 mi (136 km) south of downtown Milwaukee, reduces Milwaukee's hinterland.

Milwaukee is located near the northwestern edge of the more-or-less continuous American Manufacturing Belt, extending from the Atlantic seaboard to the western shore of Lake Michigan. Geographers consider this belt to be the "core region" of the United States and Canada, containing the highest concentration of population and economic activities. The seven southeastern counties—including Milwaukee—represent the "core region" of Wisconsin. In only 5 percent of the total area, 40 percent of the state's population and 50 percent of the tangible wealth, measured by equalized property valuation, are concentrated. Although the seven-county area had 47 percent of the state's population increase from 1960 to 1972, metropolitan Milwaukee's growth has virtually stopped. The area faces serious challenges to its future prosperity as population and economic growth shift to the Sun Belt in the southern and southwestern United States.

THE CITY'S LOCATION AND SITE

The physical setting of metropolitan Milwaukee is of primary significance because of its location on the great Central Lowlands in the heart of the North American continent, on the western shore of Lake Michigan, and astride the subcontinental divide between the Great Lakes basin and the Mississippi basin.

Milwaukee's location on the Great Lakes is both advantageous and disadvantageous. The city's location developed into a major transportation node. Although today the port function is both absolutely and relatively less important than in the past, Milwaukee is still a major lake port. With the development of direct overseas traffic, especially following the improvement of the St. Lawrence Seaway in 1959, Milwaukee became a world port. But Lake Michigan also constitutes a barrier to east-west movement. Milwaukee is separated by 80 mi (128 km) of lake from the major population concentrations and markets to the east. Interaction with the rest of the Manufacturing Belt necessitates a circuitous and delay-prone trip by rail or highway around the lake, in most instances through congested metropolitan Chicago. Cross-lake railroad and auto ferries connecting Milwaukee with western Michigan were discontinued in the early 1980s, although summer-season passenger-auto ferries resumed in 1982.

The relatively static physical characteristics of a place define its *site*. Milwaukee's most significant site characteristics include its surface landforms and drainage patterns. Surface landforms are the results of a series of massive continental glaciers, the most recent of which covered the site of Milwaukee about 10,000 to 12,000 years ago. The Kettle Moraine is a distinctive interlobate moraine, visible in the western portion of metropolitan Milwaukee, extending generally northeast-southwest (Figure 7.1), and characterized by irregular terrain with numerous depressions, or *kettles*, some of which contain lakes. Most of these lakes are scenic, and many are surrounded by residential developments. Some of these residential areas were originally summer resorts; many are now year-round communities within commuting distance of employment in Milwaukee and the satellite suburbs. The lakes themselves constitute both summer and winter recreational resources. Some well-known resort developments attract daily, weekend, weekly, and seasonal clientele from the metropolitan area as well as from the Chicago region, thereby contributing not only amenity value to metropolitan Milwaukee but also a significant economic element to the region's economy.

A series of recessional moraines formed when the front of the glacier halted temporarily in its recession, thus causing accumulation of material in ridges more-or-less successively parallel to the shoreline of Lake Michigan. In some places, the Lake Michigan shoreline cuts across these ridges at an acute angle, forming bluffs, which are receding by a few inches per year (Figure 7.2). The erosion of these bluffs threatens

houses and other buildings atop the bluffs close to the shore.

The irregular, glacially formed surface within metropolitan Milwaukee has produced an irregular surficial drainage pattern. In many places streams contain falls and rapids, which became sites for early settlements associated with textile, grist, and flour mills and later with other types of manufacturing dependent upon direct use of water power. Grafton, Cedarburg, and Menomonee Falls are examples of such sites in the metropolitan area.

Stream courses within metropolitan Milwaukee generally have a north-south alignment, although the patterns are very irregular. The most important streams are the Milwaukee, Menomonee, and Kinnickinnic rivers, which converge to form a major portion of Milwaukee's harbor (Figure 7.3). The three original settlements that subsequently became the core of Milwaukee were directly related to the access provided by these rivers. Throughout the nineteenth and early twentieth centuries much of Milwaukee's development was associated with the port function, the attraction of the railroads to the central waterfronts, and hence the localization of the city's core.

The Milwaukee River, about 75 mi (120 km) long, flows in a generally south-southeasterly course from its origin in Fond du Lac County, then southwesterly through the northeastern portion of the city of Milwaukee. The river bisects the downtown area and is joined by the Menomonee, entering Lake Michigan through an artificial channel cut in 1857 through the neck of a peninsula that is now called Jones Island. The lower 2 mi (3.2 km) of the river, below the North Avenue dam—which is located on the site of a former cascade—are actually the estuary of Lake Michigan, with the water level the same as that of the lake. This portion of the river was navigable by lake vessels from 1857 until 1959, when construction of two bridges carrying downtown freeways across the river closed it to all but small craft. For many years the Milwaukee River, traversing the

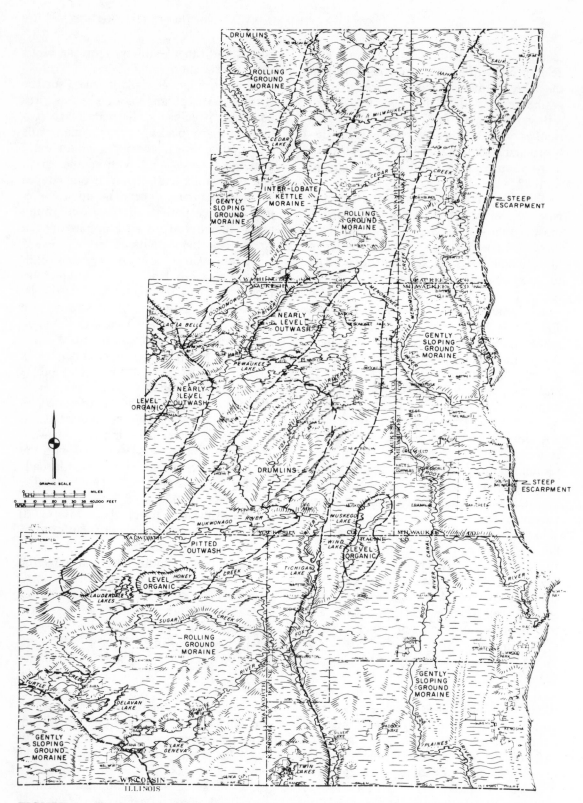

FIGURE 7.1 Physiographic features in the Milwaukee region. (Reprinted by permission of Southeastern Wisconsin Regional Planning Commission)

g the Lake Michigan shoreline at Cudahy. Recession of the bluffs
the river mouths where deposition occurs and where landfill has
(Harold Mayer)

FIGURE 7.3 The north end of the Inner Harbor. The sewage treatment plant is in the foreground, the entrance to the Menomonee River is left center, and the lower Milwaukee River is on the extreme right. (Harold Mayer)

central part of the city, was an important part of the port, but technological changes and shifts in location of industry contributed to the transfer of most port functions away from the city's center.

The Menomonee River, about 20 mi (32 km) in length, joins the Milwaukee River a short distance south of downtown Milwaukee. The lower Menomonee Valley was, and to a lesser degree still is, the locus of major industrial establishments. From the 1870s until the 1950s, it constituted an important part of Milwaukee's port, but the out-migration of industry and changes in transportation technology, including the larger size of lake vessels, resulted in a decline of activity in the valley.

The lower Menomonee Valley long constituted a barrier between the southern half of the city and its northern half, where the central business district (CBD) is located. Low-level bridges that were frequently opened for passage of vessels on the river

and canals, conflicts between street traffic and rail-switching movements, and an unattractive industrial environment discouraged interaction between the two portions of the city. Milwaukee's South Side, therefore, developed with relatively little relationship to the rest of the city until the early twentieth century, when several high-level viaducts were built to overcome the valley's barrier effect.

The third of Milwaukee's three rivers, the Kinnickinnic ("KK," as it is called by Milwaukee residents), is generally less important, having the shortest length, about 6 mi (9.6 km), and an irregular course. Its lower portion has been substantially widened and deepened to form the city's Inner Harbor, accessible to large lake vessels and to the largest ocean-going ships able to enter the Great Lakes through the St. Lawrence Seaway.

Long stretches of these rivers, as well as many other streams within Milwaukee

FIGURE 7.4 Lake Michigan shoreline. Northeastward from the First Wisconsin Center in downtown Milwaukee, a series of lakefront county parks are found partly on the morainic upland and partly on lakefront landfill. (Harold Mayer)

County—and some of the other streams within the Milwaukee SMSA (Standard Metropolitan Statistical Area)—are bordered by parks and parkways (Figure 7.4). Milwaukee County has a nationally famous system of parks totaling about 15,000 acres (6,070 ha), a large part of which is located along the floodplains of rivers and tributary streams. The parks, with their natural vegetation, regulate runoff into the streams and thus to a major degree mitigate the flood crests. Their presence prevents substantial investment in industrial, commercial, residential, and other land uses on the flood-prone sites that are now within the parks.

HISTORICAL AND CULTURAL HERITAGE

The Founding of Milwaukee

Solomon Juneau, a French Canadian fur trader who later became the city of Milwaukee's first mayor, settled in 1818 on the upland between the Milwaukee River and Lake Michigan, within present downtown Milwaukee. The permanent settlement occurred in 1833, following the formal cession of the area by the Indians to the United States. In October 1833 Juneau agreed, for $500, to relinquish to Morgan L. Martin, a lawyer who had settled in Green Bay, half of his preemptive claim to his property on the east bank of the Milwaukee River. Juneau was to manage the property and share in the profits of fur trading. Over the winter of 1833-1834 at least four white men shared a log cabin near the river mouth; in the following spring two of them started a mill and another was employed by Juneau. Subsequently, for many years, the portion of downtown Milwaukee east of the river was known as Juneautown.

The first organized settlement west of the Milwaukee River was founded by Byron Kilbourn, a Connecticut-born engineer who arrived in Milwaukee from Ohio in 1834. The area became known as Kilbourntown. The area south and southwest of the junction of the Milwaukee and Menomonee rivers developed more slowly. George Walker was prominent among the settlers of the South Side. He built a trading post and residence in the spring of 1834 and, as a squatter, laid claim to 160 acres (64 ha). By 1835 his post was the nucleus of a settlement numbering over 100 persons. Thus, unlike many other cities that began as a single nucleus, early Milwaukee had three "points of attachment," which eventually together formed the core of the growing city.

The three settlements competed with each other to attract prospective residents. In February 1837 the settlements on the two sides of the Milwaukee River were separately incorporated as towns, with Juneau and Kilbourn as the respective town presidents. Consolidation as the town of Milwaukee took place two years later, on March 11, 1839, with Juneau as president. The settlement south of the Menomonee—Walkers Point—joined on February 12, 1845, to constitute the third of the town's three wards.

The past rivalry between the settlements on the two sides of the Milwaukee River appears in the morphology of the street grids, which do not match. The distinctive platting of the settlements was deliberate. Although Kilbourn resisted the building of bridges across the river, three of them connected Juneau's and Kilbourn's settlements by 1842. They were built at an angle to the streets on either side; several of the downtown bridges today, including Wisconsin Avenue, the main axis of downtown Milwaukee, are built at an angle to the streets. But the original bridges were short-lived, as they were destroyed by the rival factions in May 1845. This event made clear the desirability of incorporation of the settlements as a single municipality. On January 31, 1846, the territorial legislature issued a charter, and Milwaukee became a single city. At the first municipal election, on April 7, 1846, Juneau was selected as the city's first mayor.

Milwaukee grew rapidly until the Civil War (Figure 7.5). Its population increased

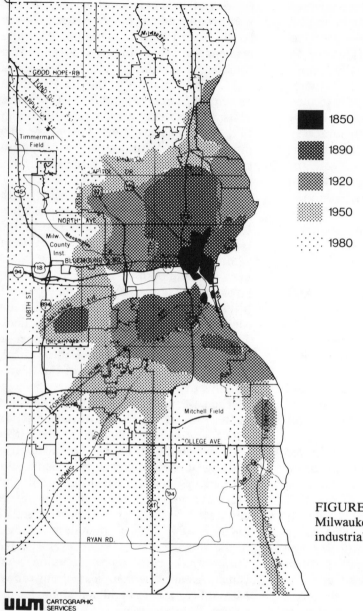

◼ 1850

▓ 1890

▒ 1920

░ 1950

⠂ 1980

FIGURE 7.5 The residential growth of Milwaukee, 1850–1980. White areas are industrial and open land uses.

UWM CARTOGRAPHIC SERVICES

from 1,692 at the time of the first census in 1840 to 20,061 in 1850 and to 45,246 in 1860 (Figure 7.5). The city's connections, both to its hinterland and to the population and industrial centers to the south and east, improved rapidly. A portion of the city's first railroad was opened in 1851, and Milwaukee secured rail connection to Chicago, and thus to the East, in 1855. Lake vessels gained access to interior waterways when an artificial channel was cut through the

sandbar across the harbor in 1857. The first horse-drawn streetcars began operating in 1860.

Milwaukee in 1860

In 1860 the area that is now within the Milwaukee SMSA had a population of 128,000, of which 45,000 was within the then city limits. This time marked the transition of Milwaukee from a gateway to a manufacturing center. At first the major manufacturing enterprises involved processing agricultural commodities, which continued to be important after the Civil War. But metalworking increased rapidly as a major contributor to the economic base of the city and region.

Flour milling was an important activity in Milwaukee during the years preceding and following the Civil War. Southern Wisconsin was then an important wheat-growing area. Some of the wheat was processed locally, some was moved through the port to eastern markets either as wheat or as flour, and some was shipped overseas. Meat packing was also important. In 1852 John Plankinton and Frederick Layton, who had started separate packing plants a few years earlier, formed a partnership and established a plant in the lower Menomonee Valley. Although much of this activity moved to Chicago following the establishment there of the Union Stock Yards in 1865, a small packing industry remained in Milwaukee until the 1980s. The meat-packing industry in Milwaukee was related to another major industrial activity, tanning, which also continues to be significant in the 1980s. Guido Pfister and Fred Vogel established a firm in 1853 that today is Milwaukee's largest tanning operation. The Civil War, with its demand for harnesses and other leather products, stimulated the industry. In 1855 Milwaukee had 9 tanneries; by 1870 there were 30. The packing industry furnished the hides, and tanbark was shipped to the city from the upper Great Lakes region.

Brewing, which "made Milwaukee famous," appeared very early in the city's history. In 1860 Milwaukee had the highest proportion of people of German origin of any U.S. city, and these immigrants not only constituted a large market but also had the skills and the traditions that supported a large brewing industry. In 1844 the Best family, who had been brewers in Germany, established a brewery in Milwaukee that was the foundation of the later Pabst operations (Figure 7.6). August Krug in 1849 founded another brewery, later to be the nucleus of the larger organization taken over by Joseph Schlitz. This company terminated its operations in Milwaukee in 1981 and in 1982, after a merger, moved its headquarters to Detroit. The largest brewery headquartered and operating in Milwaukee, and the nation's second largest, is the Miller Brewing Company, established in 1855. In 1985 Heileman (which bought out Pabst in 1984) was trying to buy out Miller.

In 1860 Milwaukee's population had a wide range in income and wealth. Lee Soltow reported that in Milwaukee County the average annual wages in manufacturing were $264. On the one hand, carpenters earned $250 to $320 and day laborers $150 to $250. On the other hand, the richest person could buy the labor of nearly 3,000 average-income workers in 1860! The wealth held by the richest 18 people equaled the wages of the 15,324 working men and women in the county that year.

The distribution of wealth, defined by the value of real estate and personal estate, revealed the class structure of Milwaukee in 1860. Eighty percent of the adult male population of the county was foreign-born, but only 8 individuals of the 46 wealthiest, or 17 percent, were foreign-born. Wealthy families employed an average of almost three servants each. Occupationally, the wealthy men were mostly lawyers, real estate developers, merchants, and bankers; only one was a manufacturer. Half the persons in the state with wealth of over $100,000 lived in Milwaukee in 1860. The top 1 percent of the wealthiest persons in Milwaukee held 44 percent of the wealth; the top 10 percent held 83 percent of the wealth. The richest man, Alexander Mitchell, a banker, owned $700,000 in real estate and personal assets, whereas the average wealth was only $2,376. Thus, both the amounts and distribution of wages and wealth in 1860 Milwaukee were striking.

Milwaukee's Ethnic Population

Milwaukee has always been characterized by ethnic and racial diversity. This diversity is celebrated by an annual Folk Fair held each fall, a lakefront Summerfest each year, and many other festivals and

FIGURE 7.6 The Pabst brewery. The architecture is characteristic of turn-of-the-century industrial Milwaukee. (Harold Mayer)

special events throughout the year. Each of the ethnic groups has retained, to varying degrees, elements of its ethnic culture, making Milwaukee a cosmopolitan city. Nevertheless, by 1980 only about 4 percent of the metropolitan population was foreign-born. Germans were by far the largest white foreign-born group, followed by Poles, whose numbers were slightly more than half those of the Germans. Other large groups of foreign-born were, in order of size: Italian, Austrian, Yugoslavian, Russian (predominantly Jewish), Canadian, British, and Czech. Each group varies in the extent to which it retains its ethnic characteristics and in where the group lives within the city and region.

The earliest permanent white residents of Milwaukee were from New England and upstate New York, but by 1848 over half of the city's residents were immigrants from abroad; by 1850 immigrants from abroad made up nearly two-thirds of the population. The 1848 potato famine in Ireland, together with a rapidly growing demand for labor in the Midwest, attracted many Irish immigrants to the Milwaukee region, but Irish immigration declined after 1850. The Germans were already predominant in Milwaukee by 1850, constituting 36 percent of the total population and 57 percent of the foreign-born population. Subsequently, the city was a center of German-American culture and was known for many years as the "German Athens." In 1860, Germans comprised 70 percent of the total foreign-born population, and the proportion remained fairly constant until about 1890 (Figure 7.7). The total number of Germans in Milwaukee peaked in about 1910. Polish in-migration to Milwaukee occurred later than the major German influx. By 1910 people born in what is now Poland constituted 22 percent of the foreign-born and 6.5 percent of the total population of the city.

The population of German origin, both foreign- and U.S.-born, has dispersed

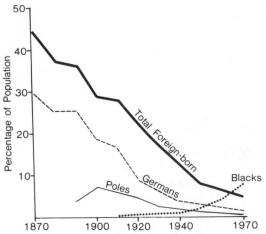

FIGURE 7.7 Percentage of foreign-born and blacks in the Milwaukee SMSA, 1870–1970 (Based on U.S., Bureau of the Census, *Census of Population and Housing* [Washington, D.C.: U.S. Government Printing Office, various years])

throughout the city and region, and coincides in location very closely with the locations of the total white population. No identifiable German neighborhood exists within the city, although numerous buildings indicate by their architecture the locations of former concentrations of Germans. In contrast, the Polish-origin population is highly concentrated, principally on the South Side. A relatively small concentration of Italians exists on the near Northeast Side (Figure 7.8).

Blacks first settled in Milwaukee in the 1830s, but their numbers did not increase rapidly until after World War II (Figure 7.7). They numbered slightly over 9,000 in 1940; in 1980, 150,000 blacks lived in the metropolitan area, of whom about 147,000 lived within the city of Milwaukee. In 1980 they constituted 10.8 percent of the population of the metropolitan area and 23 percent of the city's population. Black students outnumbered white students in the Milwaukee public schools for the first time in 1980, at which time they constituted 46.9 percent of the total enrollment.

Although housing and neighborhood conditions in the predominantly black neighborhoods were generally not as bad

as they were in some other large industrial cities such as Chicago, Detroit, and Cleveland, Milwaukee experienced racial disturbances and riots in the 1960s. Because of the rising affluence of many blacks and their consequent and effective demand for more and larger residential units and because households grew smaller as well, the area occupied by blacks increased faster than did the black population. Transition areas between the black ghetto and white neighborhoods were especially unstable. During the race riots the principal commercial area within the black enclave, along Milwaukee's North Third Street—northwest of the city's core—was largely destroyed. After 20 years, scars still remain in the form of unoccupied commercial buildings and vacant lots.

The ghetto did expand, principally to the northwest. Middle-class black areas are now extensive. Residential and school integration in Milwaukee, as in many other U.S. cities, were major political issues during the 1970s, but, unlike the preceding decade, racial violence was less common. Public housing programs and urban renewal projects replaced significant portions of the substandard housing in the ghetto. Unlike other cities of comparable and larger size, Milwaukee does not have massive high-rise public housing projects where low-income people, in large proportion black, are concentrated.

The Hispanic population represents the other distinctive racial minority in Milwaukee. In 1980, the metropolitan area had 34,343 people of Spanish origin, of which 26,111 were residents of the city of Milwaukee. They constituted 2.46 percent of the population of the metropolitan area and 4.10 percent of the city population. Six percent of the students in the Milwaukee public schools were Hispanic. Because of changes in definition, 1980 figures are not comparable with those of previous years. In 1970 the city had 11,575 persons whose "mother tongue" was Spanish; 15,606 Spanish-speaking people lived in the metropolitan area. The three distinc-

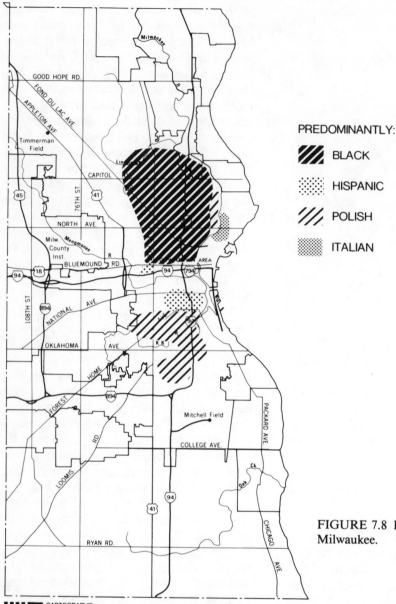

PREDOMINANTLY:

BLACK

HISPANIC

POLISH

ITALIAN

FIGURE 7.8 Ethnic and racial groups in Milwaukee.

tive Spanish-speaking groups are Mexicans, Puerto Ricans, and Cubans, all of whom live in spatially distinct clusters.

The first significant numbers of Mexicans arrived in Milwaukee in the early 1920s, brought in to replace striking European immigrants in a tannery. With the boom of the 1940s war economy, their numbers increased substantially, and they tended to cluster on the near South Side (Figure 7.8). Puerto Ricans began to migrate to Mil-

waukee in increasing numbers during the late 1940s. Like the Mexicans, they found employment in manual and semi-skilled jobs in tanneries, foundries, and other industries. Many also found employment in low-paying service industries. Puerto Ricans also tended to concentrate on the city's South Side, but to a lesser degree than did the Mexicans, and several clusters of Puerto Ricans are found elsewhere in the city.

Hispanic-Americans tend to have larger

families, lower incomes, and less formal education than do most other Milwaukeeans. They also hold more blue-collar jobs than the city average. Bilingual school programs and a higher-than-average proportion of young people somewhat facilitate the process of cultural assimilation; nevertheless Hispanic-Americans continue to constitute an identifiable, largely separate, group in the city.

Racial and ethnic groups are often associated with distinctive religions, which provide cultural identification; churches and other houses of worship are often architectural landmarks in their respective neighborhoods. Nearly 60 percent of the population of Milwaukee, or 350,000 people, is Roman Catholic. Catholics include members of ethnic groups of east European origin and Spanish-speaking people, as well as many Germans. Lutherans, who represent over 20 percent of the population, or 130,000 people, constitute the second largest denomination. Baptists, many of them blacks, account for about 30,000 people. Milwaukee is also home to about 24,000 Jews and 18,000 Methodists.

MILWAUKEE'S MAJOR AREAS

Residential Areas

A distinctive characteristic of metropolitan Milwaukee, and especially of the central city, is the low density of the residential areas. Suburban housing, constituting the greater portion of the region's housing inventory, is characteristically low in density with its associated "sprawl" features (such as factories, townhouses, and golf courses) scattered in agricultural land. Only a small proportion of Milwaukee's housing units are apartment buildings, even in the central city. A 1977 sample survey showed that only 21 percent of the city's housing units were in buildings with five or more units. More characteristic is the duplex, or two-unit building, commonly in the form of a two-story structure with an apartment on each floor (Figure 7.9). Milwaukee has relatively few residential struc-

tures that reflect the ethnic or national origins of their previous or present occupants. One notable exception is the "Polish flat": a walk-in basement apartment, typically in a one-and-one-half or two-story building.

Many of the newer residential units in the metropolitan area are located in "planned unit developments": Clusters of houses, commonly with shared walls, provide higher density than is possible with single-unit detached houses but preserve a lower overall density by making available additional open space surrounding the clusters (Figure 7.10). Some of the larger planned unit developments have small shopping centers. Many such planned unit developments involve condominium ownership, in which each unit is separately owned, but open areas used for lawns, playgrounds, and vehicle parking are owned in common. In the early 1980s some existing apartment buildings, including high-rise structures overlooking the northeasterly lakefront, were converted from rental to condominium ownership, and several new high-rise buildings were erected as original condominiums.

In general, the condition of housing, both in the city and in the metropolitan area, is better than in most other metropolitan areas, and overcrowding of housing units is somewhat less prevalent. Although 3.6 percent of the housing units in the nation's metropolitan areas in 1970 lacked some or all plumbing, the comparable figure for the Milwaukee SMSA was 2.8 percent. The extreme deterioration of inner-city areas characteristic of other large industrial cities is generally lacking in Milwaukee, where extensive areas were cleared and rebuilt during the 1950s and 1960s. The relatively few high-rise public housing structures are occupied by the elderly, the result of a federal program that was implemented in the 1960s and 1970s; many of these structures are cylindrical in shape, forming distinctive landmarks in several sections of the city.

The spatial pattern of social and economic status in Milwaukee conforms to the

FIGURE 7.9 Duplex houses in the university district of northeast Milwaukee. (Harold Mayer)

FIGURE 7.10 A planned unit development in northwest Milwaukee. This area, built around artificial Northridge Lakes, includes group housing clusters, high-rise apartment buildings, and a large regional shopping center, one of seven in the metropolitan area. (Harold Mayer)

Focus: Greendale, Wisconsin: Federal City Planning During the Great Depression

In the 1930s the Suburban Resettlement Division of the U.S. Resettlement Administration built several greenbelt towns: "rural-industrial communities on the outskirts of badly crowded cities." Every acre was to be put to its best use and the traditional division between town and country was to be broken down. Eventually, each town was to contain 3,000 to 5,000 low-rental housing units.

The justification for the greenbelt towns was the living conditions of the 1930s; 36 percent of all dwellings in the United States were substandard, and bad housing was linked to disease and crime. In Milwaukee, for example, 83 percent of all delinquent girls in 1932 came from homes in congested districts. In addition, Americans could not afford to buy homes during the Great Depression. Sixty-three percent of city families earned less than $1,500 per year, yet less than 6 percent of all new houses were valued under $2,840; in 1940 over 66 percent of Wisconsin's labor force earned less than $1,000 annually.

To alleviate shortages and to improve housing quality, 100 major cities were studied by the Resettlement Administration to decide where greenbelt towns should be built. The final list of cities, including Milwaukee, had "a long record of steady, regular growth; sound economic foundations; diversity of industry; good wage levels and enlightened labor policies; and finally an acute need for housing." The ultimate land uses in a typical greenbelt community would consist of 2,100 acres (850 ha) for farms, 1,800 acres (728 ha) for parks, 1,000 acres (405 ha) for homes, and 100 acres (40 ha) for community buildings and stores. The philosophy and plans of the greenbelt towns had a major impact, as they were forerunners of post–World War II suburbs.

Employment available in Milwaukee—Each dot indicates 100 jobs in manufacturing or major commercial establishments. There are an additional 50,000 jobs (not shown) in the central business district.

TRAVEL TIME BY AUTOMOBILE IN MINUTES FROM CENTER OF SITE

13,000 jobs . . . within 10 minutes travel time.
48,000 jobs . . . within 20 minutes travel time.
141,000 jobs . . . within 30 minutes travel time.

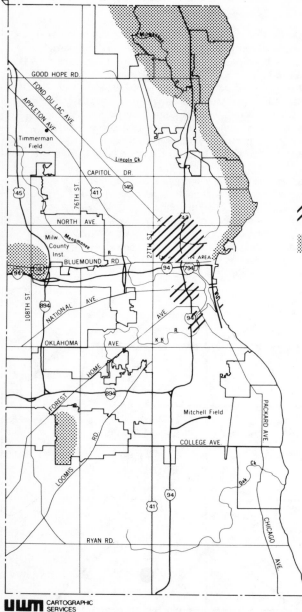

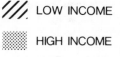

FIGURE 7.11 Low- and high-income areas in Milwaukee.

urban land-use models developed by geographers, land economists, and sociologists: a combination of concentric socioeconomic zones surrounding the downtown core, wedges or sectors radiating outward along lineal axes focusing upon downtown Milwaukee, and a series of outlying industrial and suburban nuclei. In general, residential density decreases with distance from the core except for the outlying concentrations, whereas socioeconomic status,

as measured by rental costs and housing values, income, and educational status, increases with distance. A notable exception is the northeasterly high-status wedge along the lakefront extending from downtown Milwaukee to Mequon, beyond the Milwaukee county line (Figure 7.11). The lower Menomonee Industrial Valley interrupts the continuity of the concentric-ring model (Figure 7.12). Other discontinuities occur along major railroad lines, interrupting the

FIGURE 7.12 The Menomonee Industrial Valley. On the left is the CBD dominated by the First Wisconsin Center tower; on the right is the intermodal terminal of the Milwaukee Road. (Harold Mayer)

smooth distance decay pattern (in which housing, traffic, density, etc. decline) outward from central Milwaukee, and still others are caused by extensive demolition for freeways, both constructed and aborted. Some deviations from the general pattern are also associated with racial and ethnic clusters, often of groups with the lowest incomes: the predominantly black-occupied area northwest of downtown Milwaukee, which is spreading northwestward and which exhibits its own outward rise in socioeconomic characteristics; the predominantly Hispanic-occupied area of the near South Side; and the Polish area just beyond it.

Downtown Milwaukee

Downtown Milwaukee, like the downtowns of most U.S. cities, has for several decades faced a relative, and in some respects an absolute, decline; many former central functions are being attracted not only to the periphery of the city and to the suburbs but also to other regions of the nation. Nevertheless, by the early 1980s a number of attempts were being made to

bring about a major renaissance of Milwaukee's central business district (CBD) (Figure 7.13).

Until recently, Milwaukee's downtown skyline had a picturesque quality. Few skyscrapers were very tall, and many of the buildings, dating from the nineteenth and early twentieth century, reflected in their architecture the ethnic character of Milwaukee's previously dominant population from central Europe. The City Hall and the adjacent Pabst Theater, as well as many of the office buildings, provided an aesthetic in their architecture that was a symbol of the city. Some of the buildings that remain have recently been refurbished. Several modern office buildings, constructed in the 1960s and 1970s, provide a different—and many people believe a discordant—character to the cityscape. The 42-story First Wisconsin Center, the region's tallest building, at the east end of the CBD, is the most prominent, but Northwestern Mutual's new building and the new Federal Building on Wisconsin Avenue are also part of this new look, as are the four-building complex of the Mortgage Guaranty Insurance Company and the 30-story Winmar

FIGURE 7.13 The Performing Arts Center in downtown Milwaukee. Milwaukee's "Pac," completed in 1970, includes a large auditorium, a concert hall, and a theater. (Harold Mayer)

Building, construction of which began in 1983.

Retailing has declined in the CBD, concomitant with the rapid growth of regional shopping centers and associated department and specialty stores in the outer portions of the city and in the suburbs. The only major department store east of the river closed in 1980. West of the river, the city and private developers constructed a large retail center, the Grand Avenue mall, in September 1982. It contains the two remaining major department stores, many new specialty shops, the refurbished turn-of-the-century Plankinton Arcade building, a 1,700-car parking-garage complex, and a series of continuous passageways for pedestrian movement, including second-floor routes through existing and new buildings and skywalks over the intervening streets. The Grand Avenue mall was planned as a major project to revitalize the CBD as the region's dominant retail center. Other relatively new facilities in the downtown include a medium-sized hotel, opened in 1980, and a civic plaza lined with public buildings, completed some years earlier. Among the buildings at the civic plaza are the county courthouse, an extension of the public library, the public museum, the phalanx of sport and convention facilities collectively known as MECCA (Milwaukee Exhibition Convention Center and Arena), a state office building, and a public safety building (Figure 7.14). The extensive open area around these facilities, however, constitutes an interruption to the high density of the rest of downtown and hence a barrier, especially during winter weather when pedestrians find it unpleasant and difficult to cross.

Outlying Commercial Areas

Like other metropolitan areas in the United States, the Milwaukee SMSA has been experiencing a rapidly evolving new pattern of shopping and office land use since World War II. The virtual ubiquity of the automobile has stimulated development not only in peripheral and sub-

FIGURE 7.14 Milwaukee's civic plaza. The plaza parallels and is north of Wisconsin Avenue, the axis of downtown Milwaukee. MECCA, Milwaukee's downtown convention center, is in the foreground; the Hyatt Regency, the city's newest hotel, is in the back of it; and City Hall is in the background. (Harold Mayer)

urban residential areas, but also of outlying clusters of commercial and service businesses.

During the late nineteenth and early twentieth century, a number of outlying commercial nodes developed that were based on rail transportation, including the steam railroads, but primarily on the expanding network of street railways and interurban electric lines. Older nodes, such as the commercial cores of satellite cities and towns, began to be absorbed into the spreading built-up areas but tended to keep their character as more or less independent centers until after World War II. The downtown areas of such places as Racine, Wauwatosa, Waukesha, Thiensville, Grafton, and West Bend were separated from the main urban areas of Milwaukee by extensive open countryside. As the urbanized area expanded, with widespread use of the automobile, many of these spaces filled in, and the older centers tended to be ingested more or less into the metropolitan economy and landscape. Within Milwaukee, business spread along the main arterial avenues, most of which had electric street railways, later replaced by bus lines. At and near major

intersections, commercial density was higher, reflecting higher land values, and at these points major outlying retail centers developed, such as those along Mitchell Street on Milwaukee's South Side, Greenfield Avenue in West Allis, and North Third Street on the North Side of Milwaukee. But these sites of maximum access during a time when public transportation was dominant became less accessible in the automobile era because of lack of space for parking. Outlying shopping centers, designed for automobiles, provided off-street parking. The older hierarchy of outlying business clusters—regional shopping centers, community centers, neighborhood centers, and string or ribbon developments along major streets and highways—was expanded to include newer forms, most notably comprehensively planned and developed shopping centers surrounded by parking. Some of the larger shopping centers, originally built around open malls, were retrofitted during the 1970s with roofs and climate control; the more recent centers were built as covered malls. They range in size from small neighborhood clusters to massive regional centers containing as many as four or more department stores, a hundred specialty shops, several cinemas, and, in some instances, connected or nearby office buildings containing professional services as well as commercial businesses (Table 7.1). In addition, a new regional center, the Regency Mall, was opened in 1981 in Racine County, competing to some extent with those in metropolitan Milwaukee.

THE METROPOLITAN ECONOMY

Basic employment in metropolitan Milwaukee is predominantly in the manufacturing sector; this has been true since the Civil War. The production of durable goods—especially capital goods used in the production of other goods—is the most important manufacturing category in the city and metropolitan region. In the 1980s the region's importance in industry is being seriously challenged—as is manufacturing in most other older manufacturing areas of the northeastern and midwestern United States—by the rapid growth of population and industry in the Sun Belt. In 1978—

just before the serious business recession of the late 1970s and early 1980s—among the 25 U.S. metropolitan areas with a population of over 1 million, the Milwaukee SMSA ranked third in the proportion of total employment that was engaged in manufacturing. The only SMSAs that had a greater proportion of their total workers in manufacturing were Detroit and San Jose, the former because of the automobile industry, and the latter because of the rapidly expanding computer industry. Especially noteworthy is the fact that metropolitan Milwaukee had a higher proportion of its employment in manufacturing than did the traditional manufacturing areas centered on such cities as Chicago, Cincinnati, Pittsburgh, Cleveland, and Philadelphia.

For many years production of durable capital goods comprised the three largest categories of manufacturing industries and manufacturing employment in metropolitan Milwaukee: (1) machinery, except electrical, (2) electrical machinery and electronic equipment, and (3) fabricated metal products (Table 7.2). Together these ac-

TABLE 7.1
Metropolitan Milwaukee's Largest
Regional Shopping Centers

Name	Area (Acres)	Sq. Ft. Building	Parking Spaces	Stores	Opened*
Southridge	122	1,328,000	6,700	128	1970
Mayfair	90	1,250,000	8,000	111	1958
Brookfield Square	92	1,212,659	5,300	67	1967
Northridge	170	1,089,000	8,300	142	1972
Capitol Court	56	850,000	4,500	110	1956
Bay Shore	32	550,000	2,400	66	1954
Southgate	33	500,000	3,000	56	1951

*Original opening; figures do not include, in some instances, subsequent expansions.

Source: Compiled from Directory of Shopping Centers in the United States, Vol. XXI, Sec. 2, The Midwest. (Burlington, Iowa: The National Research Bureau, Inc., 1980).

TABLE 7.2
Manufacturing Employment by Major
Industry Group, Milwaukee SMSA

Major Industry Group	Employment	Percent
Machinery, except electrical	54,048	28.4
Electrical machinery and electronic equipment	27,847	13.6
Fabricated metal products	26,262	12.8
Food and kindred products	14,843	8.4
Transportation equipment	12,930	6.3
Printing and publishing	12,557	6.1
Primary metal industries	12,543	6.1
Instruments and related products	4,630	2.3
Paper and allied products	4,360	2.1
Leather and leather products	4,354	2.1
Chemicals and allied products	3,882	1.9
Rubber and miscellaneous plastics	3,675	1.8
Miscellaneous manufacturing industries	3,321	1.6
Apparel products	2,317	1.1
Stone, clay, and glass products	1,608	0.8
Wood products	908	0.4
Furniture and fixtures	749	0.4
Textile mill products	648	0.4
Total	191,482	100.0

Source: U.S., Department of Commerce, Bureau of the Census, County Business Patterns 1977, CPB-77-51, Wisconsin (Washington, D.C.: U.S. Government Printing Office, 1978).

Note: In the analogous publications for 1978 and subsequent years, employment figures for some categories of manufacturing were given only within ranges; thus, totals and percentages were not available because of disclosure rules.

counted for several times as many jobs as the fourth-ranking category, food and kindred products, including beverages.

The importance of manufacturing to the economy of metropolitan Milwaukee is further shown in Table 7.3. In 1978, manufacturing was concentrated in metropolitan Milwaukee to a much greater degree than it was in most other U.S. metropolitan areas. On the other hand, wholesale and retail trade were underrepresented relative to the percentage of employment in these categories in most other metropolitan areas. Employment by government in the Milwaukee SMSA was very much below the national average, in large measure because

of the proximity to Chicago, which is the locus of many regional offices of the federal government. The virtual absence of large military establishments in metropolitan Milwaukee and in Wisconsin also contributed to the underrepresentation of government employment. Nearby Chicago is the principal continental focus of transportation and thus accounts for Milwaukee's relatively low employment in transportation, communications, and public utilities.

Among the large metropolitan areas in which manufacturing is the predominant source of employment, metropolitan Milwaukee normally ranks high in overall per capita income. In 1979, for example, it

TABLE 7.3
Employment by Category, Milwaukee SMSA
and All SMSAs in the United States[a]

Employment Category	Milwaukee SMSA	U.S. SMSAs	Percent Milw. SMSA	Percent U.S. SMSAs
Agricultural services, forestry, fisheries	804	184,574	0.14	0.33
Mining	(250-499)	322,276	–	0.57
Contract construction	25,525	3,292,560	4.34	5.86
Manufacturing	212,434	15,694,033	36.14	27.94
Transportation and other public utilities (except railroads)	29,052	3,631,653	4.94	6.47
Wholesale trade	35,863	4,031,192	6.10	7.18
Retail trade	107,541	11,387,981	18.30	20.27
Finance, insurance, and real estate	40,444	4,245,424	6.89	7.56
Services	134,208	13,112,714	22.83	23.34
Nonclassifiable establishments	(1,000-2,499)	267,872	–	0.48
Total	587,807	56,170,279	99.68	100.00

[a]Excludes government employees, railroad employees, and self-employed persons.

Source: U.S., Department of Commerce, Bureau of the Census, County Business Patterns 1978, Standard Metropolitan Statistical Areas, CPB-78-53 (Washington, D.C.: U.S. Government Printing Office, 1979).

ranked third among the major SMSAs of the United States, exceeded only by Washington, D.C., with its high proportion of government employees, and the Anaheim–Santa Ana–Garden Grove SMSA in southern California (Table 7.4).

The high proportion of manufacturing to total employment in metropolitan Milwaukee, and especially the concentration in the production of durable goods, made the area especially vulnerable to the impact of the recession of the early 1980s. Much of the loss of manufacturing activity in the area appears to have been permanent. Thus, metropolitan Milwaukee shares with other major urban centers in the Midwest a decline in which the so-called smokestack industries suffered from technological change, from reduced demand for their products, and from the competition of imports from abroad.

Leading Manufacturing Industries

Although metalworking and machinery production dominate the manufacturing base of metropolitan Milwaukee, the region has not had a primary iron and steel industry since the late 1920s. Its input of iron and steel comes primarily from the Calumet region of South Chicago and from

TABLE 7.4
Median Family Income for Large SMSAs

SMSA	Rank	Median Family Income ($)
Washington, D.C., MD-VA	1	29,086
Anaheim-Santa Ana- Garden Grove, CA	2	25,639
MILWAUKEE, WI	3	25,501
Seattle-Everett, WA	4	25,484
Minneapolis-St. Paul, MN	5	25,321
Newark, NJ	6	24,661
Detroit, MI	7	24,442
San Francisco-Oakland, CA	8	24,070
Chicago, IL	9	23,826
Houston, TX	10	23,068
St. Louis, MO-IL	11	22,501
Boston, MA	12	22,222
Dallas, TX	13	22,034
Pittsburgh, PA	14	21,921
Cleveland, OH	15	21,882
Atlanta, GA	16	21,878
Baltimore, MD	17	21,855
Philadelphia, PA-NJ	18	21,707
Los Angeles-Long Beach, CA	19	20,730
New York, NY	20	19,289

Source: Adapted from: U.S., Department of Commerce, Bureau of the Census, Statistical Abstract of the United States 1981 (Washington, D.C.: U.S. Government Printing Office, 1981, Table No. 736, p. 441).

northwestern Indiana. From 1866 until 1929, a large iron and steel plant was located in Bay View, just south of the present port installations on Jones Island, but obsolescence and its closeness to larger and more efficient plants only 100 mi (161 km) to the south forced the plant to close.

In 1899 Milwaukee had 101 foundry and machine-shop establishments producing $17 million of output and employing 8,468 people. By 1919 iron and steel and heavy machinery production were the leading categories of Milwaukee industry, employing over 28,000 people. Machinery, both electrical and nonelectrical, and fabricated metal

products, continue to be the three leading categories of manufacturing in the city. Transportation equipment, an important user of metal, ranked fifth in 1977, and primary metals ranked seventh. Together these industries provided two-thirds of all manufacturing jobs. Of the 16 largest manufacturing firms in the metropolitan area in 1981 that employed at least 2,000 people, 13 were in the electrical and nonelectrical machinery, metalworking, and transportation equipment categories; the other 3 were breweries, one of which subsequently closed (Table 7.5).

Many of the firms in metropolitan Mil-

TABLE 7.5
Large Manufacturing Firms That Normally Employ
2,000 or More Workers in Metropolitan Milwaukee

Establishment	Product Line
A. C. Spark Plug Division, General Motors Corporation	Emission control systems
Allen Bradley Company	Electric motor controls
Allis-Chalmers Corporation	Agricultural equipment
Briggs & Stratton Corporation	Engines, locks
Bucyrus-Erie Company	Mining equipment and supplies
Eaton Corporation	Electronic equipment
Falk Corporation	Machinery, gears
General Electric Company, Medical Systems Division	Medical equipment and supplies
Harnischfeger Corporation	Cranes and construction equipment
Ladish Company	Forgings
Miller Brewing Company	Beer
Outboard Marine Corporation- Evinrude	Outboard motors
Pabst Brewing Company	Beer
Rexnord, Inc.	Conveyors and conveying equipment
Joseph Schlitz Brewing Company	Beer
A. O. Smith Corporation	Automobile parts and supplies

Source: Economic Fact Book on Metropolitan Milwaukee
          (Metropolitan Milwaukee Association of Commerce, 1982).

Note: In some instances the respective plants produce a variety
        of products. Only the principal product line is noted for
        each.

waukee are "home grown" and date from the nineteenth or early twentieth century. Some are locally administered, although, increasingly, mergers have resulted in the absorption of local firms and operations by national and international companies, including conglomerates. These mergers have often reduced the importance of the Milwaukee operations and have, in some instances, terminated the Milwaukee plants and offices. American Motors and Schlitz are two 1980s examples. The automobile manufacturer was until the 1970s the leader among industrial employers in Wisconsin, with plants in Kenosha and a major body and assembly plant in Milwaukee. Reduced demand for its products resulted in the reduction of the Milwaukee operations, intermittent closure of the Milwaukee plant with increased production in Kenosha, and eventual control of the company by a foreign corporation. In the case of Schlitz, the Milwaukee plant was closed in mid-1981 following rapid loss of the company's market share and a strike. The Stroh Company took over Schlitz in early 1982, reduced the local office force, and then relocated the company's headquarters to Detroit. Many of Milwaukee's other industries are already divisions or subsidiaries of large companies with headquarters elsewhere.

Early in 1985 one of Milwaukee's largest industrial employers, Allen-Bradley, became a unit of Rockwell, a large conglomerate. A short time earlier, the J. I. Case plant in Racine became affiliated with International Harvester. In early 1985 other large industries that had for many years been closely identified with the Milwaukee metropolitan area were in the process of negotiating mergers or takeovers by large absentee-controlled conglomerates; among them were the Allis-Chalmers organization and the Pabst brewery. In general, the recent and prospective removal of control of such large industrial establishments to other cities threatens further losses of employment in metropolitan Milwaukee.

Another challenge to the economic base of metropolitan Milwaukee is its heavy dependence upon the automobile industry. Milwaukee is at the western end of the Automobile Belt, which extends from western Pennsylvania through northern Ohio and Indiana and southern Michigan (Figure 7.15). Reduced demand for automobiles because of the 1980s recession, imports of cars from abroad, and a decrease in the size of vehicles, as well as increasing use of robots and automation in the industry, have led to a decline in employment in automobile manufacture and in the supplier industries. Even following a general economic recovery, the automobile-related industries in the Milwaukee region will probably not provide as much employment as they once did.

Milwaukee factories also produce a wide variety of other machinery and electrical goods (Figure 7.16), ranging from huge motors, cranes, mining and earth-moving machinery, tractors and other agricultural machinery, to electrical controls, fractional-horsepower motors, outboard motors, and the nation's only plant that produces motorcycles. Tool and die makers, mostly small establishments, constitute an important part of the region's economic base.

Workers in these and other industries are heavily unionized, so that high wages characterize Milwaukee. Consequently, during hard times many industrial firms try to avoid paying these high wages by reducing their local labor force or by closing plants in the Milwaukee region. The city lacks the advantage of an attractive climate such as the growing markets in the Sun Belt and elsewhere in the nation enjoy. Milwaukee must therefore develop compensatory attractions in order to retain its existing industrial base and to maintain an adequate employment base.

Industrial Regions

Milwaukee's earliest factories were located on rivers along which falls and rapids furnished power for the early mills. The opening of the "straight cut" across the sandbar at the entrance to the Milwaukee River from Lake Michigan provided access

196

FIGURE 7.15 The General Motors plant in Oak Creek. This plant is typical of large single-story plants built in peripheral and suburban areas after World War II. The company manufactures a variety of electrical and other components for motor vehicles and aircraft in this plant. (Harold Mayer)

FIGURE 7.16 The Allen-Bradley plant in Walkers Point. One of the largest Milwaukee industrial establishments produces a variety of electrical products and components for the automobile industry. (Harold Mayer)

to the rivers by lake vessels, and many of the early manufacturing industries were then located in the heart of the present city. Tanneries and flour mills were situated on both sides of the Milwaukee River north of the city's core. Canalization of the lower Menomonee and dredging of several tributary canals in the 1870s favored industrial development on the flat-floored lower Menomonee Valley, bisecting the city and known locally as the Industrial Valley, but since the 1960s industry in this region has declined. Until the development of the highway system, industrial plants were found in two basic locations: in or near the central business district and along the railroads. Factory owners who were primarily concerned with access to local and regional markets and required large numbers of workers, and who relied on mass transit, picked central locations. Many wholesaling and light manufacturing plants, commonly in multistory buildings, also tended to cluster close to the city center. Until the early twentieth century lake vessels provided package freight service for merchandise, and the central water frontage of the Milwaukee River constituted an important part of the port. Typical of the late nineteenth and early twentieth centuries, railroads created distinctive lineal or axial industrial corridors that persist in the 1980s.

But changes in the spatial pattern of land uses by industries subsequently occurred. Pressure for land on which to expand, obsolescence of the centrally located facilities, reduced dependence on water transportation, relative freedom from local restrictions in peripheral areas, and the outward movement of the area's population combined to attract industries to the edge of the city and beyond. Already by 1893, the Cudahy Packing Company relocated from Milwaukee to a suburban site south of the city. The site, together with the adjacent prospective residential area, was incorporated as a village in 1895 and became the city of Cudahy in 1906. Similarly, the Edward P. Allis Company, predecessor of Allis-Chalmers, established a large plant

on a 100-acre (40-ha) tract west of Milwaukee which became the core of West Allis, incorporated as a village in 1902 and as a city in 1906. During the same period the Bucyrus Company—now Bucyrus-Erie—located in South Milwaukee, and the Harnischfeger Corporation in West Milwaukee. Waukesha, 20 mi (32 km) west of downtown Milwaukee, began as an agricultural trade center and resort but became an important industrial center when the Waukesha Motor Company plant located there in 1909.

The growth of industry in Milwaukee's suburban areas and its relative decline within the city has continued. Between 1950 and 1977 85 percent of the region's manufacturing establishments were new or had relocated, with a net gain of about 20 percent in number of plants during that period. Although the city of Milwaukee lost 471 manufacturing firms, it still contains about half of the SMSA's industrial plants, compared with 76 percent in 1947.

A major influence in the peripheral expansion of industry in metropolitan Milwaukee, as in many other metropolitan areas, has been the organized industrial district, or industrial park. Industrial parks have many advantages for small- and medium-sized companies. Developers may offer industries options to buy or lease land and buildings. Firms can be assured of compatible neighbors because restrictions are usually more specific than those of local zoning ordinances and building codes. Developers may offer architectural and engineering services and provide protective services, executive dining rooms and clubhouses, and recreation areas. Sites are usually offered with improved streets and underground utilities. In many instances, the companies in a park use each other's products and/or services in a chain of production and distribution. In the Milwaukee SMSA, 51 organized industrial and office park districts existed in early 1981, with a total land area of 6,298 acres (2,548 ha), of which slightly more than half were occupied (Table 7.6). Less than 20 percent

TABLE 7.6
Industrial and Office Parks and
Districts, Metropolitan Milwaukee

Location	Number	Total Land		Available Area	
		Acres	Hectares	Acres	Hectares
City of Milwaukee	10	1,221	494.1	691	279.6
Suburban Milwaukee County	14	2,216	896.8	1,186	479.9
Waukesha, Ozaukee, and Washington Counties	27	2,861	1,157.8	1,399	566.1
Total Milwaukee SMSA	51	6,298	2,548.7	3,276	1,325.6

Source: Compiled from: Metropolitan Milwaukee Industrial and Office Parks and Districts (Metropolitan Milwaukee Association of Commerce, 1981).

of the total area in these districts and only about 21 percent of the land available for further industrial occupance is within the municipal limits of Milwaukee.

Service Industries

Decline in manufacturing employment has been at least partially offset by employment in service industries. This service employment, a large proportion of which may be regarded as nonbasic or settlement-serving rather than basic or settlement-forming, in the sense of providing goods and services for use outside the metropolitan area, accounts for the largest single category of workers in metropolitan Milwaukee, as it also does in other urban areas. Nevertheless, service activities in metropolitan Milwaukee account for a smaller proportion of jobs and income than they do in most other SMSAs. Between 1960 and 1979 the proportion of production jobs in manufacturing to total jobs in the metropolitan area decreased by one-third (Table 7.7); subsequently the business recession of the early 1980s produced a further decrease in the proportion of manufacturing to nonmanufacturing jobs. Because a high proportion of service jobs are relatively low-paying, there has been a decline

in metropolitan Milwaukee's generally high incomes that will likely continue.

A major source of Milwaukee's white-collar or office employment is in finance, insurance, and real estate, but in proportion of white-collar jobs to total employment the Milwaukee SMSA ranked below all other U.S. SMSAs. Proximity to Chicago reduces Milwaukee's financial function. The Federal Reserve Bank, for example, is located in Chicago, as are many other of the financial institutions serving the Milwaukee region. Milwaukee's largest bank does not rank among the nation's 50 largest. However, several insurance companies have home offices, and others have regional offices, in Milwaukee and its suburbs. The largest is the Northwestern Mutual Life Insurance Company, ranked among the first 10 in the nation, whose home office employs about 2,300 people in a complex of modern office buildings at the east end of the city's central business district. The Mortgage Guaranty Investment Company, a Milwaukee-born institution with a large office complex in the downtown area, is another important financial institution headquartered in the city.

In both wholesale and retail trade, the Milwaukee SMSA has normally had a lower

TABLE 7.7
Total Employment and Manufacturing
Production Workers, Milwaukee SMSA, 1960-1979

Year	Employed (1,000s)	Manufacturing Production Workers (1,000s)	Percent Manufacturing Production Workers to Total Employed
1960	484	144	29.75
1965	510	145	28.43
1970	567	140	24.69
1975	612	134	19.67
1979	705	144	20.43

Source: 1960 estimated by Research Division, Metropolitan
Milwaukee Association of Commerce; 1965-1979 by Wisconsin
Job Service.

level of employment than the national average. Two-thirds of Milwaukee retail establishments employ less than 10 people each. Only three establishments—department stores—employ more than 1,000 workers each. The largest category of retail sales is food and drink, accounting for over 20 percent of the total. Although typical retail establishments are small, metropolitan Milwaukee was served predominantly by two large local supermarket chains, rather than, as in many metropolitan areas, regional or national supermarket chains. One of these chains has been instrumental in developing two of the seven large regional shopping centers within the metropolitan area and also operates a local chain of intermediate-sized department stores. In 1983, the supermarkets of that chain were taken over by a nationwide organization.

Transportation Functions

Milwaukee has been a major Great Lakes port from its beginnings as an urban settlement, although the role of the port has substantially diminished since the 1960s. The character of the water-borne commerce of the port has substantially changed, from great diversity to concentration on a few specialized types of traffic. In spite of this decline, the port continues to be a major factor in the economic base of the region. It is directly and indirectly responsible for several thousand jobs. A number of the area's industries depend upon the port for access to import and export markets.

Internal movement of *general* or *package freight* within the Great Lakes essentially disappeared in the 1930s and 1940s, and Milwaukee, like other Great Lakes ports, has virtually none. Traffic across Lake Michigan depended heavily upon ferries. The last passenger and package-freight cross-lake carrier terminated operations at Milwaukee in 1970, and railroad-car ferries, operated by two railroads between Milwaukee and western Michigan, ended in the 1980s. These changes deprived the region of its last freight, passenger, and automobile service across the lake, and necessitated movement, commonly involving substantial additional distances, around the end of Lake Michigan, principally through the congested Chicago gateway. The existence of the ferry services had placed southeastern Wisconsin on a rate parity with Chicago—in effect offering Milwaukee industries and shippers the 85 mi (137 km) of shipping between Milwaukee and Chicago on long-distance freight at no extra charge—but with the trend toward deregulation of railroad and interstate truck service, the lack of ferry service has become much less important.

With the enlargement of the St. Lawrence Seaway in 1959, large numbers of medium-sized ocean-going ships called at Milwaukee during the eight-month open navigation season. For a decade, general cargo liners, connecting Milwaukee with overseas ports on all continents, moved a large variety of materials and manufactured goods. In anticipation of the St. Lawrence Seaway, the city, from 1930 on, developed a modern complex of terminal facilities on Jones Island, including both general cargo and bulk terminals. Subsequently the older port areas downtown and in the lower Menomonee Valley declined. Eventually, however, with the development of modern highways, including the interstate highways, several of which serve Milwaukee, of large-scale intercity trucking, of intermodal containerization and rail piggyback, and because of the increasing size of ocean-going ships, many of which are physically and economically unable to utilize the Seaway, the port of Milwaukee, along with other Great Lakes ports, declined.

Nevertheless, the port remains an invaluable asset to the city and region. It is increasingly a specialized port, concentrating on a limited range of types of cargoes, including "heavy-lift" and "project" cargoes, which are too heavy or bulky to move long distances overland by rail or highway. Many industries in the Milwaukee region would be seriously handicapped, and would possibly move to more favorable coastal locations in other cities, if opportunities to ship and receive such cargo through the port of Milwaukee were eliminated. The port is equipped with a number of large cranes for handling heavy machinery, as well as containers. Entire shiploads of mining, construction, earth-moving, and agricultural machinery, as well as general cargo, are handled on Jones Island. Liquid cargoes also move through the port. Formerly, petroleum products were a major

inbound cargo. Later, however, direct pipelines from Chicago-area refineries reduced the shipment of petroleum products, and some of the tank farms in the port area have been dismantled. A liquid-cargo pier, however, continues to receive many specialized chemicals in tanker ships to and from domestic and overseas origins and destinations. Salt is another bulk cargo moving through the port, originating mainly in Canadian areas around the Great Lakes; it is stored in the port area and used to melt snow and ice from the streets and highways of Milwaukee city and county.

Milwaukee's port is one of several western Great Lakes ports that participate heavily in the export of grain. Two private grain elevators handle this product, and in the early 1980s a large public elevator was under consideration. The grain movement is mainly from southern Wisconsin, eastern Iowa, and northern Illinois. It consists principally of corn, with an increasing volume of other agricultural produce such as sunflower seeds. Overseas destinations include Europe, the Far East, and—from time to time—the Soviet Union. This traffic is handled through the St. Lawrence Seaway. The port of Milwaukee accommodates vessels of the largest size that can transit the Seaway. Such ships, "lakers," can handle up to about 26,000 tn (23,582 mt) each. Lakers transfer cargoes to larger ocean-going bulk-carrying ships in the lower St. Lawrence; these ocean-going "salties" commonly top off with additional grain in the lower St. Lawrence, because drafts are restricted above Montreal.

Milwaukee is served by three railroads, each of which is primarily a regional midwestern carrier, rather than an interregional trunk line. All three have lines that connect Chicago with Minneapolis–St. Paul and pass through Milwaukee. In the early 1980s the Milwaukee Road, which handles the greater proportion of the Milwaukee region's rail freight, reduced its route mileage by well over half, including eliminating a line to the Pacific Northwest. Its main line, Chicago to Minneapolis–St. Paul, however, was substantially rehabilitated and constitutes one of the Midwest's principal rail corridors, passing through Milwaukee. The Chicago and North Western Railway, Milwaukee's second most important rail system, is also a regional midwestern carrier. The third of the Milwaukee region's railroads, the Soo Line, is a subsidiary of the Canadian Pacific.

For many years, the principal railroad employer in Milwaukee has been the Milwaukee Road's yards and shops located in the lower Menomonee Valley. At one time major maintenance for the entire system took place there, and the shops built both passenger and freight rolling stock. More recently, with shrinkage of the rail system, employment was greatly reduced. Major freight classification was moved to the company's yards in the Chicago district. With reorganization and possible merger, the extent of future railroad activity and employment in the Menomonee Valley was uncertain in the early 1980s. If the railroad yards and shops are closed, a substantial amount of land will become available for nonrailroad use in a relatively central location.

Milwaukee was formerly a major center of railroad passenger service. The Chicago–Milwaukee–Twin Cities corridor was, between the 1930s and 1960s, a world-famous demonstration area for frequent high-speed passenger trains. These included the Milwaukee Road's fleet of "Hiawathas" and the North Western's "400s," which attracted attention similar to that given to the Japanese high-speed trains of the 1960s and later. Amtrak—the National Railroad Passenger Corporation—greatly reduced passenger service in 1972 to levels even lower than those to which it had been previously reduced. In 1983 Amtrak provided only three daily trains in each direction between Milwaukee and Chicago and one to the Twin Cities and the Pacific Northwest.

The Milwaukee region is overwhelmingly dependent, both internally and externally, upon highway transportation for the movement of people and goods; only about 4 percent of all trips are made on public transportation. Most of the Milwaukee region's express highways were constructed in the 1960s, relatively late, as part of the Federal System of Interstate and Defense Highways, 90 percent of which were federally funded.

In terms of air traffic, the Milwaukee SMSA is classified as a "medium hub," ranking about thirty-fifth among the metropolitan areas of the United States in annual passenger traffic by scheduled airlines. Milwaukee County's Billy Mitchell Field, in southern Milwaukee, is southeastern Wisconsin's only air-carrier airport. Nevertheless, air service at Milwaukee is less than would be expected because Chicago's O'Hare International Airport—the world's busiest—is only 70 mi (113 km) from Mitchell Field and draws passengers from the Milwaukee region.

THE SERVICE AND UTILITY INFRASTRUCTURE

Milwaukee is a major center of medical practice. In addition to the usual private and public clinics and medical and dental practitioners, Milwaukee County operates a large general hospital, and several large clusters of hospitals and clinics are found throughout the city and metropolitan area. The "county institutions," including public and private medical organizations as well as other public institutions, occupy an extensive campus west of the city. Recent studies have indicated that there is a large surplus of hospitals in Milwaukee County. Several of them have merged, in some instances moving to new facilities in suburban areas and closing older, obsolete central city facilities.

Residents in metropolitan Milwaukee have had somewhat more education than the national average. The 1980 census sample indicated that 71.6 percent of the metropolitan residents completed four years of high school as compared with 66.6 percent for the United States. In addition to public schools, the region has numerous private schools. Both the Roman Catholics and the Lutherans provide extensive parochial school systems. In 1980, about 63 percent of the metropolitan area's population attending school—kindergarten through high school—were in public schools and 37 percent in private schools, predominantly parochial. In the city of Milwaukee, many inner-city schools have had declining enrollments as the population has shifted to outer areas; some schools have been closed, not without considerable turmoil in their neighborhoods. During the 1970s, Milwaukee, like other northern cities, faced white resistance to racial integration.

Colleges and universities provide a considerable variety of programs. The University of Wisconsin–Milwaukee is the largest (26,000 enrollment) and one of only two public institutions offering Ph.D. programs in the state. Marquette University, a prestigious, century-old Roman Catholic institution, has about 14,000 students. Other private universities and colleges in and near Milwaukee include Carroll College in Waukesha; Carthage in Kenosha; Cardinal Stritch, Mount Mary, and Alverno, Roman Catholic colleges in Milwaukee County; and Concordia, a Lutheran institution in Mequon. The Milwaukee School of Engineering, located in downtown Milwaukee, is a well-known institution. In addition, Milwaukee has an extensive system of community colleges, the largest of which is the Milwaukee Area Technical College (MATC). Several of its campuses enroll about 70,000 students in two-year and adult education programs, mostly part-time. The MATC also operates the two public television channels that serve the metropolitan area.

Other noteworthy cultural institutions serving metropolitan Milwaukee include a world-class symphony orchestra, local opera and ballet companies, a repertory theater, and several chamber music organizations. Milwaukee's Performing Arts Center, constructed in 1970 on the fringe of the downtown, contains a large opera theater, a concert hall, and a smaller

theater—all of which are used by several of these groups. The restored Pabst Theater, built in 1893 and considered an architectural landmark typical of the period, is also used by many of these organizations as well as by touring theatrical and musical companies.

Milwaukee provides its residents and visitors with major athletic events. In addition to collegiate sports, typified by Marquette's famous Warriors basketball team, major league sports are fully represented by the Brewers baseball team, which plays in the County Stadium on the city's West Side; the Bucks professional basketball team, which uses the arena in the complex of sport and convention facilities known as MECCA; the Green Bay Packers, which annually play some of their home games in Milwaukee's County Stadium; and the Admirals ice-hockey team.

The Milwaukee SMSA has fewer problems than many other large metropolitan areas in providing utility services to its residents and businesses. Lake Michigan furnishes a virtually unlimited supply of fresh water, which is treated at a city lakefront plant, distributed throughout the municipal area, and sold to some of the suburbs. Other urban areas in the metropolitan region use water from surface streams, ground supplies, and deep aquifers. Some of the larger industries have their own access to underground water supplies.

Electric power is supplied by a utility company serving southeastern Wisconsin. In 1981 the Wisconsin Electric Power Company produced 59 percent of its energy using coal, 36 percent using nuclear power, 3 percent using hydroelectric power, and only 2 percent using gas and oil. Two of the largest coal-fired plants are on the Lake Michigan shore: one at Oak Creek in southern Milwaukee County and one north of Milwaukee, at Port Washington in Ozaukee County. A coal-fired plant is also located in the lower Menomonee Valley, and, in 1983, another was under construction and partially operational at Pleasant Prairie in Kenosha County. Coal utilized in these plants originates in central Illinois and in the western United States, brought in mainly by train, although the Port Washington plant also receives coal by lake vessel from Illinois, transferred from rail in South Chicago. The Milwaukee SMSA has no nuclear plants, although the area gets power from one at Point Beach, about 85 mi (137 km) north of Milwaukee. The local utility also sometimes receives peak-load power from the Zion, Illinois, plant of the Commonwealth Edison Company.

Concern for environmental quality is having major impacts upon collection, treatment, and disposal of Milwaukee's wastes. Solid wastes (garbage) disposal is a major problem, and the spread of urban development has greatly reduced the possible areas for landfill. In 1983 the location of additional areas for sanitary fill was a major issue in several portions of the metropolitan area. Sewage is a more immediate and serious problem. The 1982 reorganization of the Metropolitan Milwaukee Sewerage District, roughly coterminous with Milwaukee County, involved a conflict of interests between the city of Milwaukee and the suburban areas within the county. The reconstituted agency faces the problem of planning and implementing an enormous program of construction and subsequent operation of new facilities.

In a successful suit, Chicago claimed that Milwaukee sewage polluted Chicago's Lake Michigan source of water. Approximately 26 sq mi (68 sq km) of the older portions of Milwaukee and the suburban village of Shorewood are served by combined storm and sanitary sewers, which lead to a treatment plant that was opened in 1925 at the north end of Jones Island. During times of high runoff, such as during and after summer thunderstorms and spring snowmelts, the plant has insufficient capacity to treat the combined system. The resulting overflow is directly dumped into Lake Michigan, thereby creating pollution that considerably exceeds federal standards. To meet these standards the sewerage district must select one of two alternatives: either provide separate storm and sanitary sewer systems throughout the 26-sq-mi (68-sq-km) area or provide a system of deep tunnels, generally about 300 ft (90 m) below the average land surface, to store the storm runoff and release it gradually in amounts that would not tax the treatment plant, which must also be expanded.

MILWAUKEE'S FUTURE

Metropolitan Milwaukee, like most large and medium-sized metropolitan areas of the industrialized northeastern and midwestern regions of the United States, faces the prospect of little or no growth of population and employment in the foreseeable future. The challenge is to find adequate substitutes for declining industries to support a stable or perhaps declining population. In addition, emphasis must be placed on the quality of life, rather than on just making a living, which was the more characteristic approach prior to the 1960s.

If present trends continue, Milwaukee's future population will consist of more older and fewer young people. Services will be more important than manufacturing. Nevertheless, the city, and more especially the region, must attract the types of industrial and commercial firms that can furnish adequate employment and provide the facilities and amenities that the changing population demands or face a continuing long-term attrition.

Metropolitan Milwaukee continues to face some disadvantages in its geographic situation: Located on the western side of Lake Michigan, it is separated from the largest concentration of markets, industrial customers, and population; it is necessary to go around the lake to reach many complementary regions; the proximity to Chicago has a "shadow effect" on the metropolitan economy; and the climate is severe during much of the year. These negative conditions may increasingly affect Milwaukee's prospects for the future.

Milwaukee also has some outstanding advantages. Its cultural life is much more dynamic and interesting than it was a few decades ago. Its population is diversified, and cultural institutions and activities attract many people to the city and region. The city's and region's cultural and ethnic heritage is being maintained, illustrated by attempts to preserve and restore older buildings and neighborhoods and to convert otherwise obsolescent structures to new and economically productive use. Civic events such as the annual Summerfest, the Folk Fair, and ethnic festivals, have become increasingly popular. This diversity enhances not only the quality of life but also the economic base of the region.

As in most metropolitan areas, outward growth has exacerbated many physical, social, and political problems. The central city must maintain basic facilities and institutions at the same time that its financial ability to pay for these services is reduced by the out-migration of businesses and higher-income people. School closings, for example, are inevitably local political issues. The changing population of many inner-city neighborhoods has been accompanied by conflicts and tensions.

In the suburban areas, direction and control of growth is a common issue. An increasing population requires more facilities and services, but some areas resist growth. The fragmentation of the region into many local governments, both general purpose and special function, make the development and implementation of regional planning very difficult. The central city is often pitted against suburbs—as in the case of the organization of the recently created sewerage agency—and suburbs may conflict with each other. The urbanized region very often has different interests than the rest of the state, which is predominantly rural.

Several major civic bodies and official agencies have been active in studying, and in some cases implementing, policies for the future of the city and region. The city of Milwaukee's Department of City Development operates public housing projects and performs other services, and is re-

sponsible for developing and, in part, implementing a comprehensive plan for the city. Most suburban communities and counties have planning agencies, and the Southeastern Wisconsin Regional Planning Commission (SEWRPC) is concerned with the whole urban region. Created in 1960, this agency is a comprehensive planning agency for the study and development of plans for seven counties of southeastern Wisconsin. It is the designated agency under the federal Demonstration Cities and Metropolitan Development Act of 1966 and Directive A-95 of the U.S. Department of Housing and Urban Development to pass upon all major projects and proposals leading to a mandated comprehensive plan for the region. This plan includes land use, transportation, housing, air and water quality, open-space preservation, and many other mandated features. The agency actually has no real governmental powers, but it has considerable clout, especially in areas in which participation in implementing plans involves federal agencies. The federal government has provided much of its financial support, but local support sources are also important. With reduced federal funding in the early 1980s, the future of SEWRPC's many activities is in doubt.

Several civic groups have been, and continue to be, actively concerned with the future of metropolitan Milwaukee. The Metropolitan Milwaukee Association of Commerce promotes business and serves as a central agency—as does SEWRPC—for information and publicity. The Greater Milwaukee Committee, composed of business leaders, has promoted many civic improvements and supported the usual complement of service clubs and organizations. For over 30 years, the Research Clearing House of metropolitan Milwaukee has brought together the business, governmental, academic, and media people who have been conducting and utilizing research on the region. In a 2-year (1981–1982) program, the Goals for Greater Milwaukee 2000, Inc., involved several hundred professional and civic-minded individuals who, after soliciting views of the broader public, recommended policies and actions for the future of the region.

The lack of a single official government to implement regional plans is a major problem. Milwaukee's morning newspaper has long advocated the formation of a metropolitan government, but, as elsewhere, the idea is not popular among conservatives and has little support from the public. Nevertheless, the concept of metropolitanism is better known now than previously. Many public, quasi-public, and private agencies and groups are organized on a metropolitan basis.

In summary, metropolitan Milwaukee's problems are typical of other medium-sized and large, older metropolitan areas in the Northeast and Midwest, yet the special characteristics of its people and geography could result in a different future from that of other places. With successful adaptation to a no-growth future, Milwaukee and its metropolitan area must be increasingly concerned with its quality of life. If adequate employment can be provided to substitute for the declining employment in many of the area's traditional industries, Milwaukee may retain and enhance its status as a desirable place to work and live.

SELECTED REFERENCES

Alden, William C. *The Quaternary Geology of Southeastern Wisconsin*. Washington: U.S. Geological Survey, Professional Paper 106, 1918.

Anderson, Byron. *A Bibliography of Master's Theses and Doctoral Dissertations on Milwaukee Topics*. Madison: State Historical Society of Wisconsin, 1981.

Anderson, Harry H., and Frederick I. Olson. *Milwaukee: At the Gathering of the Waters*. Tulsa, Okla.: Continental Heritage Press, 1981.

Austin, H. Russell. *The Milwaukee Story: The Making of an American City*. Milwaukee: The Milwaukee Journal, 1946.

Barrett, G. Vincent, and John P. Blair. *Industrial Development Potential*. Milwaukee: Management Research Center, School of Business Administration, University of Wiscon-

sin–Milwaukee, 1976.

Beaverstock, Frances, and Robert Stuckert, eds. *The Metropolitan Milwaukee Fact Book: 1970*. Milwaukee: The Urban Observatory, 1972.

Berkman, Herman G. *The Delineation and Structure of Rental Housing Areas*. Madison: Bureau of Business Research, School of Commerce, University of Wisconsin, 1956.

Blair, John P.; G. Vincent Barrett; and Ronald L. Heilmann. *Employment-Related Industrial Development in Milwaukee*. Milwaukee: Management Research Center, School of Business Administration, University of Wisconsin–Milwaukee, 1980.

Blair, John P., and Ronald S. Edari, eds. *Milwaukee's Economy: Market Forces, Community Problems and Federal Policies*. Chicago: Federal Reserve Bank of Chicago, 1978.

Blight Elimination and Urban Redevelopment in Milwaukee. Milwaukee: Report of the Redevelopment Coordinating Committee, 1948.

Bluestone, Barry, and Bennett Harrison. *The Deindustrialization of America*. New York: Basic Books, 1982.

Boroweicki, Barbara. "Geographic Patterns of Ethnic and Linguistic Groups in Wisconsin." In *Studies in Ethnicity: The East European Experience in America,* edited by C. A. Ward et al., pp. 39–67. Boulder, Colo.: East European Monographs, distributed by Columbia University Press, 1980.

Brockel, Harry C., et al. *The Milwaukee River: An Inventory of Its Problems, An Appraisal of Its Potentials*. Milwaukee: Milwaukee River Technical Study Committee, 1968.

Canfield, Joseph M. *TM: The Milwaukee Electric Railway and Light Company*. Chicago: Central Electric Railfans Association, 1972.

Chandler, Alfred. *The Visible Hand: The Managerial Revolution in American Business*. Cambridge: Harvard University Press, 1977.

"Chicago-Milwaukee Corridor." In *Emerging Corridors*, pp. 45–51. Washington, D.C.: National Railroad Passenger Corporation (Amtrak), April 1981.

City of Milwaukee Recreational Facilities Plan 1979–1983. Milwaukee: Department of City Development, 1979.

Conzen, Kathleen Neils. *Immigrant Milwaukee 1836–1860: Accommodation and Community in a Frontier City*. Cambridge: Harvard University Press, 1976.

Cutler, Irving. *The Chicago-Milwaukee Corri-*

dor: A Geographic Study of Intermetropolitan Coalescence. Evanston: Northwestern University, Department of Geography, Studies in Geography No. 9, 1965.

Dorin, Patrick C. *The Milwaukee Road East.* Seattle: Superior Publishing Co., 1978.

Economy of Southeastern Wisconsin. Waukesha: Southeastern Wisconsin Regional Planning Commission, 1972.

Edwards, Ozzie L. "Patterns of Residential Segregation Within a Metropolitan Ghetto." In *Comparative Urban Structure: Studies in the Ecology of Cities,* edited by Kent P. Schwirian, pp. 577–590. Lexington, Mass.: D. C. Heath and Co., 1974.

Fleckner, John A., and Stanley Mallach, eds. *Historical Resources in Milwaukee Area Archives.* Milwaukee: Milwaukee County Historical Society, 1976.

Gavett, Thomas. *Development of the Labor Movement in Milwaukee.* Madison: University of Wisconsin Press, 1965.

General Mitchell Field: 50th Anniversary, A Record of Progress. Milwaukee: Milwaukee County Department of Public Works, Airport Division, 1976.

Greater Milwaukee Committee and Metropolitan Milwaukee Association of Commerce. *A Program for Wisconsin and Milwaukee: How to Create New Jobs in High Technology and Other Manufacturing.* Milwaukee: Greater Milwaukee Committee, 1982.

Greenbelt Towns. Washington, D.C.: Resettlement Administration, 1936.

Gregory, John Goadby. *History of Milwaukee, Wisconsin.* 4 vols. Chicago: S. J. Clarke Publishing Co., 1931.

Guide for Growth: Milwaukee County Park System. Milwaukee: Milwaukee County Park System, 1972.

Gurda, John. *The West End: Merrill Park, Piggsville, and Concordia.* Milwaukee: Milwaukee Humanities Program, 1980.

———. *Bay View, Wisconsin.* Madison: University of Wisconsin Board of Regents, sponsored by the Milwaukee Humanities Program, 1979.

———. *The Latin Community on Milwaukee's Near South Side.* Milwaukee: Milwaukee Urban Observatory, 1976.

Gurda, John, and Sara Sprence Spellman, eds. *A Guide to Ethnic Resources in the Milwaukee Area.* Milwaukee: Ethnic Heritage Project of the Greater Milwaukee Conference on Religion and Urban Affairs, 1977.

Hadley, David W. *Shoreline Erosion in Southeastern Wisconsin.* Madison: Wisconsin Geological and Natural History Survey, Special Report No. 5, 1976.

Hansell, Ch. R., and W.A.V. Clark. "The Expansion of the Negro Ghetto in Milwaukee: A Description and Simulation Model." *Tjidschrift voor Economische en Sociale Geografie,* vol. 61, no. 5 (September-October 1970), pp. 267–277.

Harrison, Bennett, and Sandra Kanter. "The Political Economics of States' Job-Creation Business Incentives." *Journal of the American Institute of Planners,* vol. 44 (October 1978), pp. 424–435.

Huddleston, Jack R., and Fred Schein. *Economic Change and the Urban Poor: An Analysis of Changes in the Milwaukee Low Income Area and the SMSA.* Madison: State Planning Office, Department of Administration, 1976.

Korman, Gerd. *Industrialization, Immigrants and Americanizers: The View from Milwaukee, 1866–1921.* Madison: State Historical Society of Wisconsin, 1967.

Kuzniewski, Anthony J. "Milwaukee's Poles, 1866–1918: The Rise and Fall of a Model Community." *Milwaukee History, Milwaukee County Historical Society,* vol. 1, nos. 1 and 2 (Spring and Summer 1978), pp. 13–25.

Larsen, Lawrence H. "Chicago's Midwest Rivals: Cincinnati, St. Louis, and Milwaukee." *Chicago History, Chicago Historical Society,* vol. 5, no. 3 (Fall 1976), pp. 141–151.

Levathes, Louise. "Milwaukee: More than Beer." *National Geographic Magazine,* vol. 158, no. 2 (August 1980), pp. 180–201.

Levine, Marilyn M. *Milwaukee Reports—A Bibliography.* Milwaukee: Milwaukee Urban Observatory, 1970.

Levine, Marilyn M., and Miriam G. Palay, eds. *Milwaukee Reports,* Cumulated Supplement 1970–1973. Milwaukee: Milwaukee Urban Observatory, 1974.

Malone, Frank. "C&NW: Flying High as Rival Roads Flounder." *Railway Age,* vol. 181, no. 14 (July 28, 1980), pp. 83 ff.

Mandelker, Daniel R. "Urban Conflict in Urban Renewal: The Milwaukee CRP Experience." *Law and Social Order, Arizona State Law Journal,* no. 4 (1971), pp. 634–679.

Marchetti, Peter. "Runaways and Takeovers: Their Effect on Milwaukee's Economy." *Ur-*

banism Past and Present, vol. 10 (Summer 1980), pp. 1–11.

Marshall, Ray. "Implications of Labor Market Theory for Employment Policy." In *Manpower Research and Labor Economics*, edited by G. Swanson and J. Michelson. Beverly Hills, Calif.: Sage, 1979.

Mayer, Harold M. "The Reuse of Redundant Transportational Land: The Central Milwaukee Lakefront." *Proceedings of Applied Geography Conferences*, vol. 4 (1981), pp. 6–22.

———. "The Chicago-Milwaukee Corridor," and "The City of Milwaukee." In *Landscapes of Wisconsin: A Field Guide,* edited by Barbara Zakrzewski-Barowiecki, pp. 77–116. Washington, D.C.: Association of American Geographers, 1975.

McArthur, Shirley de Fresne. *North Point South: An Architectural and Historical Inventory.* Milwaukee: Land Ethics, and Water Tower Landmark Trust, 1978.

Meadows, Richard, and J. Mitrisin. "A National Development Bank: Survey and Discussion of the Literature on Capital Shortages and Employment Changes in Distressed Areas." In *New Tools for Economic Development,* edited by George Sternlieb and D. Listoken, pp. 84–143. New Brunswick, N.J.: Rutgers Center for Urban Policy Research, 1981.

Miller, Sally. "Milwaukee: Of Ethnicity and Labor." In *Socialism and the Cities*, edited by Bruce Stave. Port Washington, N.Y.: Kennikat Press, 1975.

Milwaukee's Lakefront: A Precious Heritage, A Vital Resource. Milwaukee: Lakefront Recreational Development Task Force, March 1978.

Milwaukee River Watershed Study. 2 vols. Waukesha: Southeastern Wisconsin Regional Planning Commission, 1970 and 1971.

Mortimer, Clifford H. *The Lake Michigan Pollution Case: A Review and Commentary on the Limnological and Other Issues.* Milwaukee: Sea Grant Institute and the Center for Great Lakes Studies, 1981.

Natural Resources of Southeastern Wisconsin. Waukesha: Southeastern Wisconsin Regional Planning Commission, Planning Report No. 5, 1963.

Nelson, Daniel. *Managers and Workers: Origins of the New Factory System in the United States, 1880–1920.* Madison: University of Wisconsin Press, 1975.

"New Shortline Railroad Activity in Southeastern Wisconsin." Southeastern Wisconsin Regional Planning Commission *Newsletter,* vol. 20, no. 3 (May-June 1980), pp. 28–32.

O'Reilly, Charles T. *The Inner Core-North: A Study of Milwaukee's Negro Community.* Milwaukee: University of Wisconsin Extension Division, 1963.

Ottensman, John R. "Changes in Accessibility to Employment in an Urban Area: Milwaukee, 1927–1963." *The Professional Geographer*, vol. 32, no. 4 (November 1980), pp. 421–430.

———. *The Changing Spatial Structure of American Cities.* Lexington, Mass.: Lexington Books, 1975.

Perrin, Richard W. E. *Milwaukee Landmarks.* Rev. and enlarged. Milwaukee: Milwaukee Public Museum, 1979.

Regional Land Use-Transportation Study. 3 vols. Waukesha: Southeastern Wisconsin Regional Planning Commission, Planning Report No. 7, 1965 and 1966.

Regional Sanitary Sewerage System Plan for Southeastern Wisconsin. Waukesha: Southeastern Wisconsin Regional Planning Commission, 1974.

Residential Land Subdivision in Southeastern Wisconsin. Waukesha: Southeastern Wisconsin Regional Planning Commission, Technical Report No. 6, 1971.

Richards, Curtis William. *Differential Traffic Changes on Transit Routes in Milwaukee, 1950 to 1975.* Milwaukee: Center for Urban Transportation Studies, University of Wisconsin–Milwaukee, 1977.

Schenker, Eric. *The Port of Milwaukee: An Economic Review.* Madison: University of Wisconsin Press, 1967.

Schenker, Eric; Harold M. Mayer; and Harry C. Brockel. *The Great Lakes Transportation System.* Madison: University of Wisconsin Sea Grant College Program, Technical Report No. 230, 1976.

Schmandt, Henry; John Goldbach; and Donald Vogel. *Milwaukee: A Contemporary Urban Profile.* New York: Praeger Publishers, 1971.

Short Range Action Housing Program for Southeastern Wisconsin. Waukesha: Southeastern Wisconsin Regional Planning Commission, Technical Report No. 21, 1972.

Simon, Roger D. *The City-Building Process: Housing and Services in New Milwaukee Neighborhoods, 1880–1910.* Philadelphia:

Transactions of the American Philosophical Society, 1978.

———. "Foundations for Industrialization, 1835–1880." *Milwaukee History, Milwaukee County Historical Society*, vol. 1, nos. 1 and 2 (Spring and Summer 1978), pp. 36–56.

Soils of Southeastern Wisconsin. Waukesha: Southeastern Wisconsin Regional Planning Commission, Planning Report No. 8, 1966.

Soltow, Lee. *Patterns of Wealthholding in Wisconsin Since 1850.* Madison: University of Wisconsin Press, 1971.

Still, Bayrd. *Milwaukee: The History of a City.* Madison: State Historical Society of Wisconsin, 1948; 2nd edition, 1965.

Transit-Related Socioeconomic, Land Use and Transportation Conditions and Trends in the Milwaukee Area. Waukesha: Southeastern Wisconsin Regional Planning Commission, Technical Report No. 23, 1980.

Transportation Improvement Program for the Kenosha, Milwaukee and Racine Urbanized Areas in Southeastern Wisconsin. Waukesha: Southeastern Wisconsin Regional Planning Commission, 1981.

U.S., Bureau of the Census. *1980 Census of Population and Housing Supplementary Report, PHC80-S1-1, Provisional Estimates of Social, Economic, and Housing Characteristics, States and Selected Standard Metropolitan Statistical Areas.* Washington, D.C.: U.S. Government Printing Office, 1982.

———. *1980 Census of Population and Housing, Advance Reports, PHC80-V-51, Wisconsin, Final Population and Housing Unit Counts.* Washington, D.C.: U.S. Government Printing Office, 1981.

U.S., Congress, Joint Economic Committee. *Hearings: The Economic Future of Metropolitan Milwaukee.* 97th Cong., 1st Sess., October 8 and 9, 1981. Washington, D.C.: U.S. Government Printing Office, 1981.

U.S., Department of the Interior. *National Urban Recreation Study, Milwaukee/Racine.* Washington, D.C.: U.S. Government Printing Office, 1977.

Vegetation of the Lake Michigan Shoreline in Wisconsin. Madison: University of Wisconsin Sea Grant Communications Office, Advisory Report No. 420, 1978.

Walsh, Margaret. *The Manufacturing Frontier: Pioneer Industry in Antebellum Wisconsin, 1830–1860.* Madison: State Historical Society of Wisconsin Press, 1972.

Water Quality and Flow of Streams in Southeastern Wisconsin. Waukesha: Southeastern Wisconsin Regional Planning Commission, 1967.

Young, Mary Ellen, and Wayne Attoe. *Places of Worship—Milwaukee.* Milwaukee: Past-Futures, 1977.

Zimmerman, H. Russell. *The Heritage Guidebook: Landmarks and Historical Sites in Southeastern Wisconsin.* Milwaukee: Heritage Books, Inland Heritage Corporation, 1976.

INDEX

Acid rain, 39, 40(fig.)

Adams, Henry, 77

Adams County, 42
  Glacial Lake Wisconsin in, 38, 42–43

Agricultural products processing, 79, 142, 163, 163(table), 164, 164(table), 179, 191(table), 192
  brewing. *See* Brewing/breweries
  canning, 84, 136, 138, 138(table)
  dairy products, 79, 80, 80(table), 126, 127–128, 129, 134–135, 135(fig.), 136
  flour milling, 12, 78, 79, 80, 80(table)

Agriculture, 40, 47, 49, 127, 168
  amount/location of pastures/croplands, 16(fig.), 49, 60, 63, 84, 85(fig.), 86, 104, 106, 107(table), 110, 111, 112, 162
  in Central Plain, 43, 129, 136, 138
  and climate/storms, 28, 87, 104, 111, 130–131, 131(fig.), 132, 142
  diversified, 125–126. *See also* Livestock, -crop farming
  and early settlers, 56, 58–60, 62–67, 69–70, 72–75
  in Eastern Ridges and Lowlands, 45
  and ethnic groups, 69, 70
  mechanization, 124, 138–139, 142
  and migrant labor, 138–139, 139(fig.), 142
  and the national land survey, 59
  in northern Wis., 42, 73, 74(fig.), 85, 87, 101, 103–115, 116, 125
  in southern Wis., 73, 124, 124(table), 125–145, 152, 179
  subsistence, 124, 124(table)
  and suburban areas, 84
  in Western Upland, 44
  and wetlands, 49, 139–140
  See also Agricultural products processing; Dairying/dairy products; Soils, and agriculture; *individual crops*

Airports, 153, 161(table), 171, 201

Alcoholic beverages
  consumption, 9, 11, 12(fig.)
  and Indians, 53, 54, 56
  production, 9, 11(table), 12, 13(fig.), 14(table), 80, 80(table)
  See also individual beverages

Alfalfa, 44, 48

Allen-Bradley Company, 194(table), 195, 196(photo)

Allis-Chalmers Corporation, 169, 194(table), 195, 197

Allouez, Claude, 53

Alverno College, 202

American Breeders Association, 130

American Fur Company, 53

American Manufacturing Belt, 93, 160, 164, 165–168, 169, 170, 172–173

American Motors Corporation, 169, 195

American Protective League, 69

Amnicon River, 39–40

Antigo, 104

A. O. Smith Corporation, 169, 194(table)

Apostle Islands National Park, 40

Apple River, 119

Appleton, 160, 161(table)

Architecture, 8, 65, 68, 72, 89, 109, 180(photo), 181, 187, 197
  barns, 17, 18(fig.), 19, 20(fig.), 21, 68(photo), 76, 133, 134
  log buildings, 8, 62, 65, 76
  Prairie School of, 20(fig.), 21, 22
  See also Houses/housing; Wright, Frank Lloyd

Ariens (company), 169

Ashland, 40, 73, 76, 78, 99, 104, 115(fig.), 164

Ashland County, 41, 76, 99

Aspen, 47(fig.), 48

Atlantic Mine, 102
Austrians, 103, 104(fig.), 180
Automobile Belt, 195

Babcock and Wilcox Company, 167
Babcock milk tester, 126
Bad River (Indian reservation), 88, 88(fig.),
    90(fig.)
Baptists, 183
Baraboo, 44
Baraboo Range, 34, 35(table), 43–44
Barley, 126, 162
Barns, 17, 18(fig.), 19, 20(fig.), 21, 68(photo),
    76, 93, 132, 133–134, 134(fig.), 142,
    143(figs.)
  converted to restaurants, 19, 20(photo)
Barron County, 42
Barron Hills, 41
Bars/taverns, 11, 68, 96, 101, 102–103
Basswood, 46, 47, 47(fig.), 48
Bastian, Robert, 22
Bayfield County, 76, 86
Bay View, 194
Beans, 45, 136, 138, 138(table), 139
Beaver Dam, 138
Bedrock, 30, 34(fig.), 35(table), 36, 39, 42, 43
Beech, 46, 47(fig.)
Beer and malt beverages, 4, 9
  consumption, 9, 11, 12(fig.), 13
  production. See Brewing/breweries;
    individual brewing companies
Beets, 136, 138(table)
  sugar, 139
Belgians, 8, 69–70
  festivals, 71
Belmont, 63
Beloit, 45, 63, 66, 80, 129, 152, 160, 169
Beloit reaper, 124
Benjamin, 101
Bennett Law (1889), 68
Berge, Charles, 144
Berlin, 139
Berry, Brian, 170–171
Best, Jacob, 11
  family, 11, 179
Best brewery, 12, 179. See also Pabst brewery
BIA. See Bureau of Indian Affairs
Billy Mitchell Field, 153, 201
Birch, 46, 47(fig.), 48
Black River, 38, 39–40, 43, 72, 92, 95
Black River Falls, 58
Blacks in Milwaukee, 181, 181(fig.), 182(fig.),
    187
Blatz brewery, 12

Blue Hills, 41
Blue Mounds, 35(table), 36, 44
Bluffs and cliffs, 7, 9, 35(table), 36, 42, 48,
    173, 175(photo)
Board of Immigration (Wis.), 73, 104
Boating, 4, 5, 7–9, 116
Bogs
  cranberry, 140, 140(fig.), 141(fig.), 142
  peat, 39, 140
Bohemians, 126
Bois Brule River, 117
Borchert, John, 157
Boreal riverine empire, 51–56, 65
Boulder Junction, 5, 7
Brandy consumption, 15, 15(fig.)
Brewing/breweries, 9, 11, 11(table), 14, 79,
    162, 179, 194, 194(table), 195
  amount of, 12(fig.), 13(figs.)
  and pasteurization, 11, 12
  production, 9, 11(table), 12(fig.), 13(fig.),
    14(table), 194(table)
  and Prohibition, 12–13, 13(fig.)
  See also individual breweries
Briggs and Stratton Corporation, 169,
    194(table)
Brillion Iron Works, 167
British, 51–55, 56, 62, 63, 65, 65(table), 66,
    68, 97, 103, 104(fig.), 104, 180
  and fur trading, 51–56, 87
Brown County, 69, 164
Brule River, 39–40
Brush, John, 157
Bucyrus-Erie Company, 169, 194(table), 197
Building materials, local, 19, 34, 35(table), 39,
    44
  wood/logs, 48, 62, 64, 93. See also
    Logging/lumbering; Wood products
Bureau of Indian Affairs (BIA), 87–89
Buttes, mesas, outliers, 41–42, 43(photo)

Cabbage, 136, 138(table)
California, 11(table), 127, 131, 136
Calumet County, 167, 169
Camp Douglas
  bluffs, 35(table), 36, 42
  Castle Rock, 43(photo)
Camping/campgrounds, 4, 5, 7, 9, 48,
    116–117, 121
Canada, 4, 172, 200
  French in Upper (Quebec), 54, 56, 57
  and fur trade, 51, 53, 54, 87
  Montreal, 51, 53
  See also St. Lawrence River/Seaway
Canadians, 51, 53, 54, 103, 104, 180

Canning, 84, 136, 138, 138(table)
Cardinal Stritch College, 202
Carroll College, 202
Carrots, 136, 138(table)
Carthage College, 202
Catholics, 68, 90, 91(fig.), 183, 202
Caves, 44
  Cave of the Mounds, 44
CBD. *See* Milwaukee, central business district
Cedarburg, 169, 173
Cedar River, 72
Central Cooperative Exchange, 76
Central (Sand) Plain/lowlands region, 41(fig.),
  42–43, 84, 129, 136, 138, 172
Cheese, 17, 79, 126
  Belt/regions, 84, 134, 135, 135(fig.), 136
  processing, 79, 80, 80(table), 126, 127–128,
    129, 134–135, 135(fig.), 136
  varieties, 70, 136
  See also Dairying/dairy products
Cheney, Mamah Borthwick, 21
Chequamegon Bay, 53
Chequamegon Resort Hotel, 115(photo)
Cherry trees/cherries, 8, 45, 63, 139
Chicago, 12, 93, 107, 128, 135, 138, 155, 167,
  172, 173, 178, 181, 190, 192, 193,
  193(table), 198–201, 203
  Federal Reserve Bank, 198
  and Frank Lloyd Wright, 21, 22
  O'Hare International Airport, 201
  South, 193, 203
  tourists to Wis., 4, 5(fig.), 7, 9, 72, 85, 115,
    116, 117, 118(fig.), 173
  Union Stock Yards, 179
Chippewa County, 42, 69, 107, 110
Chippewa Falls (city), 58, 80, 96, 96(fig.)
  Cray Research in, 170–171
  Leinenkugel brewery, 11, 14
  Northern Wisconsin Tobacco Exposition,
    144
Chippewa Indians, 72
Chippewa River, 4, 43, 92, 94(photo), 95
Chippewa Valley Colonization Company, 107,
  107(table)
Chippewa Workingmen's Association, 97
Cities. *See* Urban regions; *individual cities*
Civil War, 103, 124, 125, 148, 179
Clark County, 41, 42, 110
Climate, 31(table), 42, 171, 195, 203
  and agriculture, 28, 87, 104, 111, 130–131,
    131(fig.), 132, 142
  effects of water on, 25
  precipitation, 26–29, 30(fig.), 31–33(figs.),
    111

seasons, 24–25
storms, 24, 27–29, 29(figs.), 132
temperature, 24–27, 29, 31–33(figs.)
variability of, 24–25, 27, 29–30
and vegetation, 45–46, 49
winds and airmasses, 25–26, 26(fig.), 27,
  30(fig.)
Clintonville, 138, 169
Clover/clover seed, 107, 111
Coal, 164, 202–203
Cochran, Thomas, 11
Colonization companies, 106–107, 107(table),
  108–112
Columbia County, 138
Commission of Immigration (Wis.), 65–66
Commonwealth Edison Company, 203
Concordia College, 202
Conglomerate (rocks), 34
Cooperatives, 76, 101, 129
Copper. *See under* Mining
Corn, 17, 44, 45, 48, 54, 107, 125, 130, 131,
  132, 134, 136, 138(table)
  Belt, 127, 130, 164
Coulee, 43
Cows. *See* Livestock
Cranberries, 39, 42, 43, 49, 136, 139,
  139(fig.), 140, 140(fig.), 141–142
  Ocean Spray plant, 142
  Wisconsin Cranberry Frost Warning
    Service, 142
Cranmoor, 140
Crawford County, 69, 125
Cray Research, 170–171
Crevasse fillings, 38, 45
Crops. *See individual crops*
Crystalline rocks, 34, 35(table)
Cubans, 182
Cucumbers, 136, 138(table), 139
Cudahy, 197
Cudahy Packing Company, 197
Cuestas, 44–45
Cutover region, 96(fig.)
  agriculture in, 73, 85, 87, 101, 103–115,
    136
  logging/lumbering in, 73, 92–97
Czechoslovakians, 180
  festival, 71

Dairy Belt, 127, 131, 136
Dairying/dairy products, 4, 16–17, 19, 40, 42,
  44, 45, 49, 65, 79, 80(table), 84, 104,
  107, 124, 124(table), 125(fig.), 126–127,
  127(fig.), 128, 128(fig.), 129, 129(fig.),
  130–131, 131(fig.), 132–133, 133(fig.), 134,

134(fig.), 135, 135(fig.), 136, 138, 163. *See also* Cheese; Milk
Dane, 44
Dane County, 44, 45, 63, 69, 70, 125, 136, 164
Danes, 65(table)
Dawes Allotment Act (1887), 87, 89
Deforest farm (Dane County), 125
Delavan, 63
Democratic party, 63, 68
Demonstration Cities and Metropolitan Development Act (1966), 204
De Pere mission, 54
de Souza, Anthony, 86
Devils Lake gorge, 35(table), 36
Devils Lake State Park, 44
Diseases, 49, 56, 185
Dodge County, 45, 67, 136, 138
   Horicon Marsh, 45
Dodgeville, 19
Dolomite, 34, 34(fig.), 35(table), 39, 43, 44
Door County, 5, 7–8, 45
Door Peninsula, 7, 35(table), 44
Douglas County, 76
Driftless Area, 36, 37(fig.), 60, 125
Drott Manufacturing, 169
Drumlins, 37(fig.), 38, 45, 174(fig.)
Duluth, Daniel Greysolon, 53
Dunn County, 42
Durand, Loyal, Jr., 131
Dutch, 65(table), 70
   festival, 71

Eagle River, 42, 162
Eastern Ridges and Lowlands region, 41(fig.), 44–45
Eaton Corporation, 194(table)
Eau Claire, 14, 19, 32(table), 43, 58, 69, 95, 96, 97, 148, 152, 153, 155, 160, 161(table)
Eau Claire County, 42
Economic recessions/depressions, 87, 99, 110, 112, 113(table), 115, 116, 127, 170, 185, 190, 193, 195
Edgerton, 144
Education
   amount of, 183, 186, 201
   and Indians, 87, 90, 92
   institutions and settlement building, 152, 154, 155, 157, 160, 161(table), 162
   and religion, 87, 90, 202
   schools, 87, 90, 92, 101, 105, 181, 183, 201–202, 204
   See also individual colleges and universities

Edward P. Allis Company, 79, 197
Elevation, 40–45
Emigranten (Norwegian newspaper), 69
Empire in Pine, 93
Employment, 152–154, 155, 157, 163, 170–171, 192(table), 203
   in manufacturing. *See* Manufacturing, and employment
   service-sector. *See* Service sector, employment
   and settlement-building trade, 154–155, 157, 160, 161(table)
   See also Labor; Migrant labor; *individual products and industries*
Energy, 153, 162, 164, 170, 202–203
   fuel from forests, 48, 64, 93
   nuclear power, 202–203
   waterpower, 50, 60, 95, 173, 202
   See also Petroleum/petroleum products
Ephraim, 69
   Fyr Bal Festival (Scandinavian), 71
Erie Canal, 63
Erosion, 30, 34, 35(table), 36, 42–44, 49, 140, 173, 175(photo)
Escarpments, 43, 44, 174(fig.)
Eskers, 38, 45, 45(photo)
Espionage Act, 68
Esterly reaper, 124
Ethnic/racial groups
   festivals, 70–73, 179–180
   in Milwaukee, 179–181, 181(fig.), 182, 182(fig.), 183, 187
   neighborhoods, 181–182, 182(fig.), 183, 187
   See also Immigration; Racial conflicts; *individual ethnic/racial groups*
Europe, 53, 93, 125, 130, 200
   explorers from, 49, 51–53
   immigration from, 8, 15, 45, 51, 56–58, 63, 64, 65, 66, 68, 72, 103, 104, 125. *See also individual ethnic groups*
   and New World mercantilism, 54. *See also* Fur trade
Evinrude (company), 169, 194(table)
Explorers, 49, 51–53

Faast, Benjamin F., 106–112
Faast Land Company, 106, 107, 107(table)
Factories. *See* Manufacturing
Falk Corporation, 194(table)
Farm Holiday Association, 127
Farm machinery/mechanization, 124–125, 131, 138–139, 142
   manufacturing, 79, 80(table), 124, 164(table), 167, 168, 169

Federal Building (Milwaukee), 187
Federal System of Interstate and Defense
    Highways, 153, 201
Finland, 73–74, 76
    Finnish Labor party, 74
    Finnish Socialist Federation, 76
    Helsinki, 74
Finney, 101
Finns, 66, 69, 73–75, 75(fig.), 76–77, 103,
    104(fig.), 110
    saunas, 76
Fires, 46–49
    Peshtigo (1871), 48
First Wisconsin Center, 187, 187(photo)
Fish boils/frys, 5, 8, 71
Fishing, 49, 50
    commercial, 8, 192(table)
    recreational, 4, 5, 6(fig.), 7, 7(fig.), 48, 92,
    115–117
Flambeau Ridge, 41
Flambeau River, 117
Flour milling, 12, 78, 79, 80, 80(table), 173,
    179, 195, 197
Folk Fair, 179, 204
Fond du Lac, 5, 148, 152, 160, 169
Fond du Lac County, 45, 138, 173
Fond du Lac Sandstone, 34, 35(table)
Fontana, 19
Forestry Commission (Wis.), 115
Forests, 46, 47, 47(fig.), 49, 53, 76, 84, 85,
    85(map), 93, 95, 104, 115, 119, 148, 164,
    192
    federal/state/county, 48, 115, 119
    fires, 46–49
    fuel from, 48, 64, 93
    for industry, 43, 47–48, 162, 164. See also
    Logging/lumbering; Pulpwood/paper
    industries; Wood products
    for recreation, 40, 42, 45, 48, 84, 115–117,
    119, 121
    See also Northwoods region; individual tree
    varieties
Fort Crawford, 52, 52(fig.), 55, 57
Fort Edward Augustus, 54
Fort Howard, 52, 52(fig.), 55, 58
Fort La Baye, 52(fig.), 54
Fort La Pointe, 52(fig.), 54
Fort McKay, 54
Fort Nicholas, 54
Forts, 52–55
Fort Winnebago, 52, 52(fig.), 55
Foundries, 79, 80, 80(table), 164(table),
    165–168, 182, 193–194
Foust, Brady, 86

Fox Indians, 58, 62
Fox River, 58, 63, 64, 80, 164
Fox River Valley, 44, 53, 152, 160
France, Paris, 54
French
    French Canadians, 54, 65, 65(table), 177
    and fur trading, 51–57, 87, 147
Friendship Mound, 36, 42
Fries, Robert (Empire in Pine), 93
Fur trade, 49, 51–56, 57, 85, 147, 177

Galena-Platteville cuesta, 44
Gedicks, Al, 74
General Electric Company, 194(table)
General Motors Corporation, 169, 194(table),
    196(photo)
Geologic formations. See individual types of
    formations
Geologic history, 30, 34, 34(fig.), 35(table),
    36. See also Glaciation/glacial deposits;
    Physiographic regions
Germania Mine, 99, 102
Germans, 11, 19, 63, 64, 65, 65(table), 66–69,
    67(fig.), 72, 73, 76, 97, 103, 104(fig.), 104,
    110, 126, 138, 145, 164, 179, 180–181,
    181(fig.), 183
    and beer, 11, 162, 179
    festivals, 71
Giddings and Lewis, Inc., 169
Glacial Lake Wisconsin, 38–39, 42–43, 140
Glaciation/glacial deposits, 9, 30, 34, 36,
    36(photo), 37(fig.), 38–39, 41–46, 111,
    127, 140, 173. See also Driftless Area
Goals for Greater Milwaukee 2000, Inc.,
    204–205
Gogebic Range, 34, 35(table), 40, 41, 97,
    98(figs.), 99, 100(figs.), 101–103
Gorges, 43. See also Devils Lake gorge;
    Wisconsin Dells
Government institutions, 192–193
    and settlement building, 152, 154, 155, 157,
    160, 161(table), 162
Grabens, 39
Grafton, 173, 189
Grain, 78, 79, 130, 134, 136, 200. See also
    Flour milling
Grand Avenue Mall (Milwaukee), 188
Grant County, 44, 48
Grasslands, 46, 47(fig.), 48–49, 53
Gratiots (company), 62
Gratiot's Grove, 60
Gravel, 39
Gray-iron foundries, 167
Great Depression, 87, 112, 116, 127, 185

Greater Milwaukee Committee, 204
Great Lakes, 30, 35(table), 50, 51, 63, 95,
    124, 165, 172, 176, 199, 200. *See also*
    Lake Michigan; Lake Superior
Greek festival, 71
Green Bay (city and bay), 8, 32(table), 44,
    53, 56, 69–70, 89, 92, 93, 152, 155, 157,
    160
    ethnic festivals, 71
    Fort Howard in, 52, 52(fig.), 58
    as La Baye, 52(fig.), 53, 54
    land office, 54, 64(fig.), 92
    long lots in, 54, 57, 57(fig.)
    population growth of, 148, 152, 155
    ports, 45, 53
Green Bay Advocate (newspaper), 60
Greenbelt towns, 185
Green County, 44, 70–72, 126, 136
Greendale, 185
Green Lake County, 125

Half Moon Lake, 95
Hardwoods, 46–47, 47(map), 48, 63, 73, 93,
    95, 95(fig.), 103, 164. *See also* Forests;
    individual tree varieties
Harnischfeger Corporation, 169, 194(table),
    197
Harvestores (silos), 132–133
Hay, 17, 19, 49, 63, 107, 125, 130, 131,
    131(fig.), 132, 134
Hayward, 4, 7, 104, 162
    National Freshwater Fishing Hall of Fame,
    7, 7(photo)
    office of the Bureau of Indian Affairs, 89
Health care, 161(table), 162, 171, 201
Heileman brewery, 13–14, 14(table), 179
Hemlock, 46, 95, 95(fig.)
Henry, William (*Northern Wisconsin: A
    Handbook for the Homeseeker*), 73, 104
Hibernia brewery, 14, 14(fig.)
High Cliff, 44. *See also* Lake Winnebago,
    cliffs along
Hills, mounds, and valleys, 30, 34, 35(table),
    36, 38, 39–45
Hispanics, 138, 181–182, 182(fig.), 183, 187
Hixon, Dr., 97
Hoard, William D., 127
Holy Hill, 45
Homestead Act (1862), 59, 69, 93
Homesteading, 59–60, 62
Hops, 162
Horicon Marsh, 45
Horton, Frank, 170–171
Hotels, motels, lodges, 7, 9, 43, 115, 115(fig.),
    120(fig.), 121, 188

Houses/housing, 8, 62, 65, 76, 89, 93, 95–96,
    101, 107–108, 109(fig.), 181, 183,
    184(photos), 185–187, 204
    Frank Lloyd Wright designs, 20(fig.), 21–22
    Native American, 89
    seasonal (vacation), 4, 7, 116–117, 117(fig.),
    118(fig.)
Huber, Joseph, brewery, 14, 14(fig. and table)
Hudson, 58
Hudson's Bay Company, 51, 54
Hunting
    for fur trade, 49, 51–57
    grounds, 53
    for recreation, 48, 115–116
Hurley, 40, 99, 101, 102

Icelanders, 8
Illinois, 107, 130, 160, 200, 203
    border with Wisconsin, 24, 43, 44
    Chicago. *See* Chicago
    lead mining, 56, 60, 62
    settlers to Wis., 60, 63
    tourists to Wis., 4, 5(fig.), 7, 9, 72, 85, 115,
    116, 117, 118(fig.), 173
    Zion power plant, 203
Immigration, 125, 147, 152, 169
    and ethnic persecution, 68
    and government activities, 65–67, 73, 103,
    104, 105(fig.)
    and languages, 66, 68, 69, 72, 76, 77, 104
    Old and New, 66
    and religion, 66–68, 72
    State Board of, 73
    See also Ethnic/racial groups; *individual
    ethnic groups*
Immigration Commission, 103
Income
    median family, 193(table)
    See also Labor, wages; Wealth
Indiana, 107, 194
    Gary industry, 97, 160, 167
    Wabash River long lots, 57
Indian Reorganization Act (1934), 88
Indians, 49, 85, 87, 142
    and fire, 46, 47
    and fur trading, 49, 51–57, 87
    and hunting/fishing, 49, 52, 54, 92
    lands/reservations, 57–58, 58(fig.), 59,
    87–92
    population, 89, 89(table)
    and U.S. government, 55, 58, 59, 87–90,
    92, 177
    and white settlers, 51–58, 58(fig.), 92
    See also Bureau of Indian Affairs;
    individual Indian tribes and reservations

Industrialization, 68, 77–80, 96, 148, 152, 153, 153(fig.), 169, 170
Industrial Valley. *See* Menomonee Industrial Valley
Industrial Workers of the World, 76
Industry
  heavy. *See* Manufacturing; *individual industries*
  light, 170–171
Insurance companies, 161(table), 170, 187, 192(table), 198. *See also individual companies*
International Harvester Company, 167, 195
Interstate 94, 19, 42, 45, 84, 153
Iowa, 58, 73, 107, 128, 130, 200
Iowa County, 44, 136
Irish, 63, 65, 65(table), 66, 68, 103, 104(fig.), 145, 180
Iron Belt (town), 101
Iron County, 41, 42, 76, 99, 101, 128
Iron ore. *See under* Mining
Italians, 66, 103, 104(fig.), 138, 180, 181, 182(fig.)
  festival, 71

Jackson County, Glacial Lake Wisconsin in, 38, 42–43
Jacobs, H., house (F. L. Wright design), 20(fig.)
Jacobsen (company), 169
Janesville, 45, 63, 66, 129, 152, 160, 165, 169
Jefferson, Thomas, 59
Jefferson County, 45, 67, 69
Jenson, Vernon (*Lumber and Labor*), 96–97
Jews, 180, 183
J. I. Case Company, 79, 169, 195
Johnson Wax Building (F. L. Wright design), 22
Johnston Creek, 19
Joliet, Louis, 53
Jones Island, 173, 200, 203
Juneau, Solomon, 177
Juneau County
  Glacial Lake Wisconsin in, 38, 42–43
  Sheep Pasture Mound, 42
Juneautown, 177

Kames, 38, 45
Kaukauna, 169
Kaups, Matti, 76
Kay, Jeanne, 52
Kearney and Trecker Corporation, 169
Kenosha, 66, 76, 142, 152, 160, 167, 169, 195
  Carthage College, 202

Kenosha County, 63, 126, 129, 202
Kentucky, 60, 63, 142
Kettle Moraine, 44–45, 173
Kettles/kettle lakes, 38, 42, 45, 173
Kewaunee County, 93
Kilbourn, Byron, 177
Kilbourntown, 177
King, F. H., 133
Kinnickinnic River, 173, 176
Kohn, Clyde F., 131
Korean War, 99
Krug, August, 11, 179
Krug brewery, 11, 179

La Baye (Green Bay), 54
  Fort, 52(fig.), 54
  mission, 53
  port, 53
Labor
  legislation, 116
  migratory, 138–139, 139(fig.), 142
  movement, 76
  unemployment, 74, 97, 170
  unions/unionists and groups, 68, 69, 77, 97, 100
  unrest, 66, 74–75, 77, 96–97, 182, 195
  wages, 62, 66, 76, 77, 97, 116, 195
  See also Employment; *individual industries*
Labor Advocate (publication), 97
Lac Court Oreilles (Indian reservation), 88, 88(fig.), 90(fig.), 91(fig.)
Lac du Flambeau, 53
Lac du Flambeau (Indian reservation), 88, 88(fig.), 90(fig.)
La Crosse, 44, 93, 155, 160, 161(table)
  G. Heileman brewery in, 13
  Oktoberfest in, 71
  population growth, 148, 152
La Crosse River, 43
Ladish Company, 194(table)
La Fayette County, 44, 63, 136
Lake Delton (lake and city), 9, 10(fig.), 11(fig.), 43
Lake Geneva, 5, 7, 63
  Venetian Festival, 5
Lake Koshkonong, 5
Lake Mendota, 5
Lake Michigan, 4, 8, 63, 92, 147–148, 152, 160, 172, 173, 195, 199, 202, 203
  effect on climate, 25
  and glaciation, 36, 38
  ports, 45, 47–48, 99, 153, 172, 173, 175(photo), 176, 178, 179, 199–200
Lake Mills, 132

Lake Muskego, 69
Lake Oshkosh swamps, 139
Lakes, 42, 43, 45, 60, 85, 95, 173
  effect on climate, 25
  geologic history of, 35(table), 36, 38–39, 41, 42
  and hydroelectric power, 50, 60
  and pollution, 39, 49, 50
  recreation, 4–5, 50, 116. *See also* Fishing; Recreation, water
  size/number of, 30, 49–50, 116
  and summer homes, 116–117
  for transportation. *See* Shipping; Transportation, by water
  See also individual lakes
Lake Superior, 4, 25, 39, 40
  mining regions, 97–103
  ports, 99
Lake Superior Lowland region, 39–40, 41(fig.)
Lake Winnebago, 5, 44
  cliffs along, 35(table), 36, 44
Lake Wisconsin. *See* Glacial Lake Wisconsin
Land offices, 56, 62, 64(fig.), 77, 92, 93
Land O'Lakes, 40
Land survey systems
  French, 54, 57, 57(fig.)
  U.S., 58–60
Langlade County, 93
Languages
  and immigrants, 66, 68, 69, 72, 76, 77, 104
  and Indians, 89, 90
Lannon Stone, 34, 35(table)
Lapham Peak, 45
Latitude, 24–25
Lawson Engine Division, 169
Layton, Frederick, 179
Lead. *See under* Mining
Leather. *See* Tanning/tanneries
Lefse (Norwegian potato bread), 69
Leinenkugel family, 11
Leinenkugel, Jacob, brewery, 11, 14, 14(fig. and table)
Le Seur, Pierre, 53
Lewthwaite, Gordon R., 135
Liberty (township), 69
Lighthouses, 8
Limestone/agricultural lime, 7, 34, 34(fig.), 35(table), 44
Link, Mike, 8
Livestock, 49, 65, 124, 136
  beef cattle, 44, 126, 136
  breeds/breeding, 130
  -crop farming, 125–126, 129, 130–132, 134, 138, 144

feed crops, 125–126, 129–134. *See also* Corn; Hay; Oats
  number of milk cows, 125(fig.), 127–130, 136
  See also Dairying/dairy products
Lodi, 44
Logging/lumbering, 12, 48, 50, 56, 58, 64, 65, 72–73, 76, 77, 79, 80, 80(table), 84, 85, 87, 92, 92(photo), 93, 94(photos), 95, 95(fig.), 96, 96(fig.), 97, 101, 103–105, 112, 116, 148, 152, 163, 165(fig.), 168. *See also* Pulpwood/paper industries; Wood products
Louisiana
  French in, 57
  New Orleans, 57, 60
Lumber and Labor, 96–97
Lumbering. *See* Logging/lumbering
Lutherans, 68, 145, 183, 202

McCaslen Mountain, 41
McGrevch, Arthur, 132
Machinery manufacturing, 79, 80, 163(table), 164(table), 167–169, 190, 193, 194, 194(table)
  agricultural, 79, 80(table), 124, 164(table), 167, 168, 169, 194(table), 195, 200
  construction/mining, 162, 164(table), 167, 168, 169, 194(table), 195, 200
  engines, 79, 80(table), 162, 164(table), 167, 168–169, 194(table), 195
  metalworking, 164(table), 169, 193, 194, 195
  motor vehicles, 80(table), 152, 162, 163, 163(table), 164, 164(table), 165, 168, 169, 170, 190, 191(table), 194(table), 195
MacWhyte Wire Rope Company, 167
Madeline Island, 40, 91(photo)
  mission at La Point, 53
Madison, 22, 31(table), 66, 155–156, 157, 160, 161(table), 164, 169
  population growth of, 148, 152, 155
  as state capitol, 63, 152, 155–156
  as a university town, 152, 155–156, 160. *See also* University of Wisconsin
Maguire, Charlie ("Getting in the Cows"), 15
Maine, 92
Manitou Falls, 40
Manitowoc, 45, 80, 152, 167, 169
Manitowoc Company, 169
Manitowoc County, 69, 93
Manufacturing, 77, 79–80, 80(table), 84, 152, 162–164, 164(table), 165–171, 179, 190, 191(table), 192, 192(table), 197

Belt and centers, 93, 152, 157n, 160, 164, 165–168, 169, 170, 172–173, 178, 190, 195
and employment, 77, 157, 161(table), 163, 163(table), 170, 190, 191(table), 192, 192(table), 194, 194(table), 195, 197, 198, 199(table), 203
location factors, 79, 162–163, 164(table), 168, 169, 170, 173
and settlement building, 160, 161(table), 162
See also individual companies, industries, and products
Maple, 46, 47, 47(fig.), 48, 63
Marathon County, 41, 69, 110
Marinette County, 44
Marquette, Jacques, 53
Marquette University, 202
Marshes. See Wetlands
Marshfield, 104, 162, 164, 171
Martin, Morgan L., 177
MATC. See Milwaukee Area Technical College
Mather, Cotton, 76, 145
Mauston, 42
Meadowbrook, 110
Meat products/packing, 79, 80(table), 163, 164, 164(table), 179
MECCA (Milwaukee Exhibition Convention Center and Arena), 188, 189(photo), 202
Meinig, Donald, 51
Mellen, 28
Menard, Rene, 53
Menasha, 78, 80
Menominee (Indian reservation), 88, 88(fig.), 90(fig.)
Menominee County, 88, 89
Menominee River, 95
Menomonee Falls, 173
Menomonee Indians, 72
Menomonee Industrial Valley, 176, 179, 186, 187(photo), 197, 200, 201, 202
Menomonee River, 173, 175(photo), 176, 197
Menomonie (city), 58, 160
Mercantilism (New World), 54. See also Fur trade
Mercury Marine (company), 168–169
Merrill, 42, 164
Metal industry/products, 79, 80, 80(table), 163(table), 164(table), 165–168, 168(fig.), 169, 170, 179, 190, 191(table), 193, 194
Methodists, 183
Metropolitan Milwaukee Association of Commerce, 204

Metropolitan Milwaukee Sewerage District, 203
Mexicans, 182
Michigan, 74, 75, 138, 173, 199
Detroit, 14, 179, 181, 190, 193(table), 195
mining in Upper, 97, 98(fig.), 99, 101–103
Migrant labor, 138–139, 139(fig.), 142
Military Ridge, 43, 44
Milk, 17, 79, 126–129, 129(fig.), 130–131, 131(fig.), 135–136. See also Dairying/dairy products
Millard, William, 72
Mill Bluff, 42
Miller, Frederick, 11
Miller brewery, 13, 14(table), 15, 179, 194(table)
Milwaukee, 153, 155, 157, 160, 172–205
and agriculture, 78, 93, 135, 138, 192(table), 200
airport, 153, 201
area (size), 72, 172, 178(fig.)
and beer/breweries, 9, 11–14, 79, 179, 194, 194(table), 195
buildings, 22, 187–189(photos)
central business district (CBD), 176, 187, 187(photo), 197, 204
City Hall, 187, 189(photo)
climate, 31(table), 195, 203
cultural institutions/activities, 180, 188, 202, 203–204
Department of City Development, 204
economy, 190–203
ethnic festivals, 70, 71, 177–180, 204
ethnic and racial groups, 65, 66, 70, 179–181, 181(fig.), 182, 182(fig.), 183, 187, 204
and fur trading, 53, 56, 177
Germans in, 11, 65, 70, 179, 180–181
Indians in, 89, 177
industrial and office parks in, 197–198, 198(table)
Jones Island, 173, 200, 203
and manufacturing, 79, 152, 165, 167, 168, 169, 173, 178–179, 182, 190, 191(table), 192, 192(table), 193–194, 194(table), 195
as a metropolitan area, 172, 205
North side, 181, 189
outlying commercial areas, 188–190. See also Suburban regions
population, 147, 148, 152, 155, 160, 172, 178, 178(fig.), 180–181, 181(fig.), 202, 203, 205
and railroads, 69, 77, 78, 107, 173, 176, 178, 186, 187(photo), 189, 197, 199–201, 203

recreation/sports, 173, 177, 202
residential areas/neighborhoods, 178(fig.),
    180–182, 182(fig.), 183–187
seaport, 45, 47–48, 153, 172, 173,
    175(photo), 176, 178, 179, 199–200
South Side, 176, 177, 181, 182, 187, 189
tourists from, 4, 7, 115, 116
utility services, 202–203
wealth in, 66, 179, 195
See also MECCA; Performing Arts Center
    (Milwaukee)
Milwaukee Area Technical College (MATC),
    202
Milwaukee County, 63, 84, 126, 129, 148,
    164, 172, 176–177, 179, 201, 202, 203
Milwaukee River, 173, 175(photo), 176, 177,
    195, 197
Milwaukee School of Engineering, 202
Mineral Point, 62
    land office, 56, 62, 64(fig.)
Miners, 60, 62–63, 75, 85, 112
Mining, 87, 93, 124, 168, 192(table)
    copper, 75, 97, 98(fig.), 101, 103
    employment in, 192(table)
    geologic formation of mineral deposits,
        35(table)
    iron ore, 40, 75, 76, 97, 98(figs.), 100(fig.),
        101–103, 164
    lead, 44, 56, 58, 60, 61(fig.), 62–63, 92
    towns, 99, 100(fig.), 101–103
    zinc, 44, 62, 148
Minnesota, 22, 73, 74, 75, 76, 84, 127, 128,
    129, 134
    Duluth, 66, 117, 118(fig.), 157
    Mesabi Range mining, 99
    Minneapolis–St. Paul, 7, 22, 84, 89, 116,
        117, 118(fig.), 119, 128, 153, 155, 157,
        193(table), 200, 201
    Red River Valley, 125
    tourists to Wis., 7, 116, 117, 118(fig.), 119
Missions/missionaries, 53, 90, 91(photo)
Mississippi River, 35(table), 36, 43, 44, 50,
    57, 57(fig.), 60, 63, 92, 95, 148, 165
Mississippi Valley, 53, 58
Missouri, 60, 62, 63, 138
    St. Louis, 60, 193(table)
Mitchell, Alexander, 179
Mole Lake (Indian reservation), 89(table),
    90(fig.)
Monadnocks, 41
Monocqua-Woodruff, 42
Monroe, 70, 71
    Huber brewery, 14

Monroe County, Glacial Lake Wisconsin in,
    38, 42–43
Montreal (Wis.), 101, 102, 102(fig.)
Montreal Mine, 99, 100(fig.)
Moraines, 37(fig.), 38, 41, 42, 43, 44–45, 173,
    174(fig.)
Morgan, Thomas Jefferson, 87
Mortgage Guaranty Investment Company,
    187, 198
Motor vehicles, 116, 188–189
    manufacturing, 80(table), 152, 163,
        163(table), 164, 164(table), 165, 168, 169,
        170, 190, 191(table), 194, 195
Mount Horeb Norwegian festivals, 70
Mount Mary College, 202

National Conservation Commission, 93
Nationalistic empire, 51, 77–80
Native Americans. See Indians
Neenah, 80
Neenah Foundry, 167
Nelson, Gaylord, 116
New England, 19, 56, 64, 180
New Glarus, Swiss/Swiss festivals in, 70, 71,
    71(photo), 72, 72(fig.), 136
New Holstein, 169
New Hope Township, 69
New Mexico, 131
New York, 11(table), 12, 89, 92, 126, 127
    settlers to Wis., 64, 65, 126, 180
Niagara cuesta, 44, 45
Nichols, Roland, 117
Nicolet, Jean, 53
Northern Highland region, 40–41, 41(fig.), 42
Northern Wisconsin: A Handbook for the
    Homeseeker, 73, 104
Northern Wisconsin Tobacco Exposition, 144
Northwest Company, 54
Northwestern Mutual Life Insurance
    Company, 187, 198
Northwest Territory, 54–55, 63
Northwoods region, 42, 48, 84–86, 86(fig.),
    87–121, 148, 152
    agriculture, 85, 87, 101, 103–115, 125, 152
    Indians, 85, 87–88, 88(map), 89, 89(table),
        90, 90(table), 91(photos), 92
    logging/lumbering, 92–97
    mining, 97–103
    recreation. See Recreation, forests/
        Northwoods and
Norwegians, 65, 65(table), 66, 69, 70, 73, 76,
    103, 104(fig.), 110, 145
    festivals, 71
Nuclear power, 202–203

Oak, 46, 47, 47(fig.), 48, 53, 63
Oak Creek, 202
Oats, 107, 111, 125, 129, 131, 134
Oconomowoc, 132
Ohio
    Cincinnati, 190
    Cleveland, 12, 102, 190, 193(table)
    Youngstown, 97
Ohio River, 165
Ojibwa, 109–110, 111
Old Northwestern Territory, 65
Old World Wisconsin, 68(photo)
Oneida (Indian reservation), 89(table), 90(fig.)
Oneida County, 42
Onions, 138(table), 139
Oscar Mayer (company), 157, 161(table), 164
Oshkosh, 53, 93, 97, 160, 161(table), 164, 169
    population growth of, 148, 152
Oshkosh Manufacturers' Association, 97
Outdoor Recreation Act (1961), 116
Outliers, 41
Ottawa Mine, 102
Ozaukee County, 67, 148, 202

Pabst, Frederick, 11
Pabst brewery, 13–14, 14(table), 15, 179,
    180(photo), 194(table), 195
Pabst Theater, 187, 202
Pacific Northwest, 103, 140, 200, 201
Paine, Edward, 93
Paine, George, 97
Paine Lumber Company, 97
Paper manufacturing. See Pulpwood/paper
    industries
Parks, 109, 116
    county, 5, 38, 115, 176(photo), 177
    federal, 119
    state, 5, 7, 38, 40
    See also individual parks
Parkside, 160
Pasteur, Louis, 11
Pattison State Park, 40
Peake, Ora, 56
Pearson Hill, 41
Peas, 45, 136, 138(table)
Peat bogs/soils, 39, 49, 140
Pence, 101
Pennsylvania, 11(table), 56, 92
    Centennial Exposition in, 126
    Philadelphia, 126, 190, 193(table)
    Pittsburgh, 97, 190, 193(table)
Penokee Range, 99. See also Gogebic Range
Performing Arts Center (Milwaukee),
    188(photo), 202

Perrot, Nicholas, 53
Peshtigo fire (1871), 48
Petroleum/petroleum products, 164, 165, 170,
    200, 202
Pewaukee Lake, 4
Pfister, Guido, 179
Physiographic regions, 41(fig.)
    Central Plain, 42–43
    Eastern Ridges and Lowlands, 44–45
    Lake Superior Lowland, 39–40
    Milwaukee, 173, 174(fig.), 175–177(photos)
    Northern Highland, 40–42
    Western Upland, 43–44
Pifer, Richard, 106
Pike River, 117
Pine, 43, 46, 47(fig.), 48, 72, 73, 87, 92, 93,
    95, 95(fig.), 103, 106. See also White
    pine
Pine River, 117
Plains, 39, 40, 42–43, 45
Plankinton, John, 179
Plankinton Arcade building (Milwaukee), 188
Plateaus, 43
Platte Mounds, 36
Platteville, 148
Pleasant Prairie, 202
Point Beach nuclear power plant, 203
Poles, 66, 69, 70, 73, 97, 103, 142, 164, 180,
    181, 181(fig.), 182(fig.), 183, 187
    festival, 71
Polk County, 7, 48, 69
Pollution, 39, 49, 50, 203
Polonia, 70
Population, 39, 49, 63, 73, 170, 172
    by employment sectors, 192(table). See also
        individual industries
    and goods/services, 153–160(figs. and
        tables)
    Indian, 89, 89(table)
    of mining districts, 63, 100
    of northern Wis., 73, 110, 112, 114(fig.), 115
    and recreation, 43, 48
    and settlement building, 154, 155, 157, 160,
        161(table)
    by settler/ethnic groups, 63–65, 65(table),
        66, 73, 180, 181, 181(fig.). See also
        Settlers; individual ethnic groups
    urban, 147–157(figs.), 160, 170, 172,
        177–178, 179(fig.), 180, 181, 181(fig.), 202,
        203, 205. See also individual cities
Portage County, 41, 54, 69, 126, 138
    Fort Winnebago, 52, 52(fig.)
Port Washington, 169, 202–203

Potatoes, 42, 43, 54, 70, 107, 111, 126, 136, 138(table), 139
Potawatomi (Indian reservation), 89(table), 90(fig.)
Prairie, 21, 46, 47(fig.), 48–49, 63, 124
Prairie du Chien, 54, 56, 57, 57(fig.), 58
  Fort Crawford, 52, 52(fig.), 55, 57
Prairie du Chien cuesta, 44
Prairie School of architecture, 20(fig.), 21, 22
Pratt, 101
Pred, Alan, 152
Price County, 41, 76, 114(fig.), 115
Printing/publishing, 163, 164(table), 191(table)
Prohibition, 12–13, 13(fig.)
Protestants, 68
Puerto Ricans, 182
Pulpwood/paper industries, 42, 43, 48, 79–80, 80(table), 152, 162, 163, 163(table), 164, 164(table), 166(figs.), 191(table)

Racial conflicts, 181, 202, 204
Racine, 76, 78, 160, 165, 169, 189, 195
  Johnson Wax Building, 22
  population growth of, 147, 152
Racine County, 48, 63, 126, 129
  Regency Mall, 190
Railroads, 60, 69, 73, 76, 77–78, 78(fig.), 79, 93, 95, 99, 104–105, 107, 108(fig.), 109, 112, 126, 148, 170, 173, 176, 186, 187, 189, 197, 199–201, 203
  land grants for, 73, 77, 105
Raitz, Karl, 145
Raw materials, 77, 79, 93, 152, 162, 163–164, 166–167, 169, 170
Recreation (outdoor), 48, 116–121, 171
  amount of land, 119, 119(fig.)
  areas, 86, 87, 152, 171
  forests/Northwoods and, 40, 42, 45, 48, 84, 115–121, 152, 170
  governments and, 116
  water, 4–9, 50, 115–121, 170, 173
  See also Camping/campgrounds; Fishing; Hunting; Parks; Tourism
Red Cedar River, 92
Red Cliff (Indian reservation), 88, 88(fig.), 90(fig.), 91(photo)
Red pine, 95
Red River, 72
Religious groups, 68, 89, 90, 145, 180, 183, 202
  churches and missions, 53, 90, 91(fig.), 92, 101
  and education, 87, 90, 91(fig.), 202
  and ethnic/racial groups, 66, 67, 68, 69, 180, 183

  and Indians, 87, 88, 90, 91
  See also individual religious groups
Republican party, 63, 68
Research Clearing House of metropolitan Milwaukee, 204
Reserve
  St. Francis Indian Mission, 90, 91(fig.)
Restaurants, 4, 7, 8, 9, 11, 19, 20(photo), 43, 84
Rexnord, Inc., 169, 194(table)
Rhinelander, 4, 25, 33(table), 42, 96, 96(fig.), 104, 162
  State Board of Immigration in, 73
Rib Mountain, 34, 35(table), 41
Rice Lake (city), 96, 96(fig.)
Richland Center, 21
Richland County, 125
Ridges, 43, 44, 173
River Falls, 162
Rivers and streams, 4, 30, 42, 43, 44, 58, 60, 72, 84, 92, 95, 116, 117–119, 164, 173, 176–177, 195, 197
  geologic history of, 35(table), 36, 38, 39, 41, 42
  and pollution, 39, 49, 50
  and power, 50, 60, 95, 173, 195, 202
  for recreation. See Fishing; Recreation, water
  size/number of, 49–50
  for transportation. See Shipping; Transportation, water
Roads, 58, 59, 60, 78–79, 105, 106, 110(table), 116, 152, 153, 162, 173, 176, 187, 189, 197, 199–201
  plank, 47–48, 93
Roche a Cri, 35(table), 36, 42
Rock County, 44, 45, 69, 124, 125
Rock Prairie, 69
Rock River, 63
Rock River Valley, 152, 160
Rockwell (company), 195
Roosevelt, Franklin D., 88
Rusk County, 106, 107(table)
Rusk Farm Company, 107(table)
Russians, 66, 103, 104(fig.), 180
Rye, 126

St. Croix (Indian reservation), 89(table), 90(fig.)
St. Croix County, 84, 125
St. Croix Falls (city), 96, 96(fig.)
St. Croix River, 4, 43, 72, 92, 95, 117
St. Lawrence River/Seaway, 51, 53, 57, 172, 173, 200

valley, 56
St. Nazianz, 67
Sandstone, 9, 34, 34(fig.), 35(table), 38, 41, 42, 43, 44
Sauk City, 11
Sauk County, 125
   Glacial Lake Wisconsin in, 38
Sauk Indians, 62
Savanna, 48–49, 53
Sawyer County, 107, 107(table), 108(map), 110(table)
Scandinavians, 15, 65, 66, 68, 72, 73, 74, 76, 126
   festivals, 71
   See also individual Scandinavian ethnic groups
Schafer, Joseph, 63, 64, 65, 73
Schleswig township, 69
Schlitz, Joseph, 11, 179
Schlitz brewery, 9, 11, 12, 13, 14, 14(table), 179, 194(table), 195
Scots, 65, 65(table)
Sedimentary rocks, 34
Seed, 107
Sentry Insurance, 170
Service sector, employment, 152, 153–154, 155, 156(table), 157, 158(table), 161(table), 162, 170–171, 182, 192(table), 198–199, 203
Settler empire, 51, 56–77
Settlers
   foreign-born, 104(fig.), 179, 180. *See also* Immigration; *individual ethnic groups*
   U.S.-born, 52, 56, 60, 63, 64, 65(table), 68, 73, 103, 177, 179
   white, 46, 47, 49, 63, 87, 103, 147, 177, 180
   would-be miners as, 60, 103
   See also Explorers; Indians
SEWRPC. *See* Southeastern Wisconsin Regional Planning Commission
Shale, 34, 34(fig.), 35(table), 44
Sheboygan, 45, 80, 138, 152
Sheboygan County, 93
Sheep Pasture Mound, 42
Shipbuilding, 40
Shipping, 40, 48, 62–63, 179, 197, 199–200, 203
   ports/docks, 45, 76, 124, 152–153, 160, 172, 173, 175(photo), 176, 178, 179, 197, 199–200
Ship Rock, 36
Shorewood, 203

Silage, 130–131, 131(fig.), 132–134. *See also* Livestock, feed crops
Silos, 132–133
Silsbee, Joseph Lyman, 21
Simplicity (company), 169
Sioux Indians, 72
Skiing
   snow, 48, 102, 121
   water, 116
SMSAs. *See* Standard Metropolitan Statistical Areas
Snowmobiling, 48, 121
Socialism, 68, 69, 74, 75, 76, 101
Soft-drink production, 9, 12
Soils, 30, 41, 43, 45, 48, 49, 110–111, 124, 127
   acidity, 34, 39
   and agriculture, 39, 40, 42, 43, 45, 63, 87, 104, 125
   geologic history of, 35(table), 36(photo), 39
Soltow, Lee, 65, 179
Somerset, 119
Southeastern Wisconsin Regional Planning Commission (SEWRPC), 204
South Milwaukee (city), 197
Soviet Union, 200
Soybeans, 44, 45
Spanish, in the New World, 51
Sparta, 58
Spooner, 42, 162
Spooner, John, 87
Spring Green. *See* Wright, Frank Lloyd
Squires, Guy, family, 111
Standard Metropolitan Statistical Areas (SMSAs), 190–193, 191(table), 192(table), 193(table)
State Board of Immigration, 73
Steel production. *See* Foundries; Metal industry/products; Mining, iron ore
Steven's Point, 43, 70, 73, 78, 96, 96(fig.), 160, 170
Stevens Point brewery, 13, 14, 14(fig. and table)
Stockbridge, 44
Stockbridge-Munsee (Indian reservation), 89(table), 90(fig.)
Stores/shops/shopping, 7, 9, 15, 96, 184(caption), 188–190, 190(table), 198–199
   company, 97, 101
   See also Wholesale-retail centers/trade
Storms, 24, 27–29, 29(figs.), 132
Stoughton, 144
   Syttende Mai Norwegian festival, 71

Strikes, 77, 96, 97, 127, 182, 195. *See also* Labor, unrest
Stroh Company (brewery), 195
Suburban regions, 84, 85(map), 170, 173, 185, 186, 187, 188–189, 197, 198, 198(table), 203, 204
Sugar maple, 46, 47, 47(fig.)
Summerfest, 179, 204
Sun Belt, 164, 170, 171, 172, 190, 195
Sunflower seeds, 200
Superior, 33(table), 66, 76, 104, 117, 118(fig.), 157, 160, 161(table)
  Central Cooperative Exchange in, 76
  population growth in, 148, 152
  port and shipping, 40, 76, 157
Swamps. *See* Wetlands
Swedes, 8, 65(table), 73, 75, 103, 104(fig.), 110
Swiss, 65(table), 70–71, 71(photo), 72, 72(fig.)
  cheese, 70, 136
  festivals, 70, 71, 72
Swiss Tom Farms, 132

Taliesin. *See* Wright, Frank Lloyd
Tanning/tanneries, 76, 79, 80, 80(table), 163(table), 179, 182, 191(table), 197
Technology, 147, 170–171, 190, 193, 195
Teneta, Joe, family, 111
Tennessee, 142
  Memphis, Schlitz brewery, 13
  settlers to Wis., 60, 63
Texas, 130, 138, 142, 193(table)
Textiles and clothing manufacturing, 80, 80(table), 162, 163(table), 173, 191(table)
Thiensville, 189
Three Lakes, 42
Thunder Mountain, 41
Tim's Hill, 34, 35(table), 41
Tobacco, 44, 54, 69, 70, 126, 136, 142, 143(figs.), 144, 144(fig.), 145, 145(fig.)
Tomah, land formations, 42, 43, 44
Tomahawk, 42
Tools/instruments/hardware manufacturing, 80, 163(table), 164(table), 166, 167, 169, 191(table)
Tourism, 4, 5(fig.), 6, 7–9, 39, 40, 42, 43, 44, 48, 84, 101, 102, 116, 162, 165
  amusements/attractions, 9, 43, 44, 134
  and ethnic groups, 8, 62, 70, 72
  Northwoods and, 115–117, 117(fig.), 118(fig.), 119, 119(fig.), 120(fig.), 121
Tourists, out of state, 4, 5(fig.), 6(fig.), 7, 9, 42, 72, 85, 115, 116, 117, 118(fig.), 119
Townsend Act (1767), 62

Township and range survey, 58–60, 59(fig.)
Trade areas. *See* Wholesale-retail centers/trade
Transportation, 147, 152–153, 161(table), 170, 171, 172, 192, 199–201, 204
  by air. *See* Airports
  employment in, 192, 192(table), 199, 201
  equipment manufacturing. *See* Motor vehicles, manufacturing
  public, 189, 197, 201
  by rail. *See* Railroads
  by roads. *See* Roads
  by water, 50, 51–52, 53, 60, 62–63, 65, 72, 73, 94(photo), 95, 147–148, 152, 160, 165, 172, 173, 178, 197, 199–200. *See also* Shipping
Treaty of Ghent (1814), 54–55
Treaty of Paris (1763), 54
Trewartha, Glenn T., 131
Troy Lake, 63
Tyomies (Finnish newspaper), 76

Unions/unionists, 68, 69, 77, 97, 195
United States
  American Manufacturing Belt, 93, 160, 164, 165–168, 169, 170, 172–173
  Automobile Belt, 195
  beer consumption, 9
  beverages production, 9
  Cheese Belt, 135, 136
  Corn (-Soybean) Belt, 127, 130, 164
  croplands, 16(fig.)
  Dairy Belt, 127, 131, 136
  dairy industry, 127, 127(fig.), 128, 131
  Spring Wheat Belt, 127
  Sun Belt, 164, 170, 171, 172, 190, 195
  tobacco growing, 142, 144(fig.), 144
  See also U.S. government; *individual states*
University of Wisconsin, 21, 152, 155–156, 160, 161(table), 202
  Agricultural Experiment Station, 111–112
  College of Agriculture, 104, 110, 111, 126, 127, 133–134
Upper Great Lakes region, 75–76, 179. *See also individual states*
Upson, 101
Urbanization. *See* Urban regions; Population, urban
Urban regions, 60, 84, 85(map), 147–171
  development patterns, 147–154(figs.)
  manufacturing and, 162–170(figs. and tables)
  spacing and size, 154–160(figs.)
  See also Population, urban; *individual cities*

U.S. Agricultural Adjustment Act (1933), 144
U.S. Department of Agriculture, 144
U.S. Department of Housing and Urban
    Development, 204
U.S. Department of the Interior, Bureau of
    Indian Affairs (BIA), 87–89
U.S. government
    and control/possession/statehood of Wis.,
        55, 58, 63
    Declaration of Independence, 59
    forts, 52, 55
    and fur trade, 55–56, 87
    and homesteading, 59–60
    and Indians, 55, 58, 87–89, 177
    and lumbering, 92
    and mining, 62
    national land survey, 58–60
    and urban development, 204
    See also individual government
        departments/agencies/acts (legislation)
U.S. Immigration Commission, 103
U.S. Public Health Service, 89
U.S. Resettlement Administration, Suburban
    Resettlement Division, 185
U.S. War Department, Bureau of Indian
    Affairs (BIA), 87

Vegetables, 45, 54, 84, 136, 137(map), 138,
    138(table), 163, 164(table). See also
    Agricultural products processing, canning;
    individual varieties
Vegetation, 30, 45–49, 177
    and climate/distribution, 45–46, 47(fig.)
    evolution of, 35(table), 46–47
    and pollution/development, 39, 50
    See also Forests; Grasslands; individual
        plants/trees
Vernon County, 69, 70, 144
Vilas County, 42, 86, 117, 128, 170
Vogel, Fred, 179
Vogeler, Ingolf, 86
Volcanic activity, 34, 35(table)

Walker, George, 177
Walkers Point, 177, 196(photo)
Walters brewery, 14, 14(table)
Walworth County, 63, 126, 129
War of 1812, 54
Washington, George, 55
Washington County, 44, 148
    Holy Hill, 45
Washington Island, 8, 44
Water supply
    geologic history of, 34, 35(table), 39, 44

Lake Michigan, 202, 203
    underground, 34, 39, 202
Waukesha, 77, 167, 189, 197
    Carroll College, 202
Waukesha County, 69, 84, 148
    Lapham Peak, 45
Waukesha Motor Company, 197
Waunakee, 138
Waupaca County, 7, 69, 126
Wausau, 42, 96, 96(fig.), 148, 152, 154, 155,
    160, 161(table), 167
    land office, 64(fig.), 77
Waushara County, 126
Wauwatosa, 189
Wealth (income), 65–66, 74, 77, 89, 90,
    91(photo), 97, 112, 115, 116, 172, 179,
    183, 186(fig.), 192–193, 193(table), 195,
    198, 204
Weather
    forecasting, 28(fig.), 29, 30
    See also Climate
Weeks, L. W., 132
Welsh, 11, 63, 65, 65(table)
Wesby, 70
West Allis, 189, 197
West Bend, 189
West Blue Mound, 44. See also Blue Mounds
Western Upland region, 41(fig.), 43–44
West Indies, 93
West Milwaukee (city), 197
Wetlands, 39, 42, 43, 45, 49, 53, 60
    and agriculture, 49, 139–140
    history of, 35(table), 38, 39, 41, 42, 47(fig.),
        49
Weyerhauser Company strike, 97
Wheat, 65, 66, 72, 73, 77–78, 79, 107, 124,
    124(table), 125, 125(fig.), 126, 179
    Spring Wheat Belt, 127
White pine, 46, 72, 87, 95, 106, 164
Whitewater, 63, 160
Wholesale-retail centers/trade, 157, 158(fig.),
    159(fig.), 160, 161(fig.), 162, 170, 188–190,
    190(table), 192, 197, 198–199
    employment in, 192(table)
Wildlife, 45, 47, 48, 49
    and pollution/development, 39, 50
    See also Fishing; Fur trade; Hunting
Wild rice, 49, 54
Wilson, Woodrow, 68
Winmar Building (Milwaukee), 187
Winnebago (Indian reservation), 89(table),
    90(fig.)
Winnebago County, 69, 167
Winnebago Indians, 62, 72

Wisconsin
  state capitols, 63
  statehood, 58, 63
  as U.S. possession, 55
Wisconsin Arts Board, 19
  Dairyland Graphics Project of, 19
Wisconsin Colonization Company, 107,
    107(table), 108–110, 110(table), 111
Wisconsin Dairyman's Association, 126
Wisconsin Dells (city and geologic
    formation), 5, 7, 8–9, 10(fig.), 11(fig.), 43,
    162
  geologic history of, 35(table), 36, 38–39, 43,
    140
Wisconsin Department of Agriculture, 17
Wisconsin Department of Natural Resources,
    92
Wisconsin Department of Public Instruction,
    76
Wisconsin Division of Tourism, 4, 6(fig.), 134
Wisconsin Electric Power Company, 202
Wisconsin National Guard, 97

Wisconsin Rapids, 43
Wisconsin River, 4, 10(fig.), 44, 64, 148, 164
  geologic history of, 38, 43, 44, 140
  gorge. See Wisconsin Dells
  and lumbering/pulp/paper industries, 42,
    72, 80, 92, 95
Wolf River, 117
  and lumbering, 72, 92, 95
Wood County, 41, 42, 140
  Glacial Lake Wisconsin in, 38, 42–43
Wood products, 76, 80, 80(table), 93,
    163(table), 164, 164(table), 191(table)
World War I, 69, 99, 110
World War II, 99, 138, 182
Wright, Frank Lloyd, 4, 20(fig.), 21–22,
    22(fig.)
  Spring Green, 21
  Taliesin, 21
  See also Prairie School of Architecture

Yellow birch, 46, 47(fig.)

Zinc. See under Mining